A Pained Life

A Pained Life

A Chronic Pain Journey

Carol Jay Levy

This book was printed in the United States of America.

DISCLAIMER

This is a true story; all events are directly taken from or based on medical records, legal documents, personal and/or private correspondence. All conversations are based on the above and/or the author's best recall.

Asterisk indicates a name has been changed.

To order additional copies of this book, contact:
Xlibris Corporation
1-888-795-4274
www.Xlibris.com
Orders@Xlibris.com
18435

DEDICATED TO THE MEMORY OF DR. MARY VIERNSTEIN

CHRONIC PAIN

THE MEDICAL APPROACH

The everyday fact of dealing with pain is a difficult job. When pain is constant, it is the first sensation in the morning. It is the last at night. In the interim, it is the most demanding.

The support systems around the patient—physicians and therapists, societal and governmental, family and friends—can either help or hinder the process.

One way in which we, the pain patient, can help ourselves is by knowing the rules of the "pain game."

Unlike most games, there is an aura of mystery surrounding them. The suspense, however, is one sided. The doctors know what the tenets are. The patient must depend on her/his luck and intelligence.

The first code is that pain is a psychological maneuver. This principle is the most important. For many medical service providers, it is the decisive factor in deciding what, if any, treatment will be given.

Dr. Anita Avilon, in *Chronic Pain. Psychosocial Factors In Rehabilitation,* discusses what she terms, "pain proneness." She reports that "no single theory or work has given an adequate model of why persons become chronic pain patients. However we get some pieces of the puzzle, i.e., the conversion of pain into unconscious emotion . . . the use of pain complaint as a way of neurovegetative and behavioral conditioning."[1] Once we get past the obfuscation of her language, the assumption is clear. The first, that pain is not the sole criterion in becoming a chronic pain patient. Her second, that pain is used first and foremost as a means of conscious, or unconscious, manipulation.

Helen Neal, in her book *The Politics of Pain,* states, "Pain ranks almost with money in the power it invests people with to tyrannize others."[2]

This tyranny is accomplished a number of ways. One way is monetarily: insurance, social security, workman's compensation, and medical malpractice litigation.

One can receive non-financial profits: medications—I have my narcotic supplier; dependency—I can't do it myself, or martyrdom—I can do it, it only hurts for a little while.[3]

It is done through specific games: one-upmanship—my pain is worse than yours; love moves—he (she) will pay more attention if I am sick; confounding of physicians—he has never seen *this* before.

Certainly, some people will use their pain as a device. Most of us do not. It hurts. We only want to make it stop.

When we are challenged to defend the various actions we have taken to help live with, or because of, the pain, it becomes the source of additional hurt. There are pain centers and doctors, for instance, who refuse to accept, as patients, anyone who is involved in litigation. I, personally, am a plaintiff in two lawsuits. The cases have nothing to do with the pain. Nonetheless, a psychiatrist and a neurosurgeon told me, "If you drop your lawsuits, we will do the surgery."

One reason behind the refusal of many doctors to accept chronic pain and its effects lies in the definition. Any pain becomes chronic if it lasts beyond six months. If a pain has lasted that long and has not responded to therapy, the probability is that the correct diagnosis cannot be found.

It is often said in our society that M.D. stands for Medical Deity. With chronic pain, the doctor who helps is the one who understands that M.D. means Medical Detective.

Dr. Nelson Hendler, in *Coping with Chronic Pain,* tells the story of Harriet.

Harriet was a nursing student. She knew how a medical complaint should be handled. Yet, she was forced to go through what I call the "psychiatric syndrome."

One day, while working on the ward, she wore a pair of shoes that were too tight. The following day, she experienced severe pain in one of her legs. Initially, she chose to ignore it. After a few weeks, the pain had not relented. She was forced to resort to using crutches. Finally, she felt she had no option but to go to the student health center. They examined her leg on X-ray. The doctor on duty advised her to spend a few days on bed rest. He gave her a prescription for narcotic painkillers and sleeping medications. All were to no avail.

Because she had no relief, the school doctor arranged a consult with an orthopaedic surgeon. He, too, found no evidence of disease. His treatment consisted of referring her to the campus psychiatrist.

Before the orthopaedic exam, she had related to the university physician that she felt depressed. She was very worried about her upcoming exams. The doctor listened. Since both he and the orthopaedist could not find a physical cause for her problem, they decided the difficulty must lie in her psyche. Her distress over the exams and her sadness were being expressed through her leg pain. Thus, the rationale for the psychiatrist.

Harriet's luck changed with him. He knew that chronic pain is a disease in and of itself. In fact, his office was located in a pain clinic. Finally, she received a test specific to her complaint of pain. The test, called a thermogram, measures heat in an X-ray–type procedure. It can show damage not visible on a regular X-ray. These films showed that Harriet had injured her sympathetic nerve. Now that they had visible proof, counseling could give way to medical (body) therapy.

A surgeon performed a nerve block on Harriet's leg. He injected local anaesthetic, hoping to provide temporary relief. If successful, it would provide evidence that the nerve could be cut surgically to permit permanent relief. It was successful. She chose to go ahead with the operation, and it worked. She went on to complete her nursing course. All her complaints of leg pain were gone.

Harriet was lucky in that she stayed a victim of the psychiatric syndrome for only a short period. Had her problem been related to a more unusual disorder, she might not have been so fortunate.

My story is similar to Harriet's. However, the cause of my pain is not as common. As a result, I found myself a pawn in the psychiatric/medical scenario for a much longer time.

My disorder is the result of a neurovascular birth defect. It did not announce itself until 1977, when I was twenty-four. It made itself known via a pain syndrome called trigeminal neuralgia.

Although I did not know for a few years, and then only after research of my own, that my symptoms were stereotypical, I still went through a myriad of tests and psychiatric evaluations. Compared with the textbooks, my pain differed in only two aspects: (1) Trigeminal neuralgia (or tic douloureux) normally occurs after fifty years of age. If it occurs after forty, it usually does so in conjunction with multiple sclerosis. It rarely appears before the age of forty; (2) Tic most often claims the lower cheek and jaw. Aside from those—age and location—my story went by the book.

Well, almost.

CHAPTER ONE

I awakened about 8:00 A.M. on that beautiful May morning in 1976. The sun was shining. Leaves floated through the air, held aloft by slight breezes.

I was where I wanted to be, where I felt I was meant to be. In Soho, New York City, my dream of singing and acting was an audition away. My apartment mate, Danny, was in his room.

I took my habitual morning shower and washed my hair. After drying it, I combed it out and tried to force it into some semblance of a style. I put on a flowered short-sleeved blouse and blue jeans. I walked into the living room. Out of habit, I turned on the TV. I sat down on the couch. The sounds of the show flitted in and out of my consciousness. It was a perfectly normal and lovely day.

Suddenly, a pain, the likes of which I had never before felt. It sliced through the side of my left temple. A lightning bolt, the thwack of a sharp knife, the splintering of my skin, the rending of my soul. Consciousness became pain. I stared into nothingness. I waited the twenty seconds or so it lasted, which filled the span of an eternity.

I stayed stock-still, my hands gripping at the couch. I was afraid to move, to speak, to breathe. I was terrified that any movement would make it come back. The idea that it could return was too awful a thought. I had not a clue of what I could have done to make such a terrible thing happen. I had done nothing of which I was aware, nothing but sit and think. I decided, *If I can just*

*stay still, immobile as a statue, maybe, please God, maybe, it would
not come back.*

I stayed that way for about fifteen minutes. When it finally
seemed safe, with no return of the pain, or even a hint of it, I
carefully rose from the couch. Still fearful, making a concerted
effort not to move my head, I walked into the bathroom. Surely,
something that horrendous must have left a mark.

Reluctantly, I stood before the mirror. I averted my eyes for
fear of what I might see. I did not know what I thought I might
find. Anything that stupefyingly overwhelming had to have left
some proof of its existence. A bright red and swollen left eye
looked back at me. Amazingly, there was no other evidence that
the lightning had torn through me. The pain felt as though it had
literally sliced a thin line through my left temple. I looked harder
into the mirror. "There's nothing there," I said out loud in total
befuddlement. It was incomprehensible to me that there was no
physical sign of the pain.

I wanted to pretend that it had not happened. Without any
visible proof, it might be something I could do. But pretending is
supposed to make things better, not worse, not terrifying.

And I was terrified. Terrified that it might come back. Terrified of what it might mean. It was the latter fear that decided my
plan of action. As long as the pain did not return, I would ignore
it. If I could succeed in doing that, then, hopefully, I could make
the pretense of it never having happened into my reality.

But the pain had a plan of its own.

The spontaneous pain, so much worse in its intensity, took a
backseat. Not long after the first pain came and went, one came
that refused to leave. It enveloped the entire upper left half of my
face and the top left side of my scalp. There was no longer a time
when I was pain free.

Usually, when I have a headache or a cold, I can make it
better, at least for a while, by resting or taking an aspirin or a
cold pill. This was different. Nothing made it better. So many
things, the normal everyday things, made it so much worse.

I always loved reading. Now, I could only read for ten or fifteen minutes. The movement of my eye, from left to right, or up to down, would make the "normal" pain—an awful combination of soreness, aching, heaviness, pulling, and other sensations for which I had no words—worse. If I forced myself to read longer or do any other activity that required moving my eyes, including talking to more than one person at a time, the pain became so fierce that I became nauseated.

It was reasonable to think that all I needed to do was close my left eye. After all, that was where the pain started. It is not something that most people think about, how our eyes work. I certainly had not thought about it before this happened. I found the answer to the question very quickly: It is not possible to move one eye without the other tagging along.

A light being turned on, or off, made me flinch. My eye involuntarily closed to keep the light out, but it was never fast enough. It was as though a torch was being held to the inside of my eye. The sun, something so innocent, something that makes a day so much more beautiful, was an evil now.

The strangest part was that any touch to that area—the left front scalp, forehead, or upper cheek—would trigger the original lightning.

Since I could not touch, I was no longer able to wash that part of my face or my hair in that area. Going outside, such a simple thing, was no longer simply a matter of leaving the apartment building. A little wisp of wind, or the breeze made by someone passing by too closely, changed the baseline pain into horrific pain. I could not protect myself from the shining of the sun by wearing sunglasses. The touch of the frame against the left side of my nose and temple increased the pain. Almost everything I normally did with little or no thought now required a decision. Is it sunny today? Is someone going to turn a light on or off without my knowing in advance, giving me time to prepare? Is there a breeze outside? Is there a fan? Is an air conditioner on? The choices were simple. Yes, I think I can go there. No, I cannot take the chance, the pain will be too great. Within a week,

I found myself answering *No* much more often than *Yes*. I had become almost totally disabled.

I found myself developing strategies to get through each day. I had to force myself to go outside. Instead of shopping for enough groceries to last a week, I would buy a day or two's worth at a time. That forced me to go out to buy food. I would not keep more than $10.00 in the house. That would force me to go to the bank. I had been seeing a psychologist once a week. Since the pain, the main benefit of the therapy was that I was forced to go outside if I wanted to keep the appointment. The pain took over my life. It made my choices for me. There was no option. I had to see a doctor.

I could not go back to my doctor in Philadelphia. I did not have the money. I barely had the funds for anything.

In 1970, at age eighteen, I entered Temple University. Three and a half years into the completion of my B.A. in psychology, I left for a semester to start a physician's assistant program at Hahnemann Medical College, also in Philadelphia. I left after three months into the two years it would have taken to finish. I returned to Temple to finish the B.A. I really did not want to do either as my life's work.

I was programmed that college automatically follows high school. My parents always expected me to become a psychiatrist or psychologist. As much as my secret desire was to perform, it seemed like something only other people do. It never occurred to me that all the actors and singers I saw, on stage or screen, had to come from someplace else first, too. To my parents, it did not matter if I had a dream or succeeded at it. They thought I had a good voice, but I was meant to be a professional . . . something. Something white collar, not grease painted.

I loved to sing, I loved to be on stage. There was one problem: terrible stage fright.

To help me with it, my high school choir director suggested I take voice lessons. My parents had turned down my requests earlier in life to take ballet. I would have liked to have learned to play an instrument, but I never had the opportunity to do that either. However, Mr. DePolis making the suggestion was different. He was a person of, and in, authority. My parents agreed and sent me off to the local singing teacher.

One day, I noticed an ad in the local newspaper. Auditions were being held that afternoon. The Downingtown Dinner Theater was casting for *Carousel*.

In a behavior that I oft repeated, I decided it was now or never. I would go to the tryout. If I was cast, then maybe I could go forward with trying to be a professional singer/actor. If I was not, then it was not meant to be.

My audition was awful. I stood on the apron of the stage. My hands were clasped together in front of me. I sang without any movement, action, or emotion (other than fear). To my absolute amazement, I received a call two weeks later. "Are you still interested in being in the chorus of *Carousel*?" Was I? You bet. "Yes, I am," I said in an attempt at a calm voice. "The pay is twenty dollars a weekend." Pay? I had almost forgotten. Heck, I would have paid them to let me be in the show.

It was just as I always imagined. Normally shy, I was a completely different person. Not at first, but within a few weeks of singing, dancing, and acting on weekends, I was the person I always felt was hiding inside me. Someone outgoing, funny, happy. I stayed that person as I went on to be in the chorus and played a character role in the next production, *Hello, Dolly*.

Sacha, one of the *Hello, Dolly* leading ladies, wanted to sublet her New York apartment. The rent was cheap. And how often might an opportunity like this come along?

My six months in the dinner theater was all of the acting experience I had. I had first "dibs" on the apartment. Then I found out that Danny, one of the leading men from *Hello, Dolly*, wanted to take it. When I found out, I felt guilty. He was a real professional, having worked in the theater for years. It seemed to me he had more of a right to be in New York than I did. "We could share it," I offered. We barely knew each other. I never expected him to accept.

The two of us moved into the two-bedroom apartment on a tree-lined street in Soho, a few blocks down from Greenwich Village. We had a nice big kitchen, living room, and bathroom with a shower—no tub. Somehow, we never got around to sprucing it up, but we were both where we wanted to be.

Danny was already working in an off-Broadway show. I had hopes I would succeed as well.

I think few, if any, would dispute the fact that I am not a dancer. Any doubts I might have had were laid to rest in dance class. It did not help that most of the other students had been studying dancing for years. Many were working as dancers.

Phyllis, a young girl from the dinner theater, had also moved to Manhattan. She and I went to class twice. She, an accomplished dancer, stuck it out. I was so far out of my element, I never went back.

I looked for work, preferably in the mental health world, in case I failed to be cast in anything. That way, there might be an opportunity for training. The clinic address I had must have been wrong because I could not find the office. I went into another building and knocked on a door. It turned out to be a psychotherapist's office.

The secretary opened the door. As soon as I told her what I was looking for, she said, "Our secretary quit this morning. Come on in."

I met the therapist. A large man, in height and presence, he had a thick black mustache and untamed, chin-length, black hair. I was not totally impressed. Not because of him. Because of the form of therapy he practiced. His specialty was primal scream therapy, to my mind a pseudo-therapy at best. He asked me a few questions about my experience and who I was. I replied, and he offered me the job. I told him I had one condition that had to be met—I had to be given time off for auditions and classes. "No problem," he said.

My life in New York City was starting on a high note. I had a job. I had hopes.

I went to a few auditions and took some voice and acting classes. Then my boss told me he could not spare me for the time I was taking off.

I hated the job since I could not do what I had come to the city to do. I could not quit because I needed the money. Although I did not like him, he liked me, at first. Towards the end, I think his feeling for me was one of hate. "I can't take the contempt I see in your face anymore," he said four months later, right before Christmas, when he fired me. I no longer had a job. But I still had hope.

One audition was something right out of a movie. A bunch of men and women awaited their turn, stretching, dancing, doing vocal warm-ups, singing, or sitting. A number of them, including me, were gnawing their knuckles. We were in a gym-type locker room where the dancers were changing into leotards. The singers were called, one by one, into the large room next door.

The room was what I had always imagined: A big studio with a brilliant hardwood floor. A large window, letting in the sight of people walking along the street, helped to reduce my fear by reminding me I was not alone. Sun streaking through the trees and into the room. The pianist sitting at a beautiful black grand piano. I gave her my music, "How Are Things in Glocca Morra?" from *Finian's Rainbow*. At her nod, I began to sing.

I missed a note, thinking it went up instead of down. To my very pleasant surprise, I was asked to stay for the dance auditions. Eight of us were in the room. Seven of us could dance. As soon as they saw me dance, "We're calling you back for the dance audition" became "Thank you very much, you can leave."

That was such a happy and sad day for me. It could have gone one of two ways: I would take more classes and do more auditions until I succeed—the life I envisioned for myself, or something totally unexpected could happen—a life I could never have pictured, instead. The pain and my poverty were the start of that life.

I expected that my unemployment benefits would hold me
for a while.

When I got to the unemployment office, I found out that I
had been making far less money than I realized. John*, my boss,
had told me he would pay me $116.00 per week or $5.00 per
hour. I took care of his checkbook, which included writing out
my own paycheck. My hours, determined by him, were erratic.
In an attempt at fairness, I used the hourly wage to compute
each paycheck. It turned out to be much less than $116.00. My
pay averaged out to only $82.00 per week. Unemployment paid
half a week's normal salary. That gave me $41.00. I was not sure
how I was going to get by.

The rent would not be a problem. My portion was $90.00 per
month. Between my savings, $164.00 per month unemployment,
and my father's help when necessary, my shelter was assured.
Phone bills were minimal. We mistakenly believed that the rent
included electricity. Danny had decided to move back home, so
I was alone the day the lights went off. Although we had never
seen an electric bill, it turned out it was not included in the rent.
They wanted $212.00 to turn it back on, money I did not have.
My father paid to have it turned back on. Once the pain started
and light was a problem for me, I kept the new bills down using
a very low wattage.

There was only one other expense that was essential. It was
the fee of the psychologist I began seeing shortly after I arrived
in New York. I started seeing her because of depression. Some of
it was from my normal state of being. The rest was a reaction to
my move and to my employer, John. And then to the pain.
Carolyn's compassion evidenced itself by her willingness to reduce her fee to $15.00 a session. That I could afford. A private
medical doctor for the pain was another matter.

When I was twenty, I worked in a volunteer program for college students considering a career in medicine. One day, I
accompanied a surgical resident on his clinic rounds. After he
introduced me to one of the patients, he showed me the stitches

that needed to be removed from the patient's head wound. "Ms. Levy will be taking those out for you," he said. Then he left the room.

The patient now believed I was a medical person who knew how to remove sutures. I did not know what to do. It seemed wrong to tell him that I was not a doctor, resident, nurse or medical student, since the resident had left him in my hands.

My parents passed on to me their acceptance of the word of all authority figures, whether what they said made sense or not. I was not the type of person to say "no" or to question things. I was wearing a white coat. My name pin read, "Premedical College Student Volunteer." The patient should have seen it. Whether or not he read it was a different matter . . . I had seen stitches taken out before. I knew, as I cut each suture, that what I was doing was wrong. I did it anyway. *Thank God*, I thought, *I will never be subjected to this type of treatment.*

I had medical insurance, but it was a reimbursement plan. Every doctor I called wanted me to pay them up front. I did not have the money to do that. New to being poor, I had no option. I had to go to a clinic.

At first, the staff of the clinic at New York's St. Vincent's Hospital was kind and concerned. I did not have to wait overly long. Each resident who saw me felt it was incumbent upon him to present me to another. After a couple of visits, things changed. I was no longer interesting. I was merely frustrating and old news.

One problem for the staff was my medical knowledge and experience. My information came from the Physician Assistant Program and years of working as a volunteer and ward clerk in a local emergency room. Scarce as my knowledge was, it was often seen as a threat. When I would use appropriate terminology, I was often asked, "Why do you talk like that?" Without medical letters after my name, my knowledge was suspect. The fact that pain is a wholly subjective complaint did not help.

The problem from my side was that, in a clinic, patients only see residents. Some of them were closer to the beginning than to the end of their training. Only as a last resort would you see an attending physician.

The difficulty was that the residents were accustomed to the diseases they read about in their textbooks. When patients like me did not correspond to a particular chapter, efforts were made to make us fit.

My complaints were adapted by ignoring my complaint of pain. I had a blood vessel visible in the left corner of my eye. Since it could be seen and examined, that was where they directed their attention.

CHAPTER TWO

For six months, I traveled back and forth to the clinic. I was seen primarily in the Ophthalmology Department. Other specialties were soon involved: I was seen in the General Medicine, Cardiology, Rheumatology, Neurology, and, as a last resort, Neurosurgery, clinics. In a period of twelve weeks, I visited the peripheral clinics fourteen times. I was seen eight times in Ophthalmology. In between, I underwent blood and X-ray studies. These were done at St. Vincent's, whenever they had the machines. When they did not, I was sent elsewhere.

All the tests came back with the same answer: negative. There were the unusual blood vessels within the eye, but they were nothing to get excited about. Or to use as explanation.

Cardiology tested my heart. General Medicine tested my blood and organs. Rheumatology tested my blood and joints. The results were obvious. I was exceptionally healthy. I just had pain.

The heart study was no problem. I just had to lie still. The blood studies were no problem. I just had to sit still. The eye studies were a problem.

There was always a chance that one of the eye examinations would nail the diagnosis. I constantly rationalized agreeing to things I knew would cause me pain. *Just in case*, I would tell myself. The normal inspection with an ophthalmoscope pained me because of the light and the requests to move my eye. Dr. Lanning, one of the residents, looked into my left eye with a magnifying lens to increase the intensity of his light. The light blinded me with pain. The harder I tried to keep my eye open, the more it struggled desperately to stay shut. Dr. Lanning was not empathetic. "If you want me to examine the eye and help you, you would cooperate!" he hissed through gritted teeth. "Now hold still!"

Once I agreed to hold still for one exam, it opened the door for worse. One study tested my retina. It was similar to an electroencephalogram in that the results were visualized on a graph recording. It differed in that the leads were not attached to my scalp, which would have been difficult enough for me. They were placed on my eye. The pain was horrific. The test revealed no new data. The next study was even worse. Ultrasound can be a good way to study the eye, but even to a patient without facial pain, it has to be an uncomfortable procedure.

Ultrasound waves are conducted through water. A normal patient is studied by having a chamber with water in it placed over their eye. I could not tolerate that. Instead, they placed me on a litter and told me to put my head back into a plastic container. It held enough water to cover my eyes and mouth but leave my nose free for breath. Then they moved a sensor back and forth on my eyes. "Please," I would say when I could sit up. "Don't make me do it anymore." The pain was so bad. The technician had a job to do. She insisted that the test was necessary. She did it twice before they obtained an acceptable result. Once again, negative.

I could not understand how someone could have such a pain. I could not understand how someone could have such a pain and no reason could be found.

I really should not have been surprised. After all, this was not the first time it had happened.

When I was nineteen, I had an occlusion in my left leg. The doctors I saw never determined whether it was caused by a blood clot or some type of spasm in the knee artery. When I was twenty-two, I had a pain problem in my left shoulder. It was ultimately linked to an inversion of two blood vessels. Both times, one of the problems in diagnosing me had been my age. Neither problem should occur in someone younger than their forties. Subjectively and objectively, I had the correct symptoms. But, because of my youth, they told me my pain and disability were psychological. In the second instance, one of the physicians insisted I undergo a sodium amytal (truth serum) interview before he would countenance the surgery. The initial therapy offered in both instances was Valium and a supportive physician. The leg problem slowly abated by itself. The shoulder pain disappeared after the operation. Even though both problems were objectively seen on X-ray (for the leg) and surgery (for the shoulder), it took over two years for me to find the doctors that were able to diagnose and help me.

I had little doubt that I was headed in the same direction now. The pain and disability were too overwhelming. I could not wait two years.

A doctor, a hospital. I still believed this was where you could go and find relief, to find a sense of comfort. *But where was the comfort zone for me? When will I find it?* I wondered. *Where is it?* I cried to myself. *Maybe,* I told myself, *just maybe, the next test, the next exam, the next doctor . . . That'll be the one to do it.*

The next thing the resident insisted upon was photographs of the inside of my eye.

St. Vincent's did not have the cameras, so they sent me over to Cabrini Hospital. I was on the bus, my long hair down, wearing jeans and a button-down denim shirt open over a white blouse. As always, at least since the pain started, I was wearing sunglasses.

The lady in front of whom I was standing smiled up at me. "Are you a model? Or an actress?" Her question made me feel so very good, especially because this was an appointment I was definitely dreading.

I did not know anyone at Cabrini, so the sense of familiarity was gone. That would have helped to make the test a little easier. I knew it would be horribly painful. The technician, or doctor, would be using a flash camera. I knew what that meant. Each time the bulb went off, so, too, would the pain.

I was sitting in the waiting room. My stomach was doing wheelies in anticipation. A white-smocked man walked past the door a number of times. I assumed he was a doctor. Each time, I looked up and smiled. Each time, he smiled back and kept walking.

Finally, still smiling, he walked into the waiting room. He held out his hand. "I'm Dr. Carlin. I'll be taking the photos."

His smile was kind. I felt I could trust him.

"You need to put your chin in the strap there," he instructed. "Look to the right. Look to the left. Look straight ahead." All the kinds of eye movements that increased the pain.

I made him promise me, "Please, you have to tell me before you are going to set off the flash. Because of the pain, you have to warn me." He said he would. He kept his promise, but it made no difference. It was as bad as I had expected. The pain was unspeakable.

He was sweet through it all. He stopped when, either I said or he felt, that the pain was too severe. To help me through it, he talked. He asked questions about me, told me things about himself, made quiet jokes. Little by little, he endeared himself to me. When he saw or felt that I was unable to take any more of the pain, he would put his hand on mine. The pressure of another hand, of human touch, helped me tolerate the pain the camera caused. His warmth soothed the cold icy dread and fear.

Dr. Carlin—Jamshyd—and I started seeing each other. I was surprised that he wanted to date me. After all, the major moods and personality he saw came from the pain. Anger, fear, sadness, terror, and more fear. Not particularly the kind of qualities that were attractive. And yet Jamshyd found me interesting enough to date.

An attractive man, he was short, with somewhat shaggy black hair, dark deep-set eyes, and an olive complexion. A Jewish man from Iran.

I learned early in life not to say "no" no matter what I was feeling. This was a problem in many of my medical relationships. It was true in my personal ones as well. My personal relationship with Jamshyd was not a particularly good one. But medically, he was my savior.

Most evenings we spent at my apartment. On our first date, we went to a nightclub. We got back late. Jamshyd was very tired. Since he lived far from the hospital and I lived only five minutes away, he asked if he could stay over, just to sleep. On his fifth request, I gave in.

Often, I agreed to do things that I knew he knew would cause me pain. He drove a motorcycle. He repeatedly asked me to ride with him. I felt I could not continually refuse. He knew from our hospital interviews that riding on a motorcycle and wearing a helmet would worsen the pain. Nevertheless, he always asked me. After the first "no" he would ask me again. I usually ended up agreeing. If we went out for a picnic in the park or a walk, the breezes would set me off. Much of my energy went to pretending I was just fine.

Late one evening, he finally understood.

We were at my apartment. We were sitting on the couch and touching each other. It was very pleasant. Then his hand went to the upper left side of my face.

"Don't do that. Don't touch me there!"

"What's wrong?"

"You're setting off the pain!" I cried as he tried to touch me again.

"Please. Don't do that."

"Where can't I touch you?"

I mapped out the area for him. Suddenly, he straightened up. A look of recognition crossed his face.

"I know what you have. You have trigeminal neuralgia."

"Tic douloureux! No. I can't have that. That is NOT what I have."

I could not have been more emphatic. I knew about tic. What I knew scared me silly.

My knowledge came from an old television show called *The Bold Ones*. The program revolved around three different professions. I recalled one of the medical dramas. The disease of the week that Sunday was trigeminal neuralgia.

The main character was a model who suffered from tic. Each attack would send her into screaming fits of agony. She threatened suicide if she could not find relief. In came the surgeon. He could perform an operation on her. He would implant a little box in her body. She would wear another box on her belt. Each time the pain came, she triggered the unit on her belt. It would send a message to the device in her body. That, in turn, emitted an electrical impulse which somehow interfered with the pain. After much histrionics, she agreed to the surgery. It worked. At the end of the hour, she walked into the sun, smiling and pain free.

The show aired in 1971. Why I could still recall that specific episode five years later, I did not know. I did know that I hoped the writer had used poetic license. I tried to convince myself that the actress had been directed to overact. My pains were horrendous. If the author and Jamshyd were right, I was in big trouble. The pain would not miraculously disappear. It would return again . . . and again . . . and again . . .

My reality was a nightmare. I continued to agree to more and more painful tests. All had the same results—negative.

I knew my current pain met the criteria for trigeminal neuralgia. I was so terrifically appalled by that idea and truth that I needed to find a way to undo it. That could only happen if I tried to blame myself, consciously or unconsciously. Maybe the torture of the pain was not in my body. Maybe it was coming from my mind. *No sane mind could make up this kind of pain. Could it?* I tried hard not to ask myself.

No one ever said directly, "It's psychosomatic." They often said, "You're overreacting." That was why I had to fight tooth and nail to get pain medication.

No matter how often or how hard I told them how bad the

pain was and how disabled I was by it, the resident told me to wait. He alone would decide if and when the pain required drugs. When I broke into sobs on the phone one afternoon, Dr. Lanning finally gave in. He offered to give me a prescription. Instead of trying me on increasingly strong types of pain relievers, he went right to the hard stuff. He gave me a prescription for codeine.

I had never taken a narcotic before. He prescribed a small dose, only half a grain. Half an hour after taking it, I felt very strange. My mouth was filled with cotton. My head was made of wood. When I talked, I was not sure I made much sense. It did not affect the pain directly. It made me feel as though the pain stood outside of me. I felt a step away from reality.

I tried hard to pretend that Jamshyd was wrong. After all, if the area of the pain defined the diagnosis, it could not have been missed. It would have been picked up by any resident. Since none of them had, it could not be tic.

The reality was that it was the correct diagnosis. The reason it had not been realized was simple. No one had taken the time to give me a good exam. No one had been able to sit down with me and take a detailed history. It was not the doctor's fault. With twenty to thirty patients waiting to be seen, there was not much time available for each patient. Every visit, I mapped out the area of pain the same way I had done for Jamshyd. I told them repeatedly how bad it was. They did not hear me. Had Jamshyd not had such a nice smile, I would not have gone out with him. Had it not been for sex, I would not have been diagnosed.

Try as I might to deny it, I knew he was right. Trigeminal neuralgia is pain (neuralgia) in the fifth (trigeminal) cranial nerve. One of the mnemonics I remembered from school was the one for the cranial nerves: On Old Olympus Turning Top A Finn And German Viewed A Hop.

Each first letter stands for a nerve. The T in Top (number five) is for the trigeminal. The fifth nerve is responsible for the sensation of touch in the face. The addition of neuralgia means that touch is no longer interpreted as touch. Its sensation becomes pain. I tried to hold on to the hope that he was wrong. I knew I would never allow somebody to sew a box into my body. Of course, I had no worry about that, or anything else. Not until I could get the diagnosis legitimized at the clinic.

CHAPTER THREE

Since it is unethical for a doctor to date a patient, Jamshyd and I had to hide our relationship. He worked at the St. Vincent's clinic as well as in Cabrini, the other hospital. Since he did not diagnose me during a regular clinic visit, he could not simply write the diagnosis in my chart. The rest of the staff in the Ophthalmology Department had given up on me. The Neurology Clinic had become my primary habitat. Each visit there had become distressingly similar. "Here's another drug we can try. I don't know what you have. It might help. Then again, it might not."

I knew the next visit to Neurology, following my diagnosis via romance, would be tricky. I had to introduce the idea of trigeminal neuralgia without divulging my source. I worried about the possibility of compromising Jamshyd.

"A friend of mine had a suggestion," I said. "He thought I might have something called trigeminal neuralgia. Could that be what this is?" I asked with my most innocent air.

The doctor got a funny look on his face. He was in the process of escorting me from the room. He stopped in mid-step. He looked at me. He walked back to his chair. He sat silently for a moment. "That's what it is. That's exactly what you have."

For the first time, I was filled with hope. Hope that came in the form of a prescription.

He started me on the drug Tegretol. Although an anticonvulsant, it is also specific for trigeminal neuralgia. Unfortunately, it was not specific for my trigeminal neuralgia. I thought all I needed was a name for the pain. Once identified, it could be stopped.

When it continued, my level of disappointment and frustration increased a hundredfold.

Even with the diagnosis, Ophthalmology continued to be attracted to the blood vessels in the corner of my eye. I had no way of knowing whether or not they were important. I continued to let them examine the eye. More to the point, I continued with them because I had trouble separating emotionally from the clinic.

I had been going there long enough to have developed a sense of loyalty. It was a misplaced fidelity. Although it did not help me in this situation, it did not, as would happen in other medical relationships, hurt me either. I vacillated for another month. Finally, I accepted the fact that I was getting nowhere. There was no other option. I had to find another doctor.

I could not go to Jamshyd for a referral. As a resident, he would be most familiar with people at the hospitals I currently visited. As my boyfriend, he often told me, "When we are together, I am not your doctor."

I called doctors on my own, including one, a resident I liked and trusted, who was now in private practice. Each office gave me variations of the same line, "Even though you have insurance, our policy is for you to pay us directly and have the insurance reimburse you." If I could work and/or had money, that would not have been a problem. Since I had neither, I had to find a physician who would not insist on the money up front. The best idea seemed to be to return to the Philadelphia doctor I had seen years before for my arm and leg problems. I liked him. I trusted him. And, best of all, he accepted my insurance.

I was having a very difficult time financially. When the lease expired on the two-room apartment, I moved to a studio apartment two blocks away. At half the size, the rent doubled. Actually, it was $5.00 less per month ($175.00), but with no roommate, I was responsible for the entire amount. I had to rely totally on my father for the rent. I could not expect, nor permit, him to pay my other costs. I could think of only one other option: public assistance.

Coming from an upper-middle-class family, I was unprepared for what awaited me. A sign on the door alerted me to what I might expect. No Illegal Drugs or Weapons Permitted in This Building. As I was standing in line, waiting to be interviewed, a man cut in front of me. I asked politely if he had been there before. He responded by threatening me with a knife. When I went to complain to the guard about the knife, he told me, "Get back in line and keep quiet." Obviously, I was out of my element.

I stood in line for over an hour before I reached the interviewer. She glanced down at my application form. Then she glanced up at me. She had no questions. "You don't qualify," she said curtly. I tried to ask her, "Why not?" but all she would say was, "Next."

I had called beforehand. I knew that I met the financial requirements, i.e., I was poor enough. I returned a week later and spoke with a supervisor. She, too, just glanced at my papers. Her response was just as quick. "You do qualify."

Along with the welfare, I received Medicaid. It paid all my clinic costs. I had been paying $7.00 per visit. That was a small fee, but it was quickly adding up. The clinic went on a "Medicaid first" plan. The clinic used the state money to cover my medication and test costs as well.

To qualify for the Medicaid, I had to be declared disabled by the state physicians. The examinations were conducted in a large building. The halls were teeming with people. We would be shepherded from one line to another. At one station, they checked my eyesight. At the next, they took my blood pressure. At the third, they took my blood. Next, we were directed to leave a urine sample. All of these were done without the slightest regard for privacy. The last line was for diagnosis. I entered a little room. The doctor asked me what I had. I told him "trigeminal neuralgia." Even without the benefit of hearing the other conversations,

I knew ours must have been unusual. The doctor asked me, "What is that?" I explained. "How is it spelled?" I told him. He agreed with my assessment that I was disabled.

The assistance and Medicaid were rounded out by food stamps. In a way, I found this the most humiliating. With the first two, you were among people in the same situation as yourself. With the food stamps, I announced to the public at large—at least those buying at the same supermarket—that I was impoverished. *Surely*, I thought, *they wondered about me just as I had always wondered about those before me.* Becoming self-sufficient was almost as great a driving force as stopping the pain. To a degree, they were synonymous.

Feeling choiceless, I gave in and phoned my father. He agreed to help me pay to see a private physician. I decided to see a neurologist I had seen years before for a problem with excessive tiredness, following a bout with mononucleosis and hepatitis. I thought it made the most sense to see him since the clinic had identified my problem as neurological. If not, then I would make an appointment with Dr. Perilstein, the vascular specialist.

I recalled Dr. Mandel, the neurologist, as a very kind and gentle man. Either the years or my memory must have caused the changes. I sat on a litter as he alternately questioned me and spoke on the phone. I told him my story. "My face is very painful to the touch. I don't have headaches. I can't tolerate bright light." The visit resulted in a letter to my gynecologist. He had been the original referent for the first visit when I was sixteen. The letter read that I had headaches, could touch my face with no difficulty, and had probable "psychosomatic" eye-closing reaction to light. His diagnostic paragraph began, "I do not believe she has trigeminal neuralgia." His treatment proposal consisted of Valium and a "supportive physician." As before, I knew that my pain required more than that.

It had been only two years since I had last seen Dr. Perilstein. I did not think my memory of him would be as errant. He listened to my story and knew fairly rapidly that I no longer fit into his area of expertise. Instead of fooling around, as we had done in the clinic, by saying "maybe this, maybe that," or ignoring my complaints like Dr. Mandel did, he sent me directly to a neuro-ophthalmologist. I felt it was the right direction. Even if the ophthalmologist in him wondered about the blood vessel in my eye, the neurologist could still hear me when I talked about the pain.

My first appointment with him did not leave me enthused. Dr. Schatz is a short, dapper man, leprechaunish in his behavior, earthy in his talk, impressive in his medicine. He came out to the waiting area to greet me. We walked back to the consultation room. I did not see an examination area until after he fully understood my entire story. His interviewing technique was antithetical to that of Dr. Mandel and the doctors I had seen in the clinic.

Dr. Schatz's concentration centered on only one thing—me. He did not want my history in piecemeal fashion. When I forgot certain incidents, or skipped ahead in my chronology, he became annoyed. "Don't be schizophrenic," he admonished when I returned to parts of the story out of sequence. I knew he referred to the scattered way I was telling him about what had happened. Immediately, though, my mind flashed on other doctors and other words, "It's all in your head." After the conversation, we spent half an hour in the examining room. That reassured me that he was not giving me the brush-off.

I came to him for face pain. He made sure he did every neurological test for every part of my brain. "Close your eyes. Show me your teeth. Remember the three words I am going to say. What were they? Move your fingers, one at a time, against your thumb. Do it as rapidly as possible. Walk a straight line." He picked up a tuning fork. He slapped it against his palm and held it to each ear. "Can you hear that? Tell me when it stops." He bent my big toes. "Which direction am I pointing your toe?" He scratched my leg with an open safety pin. "Do you feel that?

Where do you feel it?" He held out an open book. Numbers were hidden, somewhat, within a colored block. "Tell me if you see numbers on these pages. What are they?"

He also did the most important tests. The ones that hurt so bad. "Close your eyes. Tell me what you feel." He was touching the upper left side of my face. *Oh God,* I said to myself. To him, working to control the pain in my voice, I answered, "My left forehead." I cleared my throat noisily in an effort to force away any pain sounds that were trying to get through. He touched my open eye with a cotton swab. I blinked and swallowed hard. "Yes. It hurts there, too." He touched other areas of my face. I had no trouble telling him when and where. The rest of my face, he could touch forever. "Okay, come back to the office so we can talk." *Oh good,* I thought. *Now I'll be fixed!*

I left the office with two prescriptions. One for Sansert. The other for Stelazine. The first is a drug for vascular disorder. The second is a psychotropic. I could understand the reason for the first, given my past history. I did not know why he added the second. If he thought I had a physical problem, why would he give me a drug for the mind?

It was the first drug, ironically, that caused me a problem. Two days after starting it, I developed terrible cramps in my left calf. When my leg had gone bad years before, cramping had been the first symptom. I was afraid it was happening again. I called Dr. Schatz.

"You can't be having cramps in your leg from this drug. It's not a possible side-effect," he said. "They're really bad," I responded. "I'm afraid to walk. I'm afraid that another cramp will start."

"This drug does not cause cramps," he replied, "at least not this early in the therapy. If you really think you can't tolerate it, you can stop the drug. But, I don't think your cramps are drug related."

I had no question that the drug was the culprit. He is telling me it is not possible. *Great,* I thought, *he thinks I'm making this up.*

I was very tempted to break the next appointment with him. I had a month in which to make up my mind. With no change in the pain, I returned to what seemed to be becoming a chronic thought—*I have no choice.* I kept the appointment. Every aspect of my life was being orchestrated by the pain and my attempts (often futile) to minimize it.

Because the lightning attacks were triggered by cold, light breeze, or a touch, I found myself staying in my apartment for all but an hour or two a day. Then I would go out for necessities. It was a beautiful autumn. The sun glowed constantly. Instead of lifting my spirits as a sunny day usually would, it was now another source of pain. I had to stay home in the mornings and at night. The sun was too bright in the morning. My eye could not adjust to headlights at night. I loved to walk in the rain. Now, I was afraid to leave the house without an umbrella, no matter how slight the chance of precipitation. It might touch my face and set off the pain. I could not take the chance. I adored the colors and mien of the fall. Now, it was discolored by the very dark sunglasses I had to wear. To add insult to injury, my face was horribly dirty. I could clean three-fourths of it, but the area encompassing the pain—the upper left forehead, cheek, and scalp—were untouchable, and therefore, unwashable. The same was true of the hair on that side. The pain imprisoned me. How could I not keep the appointment?

I felt nervous about seeing Dr. Schatz again. There had been a change in the pain. I still had the spontaneous attacks, but the pain, always lightning sharp in its intensity, had now become "pins and needles." Not the kind that happens when your leg "falls asleep." It felt like an electric shock taken to its ultimate strength. I worried most about the second change. The normal sequence was touch and then immediate pain. The first time the new order occurred, I thought the pain was gone. Someone accidentally touched my face, and the pain did not come. Just as I started to breathe a sigh of relief, it started. This was the new sequence. Touch and then, a break of twenty seconds or so. Then pain. I could find only one explanation. It *is* psychological. My mind needed the time to remember that it was supposed to have the pain.

I entered the office. Dr. Schatz asked how I was. I told him, as I tell everyone, "Fine." Then we got down to medical talk. We discussed the drugs. He mentioned that, at some point, he would want to do some tests. Then he wanted to know if there had been any changes. When I told him about the "pins and needles," he looked interested. My comment that I had almost thought it was over commanded his attention.

"What made you think that?" he asked. I explained about the time lag. His response surprised me. "It's time we brought you to the hospital. When do you want to go?"

When I had the leg problem, the doctor told me it was urgent that I be hospitalized. I waited two weeks for a bed. "As soon as possible," I answered. "I just want this to be over." He walked me to the secretary's desk. "Get Carol a bed for tomorrow," he told her.

"Wait," I said, "I can't go in tomorrow. I don't have any clothes with me, or anything."

Dr. Schatz looked at me. "You said as soon as possible." "Yeah but," I intelligently replied, "it always takes two weeks to get into the hospital."

Not this time, it didn't.

I spent the next morning taking the train back and forth to New York to get some clothes. That afternoon, I entered the Thomas Jefferson University Hospital in Philadelphia. With the exception of two days, I would not be in the outside world until fifty-six days and one brain surgery later.

CHAPTER FOUR

The next morning, Dr. Schatz came to my room. Fourteen medical students, interns, and residents followed. No women, only men of varying sizes and appearance. The interns and residents wore white coats; short for the former, long for the latter. The students were neatly dressed in pressed slacks and button-down shirts. Some wore ties. All had a look of anticipation. Most carried notebooks. The more industrious had tape recorders. I suspected all along that I was not the typical patient with a typical problem. It did not occur to me until then that there might be something seriously wrong with me.

"No." Dr. Schatz said when I asked him. "There's nothing terrible. I just wanted to get you in, so we can run the studies." I knew he had to be looking for something in particular. I had no idea what it could be.

I was scared of what was to come. I was petrified with the thought that the pain would not end.

"Wait. Dr. Schatz," I cried out as he started towards the door. My eyes were imploring, I was fighting back tears, and my voice was trembling. The question had to be asked. "Will this ever go away?"

He came back over to the side of my bed. "Don't you worry about that. That's my job."

At first, it seemed like I had been admitted only to repeat most of the tests that had already been done at St. Vincent's. The blood tests remained negative. Nothing new was found on the X-rays. The really painful tests were yet to come.

The first was an arteriogram. This is an X-ray requiring an injection of iodine dye through a catheter. The catheter is inserted into a surgically cut hole in the groin. The dye lights up the blood vessels. In my case, the dye is used so that those in the brain could be studied. It is an uncomfortable and potentially painful test to all testees. For me, the pain started outside the radiology suite.

The radiologist insisted I wear the shower cap given to patients to keep hair from flying into the sterile surgical area. I tried to explain to him that I could not put anything on my head. "If I put it on, it'll set off the pain."

He refused to listen. "You have to wear it," he insisted. "I can't start the procedure until you put it on," he said, pointing at the hat.

I pleaded with him. "Please, I can't. It'll set off the pain!"

He did not want to hear me. Turning to the nurse, he barked out his order. "Nurse," he directed, "put that cap on her." She did not want to do it. I could see the battle and then the defeat within her eyes. He was the doctor. She had to do as she was told. As I knew only too well it would, the pain became much worse.

Sometimes, the sharp pains were spontaneous. When he injected the dye for the first time, something triggered the lightning. I had no way of knowing if it was the dye, the pressure of the hat, or nothing that set the pain in motion. All I knew was the pain. "Oh my God!" I screamed. The doctor yelled at me from across the room. "What's the matter?"

I started crying. "You set off the pain," I sobbed.

In a nasty voice, he replied, "The injection [of the dye] cannot trigger the pain. Now, stop crying. You're moving every time I try to take a picture." The more he insisted I stop crying, the harder I cried. My body shook from a combination of the pain and the fear that there would be another bolt. Trapped by both, the ability to stop was beyond me. Finally, we reached a compromise. "Tell me when you're going to take a picture, and I'll hold my breath," I said, weeping. "That's the only way I can stop crying."

When he realized there was no other way to finish, he agreed. He warned me when to stop breathing. Then he took a picture. I held my breath for the few seconds necessary. Then I continued my crying. Finally, the process was completed. We both left the radiology suite miserable and angry. He got his pictures, and I got the results—negative.

I knew the immediate cause of my tears had been the pain. My inability to stop was due to more than that. I had gone into the hospital virtually alone. Since the pain started, I had an increased sense of the isolation that I had felt most of my life, except for the six months I worked in the dinner theater.

Shortly before the pain started, I acquired another roommate. Frank was a friend of the woman from whom I had sublet the apartment. After the pain started, it was obvious that something was wrong with me. He and his sister, Mary, who stayed with us for two weeks, tried to befriend me. Even though they asked, I found it too difficult to confide in them. One reason was my inability to confide easily in anyone. More importantly, I could not understand what was happening to me.

The depression I knew. It was a familiar feeling. The pain and inability to touch my face was something else. I found it too hard to explain to myself why I could not do anything without pain. How could I explain it to someone else? They tried very hard. Often they asked me if I wanted to join them on a walk or go for a cup of coffee. I said "okay" only after I had used up all the excuses I could think of to say "no." My reticence to go out and do things was not only with them. It extended to other people as well.

Before the pain started, I enrolled in an acting course. Meredith, a classmate, and I became friends. We spent time together at her apartment, talking about our hopes, dreams, and lives. Sometimes we went out to a café or to shop. I enjoyed her and our time together. Now, I made no attempt to contact her. A few of the people I worked with in the Philadelphia theater had also moved to Manhattan. I called none of them. No one could understand, I was certain. It never occurred to me to try. It never occurred to me to give them a chance.

I did not realize how antisocial I had become until I was on the train to New York to pick up my clothes the day before I went to the hospital. Sitting a few seats back, I noticed a woman I had not seen since college. Leslie and I had been good friends then. In any other situation, I would have been eager to go back and find out how she was. Now, my face was dirty. The pain was intense. I sat turned toward the window. I fervently prayed that she would not see me.

Fortunately, there was still one person to whom I felt close enough to share what was happening.

Edna and I met in college. After graduation, we moved into an apartment in Glenside, Pennsylvania. She was working for the Philadelphia school district, and I was in the Physician Assistant Program.

One afternoon, about nine months into our yearlong lease, she came home and made a surprise announcement. "I wanted to wait until everything was in place before I told anyone. I'm going into the air force." After I was able to close my mouth, which hung open from the shock of her news, we talked about her plans. A big part of her decision came about as a result of the benefits the service could offer. The more we talked, the better and better it sounded. A week or so later, I went in to talk with Sergeant Sanders, the recruiting officer.

There was a rather simple test that had to be taken which both of us easily passed. It was a feather in the sergeant's cap to add two college graduates to his enlistment roster.

Edna and I hoped, once all my paperwork was done, that we could be stationed together. It looked like that could happen. Until I had to ask Dr. Perilstein, the doctor for both my arm and leg problem, if he would sign the medical release. He refused.

He did not feel that there was enough information about why I had had the problems to make me a candidate for the physical rigors of military life. Neither my father nor Sergeant Sanders was dissuaded. Both told me they could find a doctor who would give the necessary permission.

The more I thought about it, despite the advantages offered by the air force, I realized that Dr. Perilstein had a point. He had my best interests at heart, as did neither my father nor the sergeant. Each of them had agendas that only peripherally, at best, considered what was best for me.

Edna was sent to the Shepard Air Base in Texas for basic training. I remained in Pennsylvania. I moved to a new apartment and took a job at the local psychiatric hospital as a receptionist/switchboard operator.

My friends from high school and I lost touch with each other almost as soon as we left school. Most of my friends from college had gone off to live their own lives. Edna was all there was, and I missed her. Our contact now could only be through letters and telephone calls. The thing lacking was the physical connection. I needed the eye-to-eye relationship, which I no longer had with anyone.

Unfortunately, that included my family. We were never very close. As I entered college and matured, the schism deepened. Although I have two half sisters and a half brother from my mother's first marriage, I felt like an only child. The rift between my parents and me was so great that I often felt like an orphan. My brother, David, eight years older than I, lived with his family in Florida. That gave him a legitimate reason to be uninvolved.

Leslie, the oldest, and Cathy, four years older than I, lived with their families in suburbs outside of Philadelphia. Except for occasional birthday cards, they had not been in contact with me since before my move to New York. I heard from none of them while I was in the hospital.

My father tried to visit almost every day. He believed my problem was psychiatric which made his support ironic. He preferred to think of me as a malingerer rather than physically ill.

One afternoon, he asked me why I could not read. I explained to him, as I had done a number of times before, that any eye movement caused me pain. "I can read for ten to fifteen minutes, but then the pain becomes intolerable." He had a quick answer. "I've seen you read, so I know you can." He needed to think I did not want to work. He preferred to think that rather than accept the idea that the pain and disability were physical.

The visits themselves were a problem. Our relationship could be defined by our political leanings. My father, a staunch Republican, disagreed with almost everything I, an equally staunch Democrat, held dear. No matter the topic, his black was my white. Most visits went one of two ways. Either we had nothing to say to each other or we teetered on the verge of disaster. We did not get along, but that did not mean that he did not care in his own way. He thought about it and came up with a good idea. He brought a game of checkers. That required no discussion once we each picked our side of the board and decided whether we wanted to be red or black.

My mother visited a few times. She always had trouble with my being ill. This time was no exception. When I went into the hospital with my leg problem years before, she was the one who drove me. She was unable to deal with her feelings about it. Instead, she threatened to kill us both. "I could just drive us into that tree," she said as we drove down the expressway. While I was hospitalized that time, she went into a psychiatric facility. She repeated the behavior during this stay. It was my father who suffered most from this. He would call and say, "I have to visit your mother today, and I can't make it up to see you." No matter whom he decided to visit, he would feel guilty about "neglecting" the other.

There was one other visitor.

When I worked at the dinner theater, I was an entirely different person. I was outgoing and exceptionally friendly. Normally uncomfortable with people, at the theater I was in my prime. I was everybody's buddy. I had made one good friendship in particular. It had been a year since we had last seen each other, but

I called him anyway. As soon as I told Paul where I was, despite the fact that he lived quite a distance from Philadelphia, he immediately agreed to come. I loved seeing him again, but all the camaraderie was gone. Not only did I have pain, I was back to the normal uncomfortable Carol Paul had not known. We were now only acquaintances.

I felt bored, anxious, angry, and emotional. I was almost totally alone. I had severe pain constantly. No one had the time to delve into my emotional reactions to all that was happening. The hospital is a place where one expects to get better. I was getting nowhere. Even the one person who visited consistently, my father, denied my pain.

Actually, there was one person who I was sure would care if she knew what I was going through. The problem was that I had no idea where she was. We had not talked with each other for at least four years.

Maria, a short, very pretty, dark-haired Brazilian, lived with our family during my senior year in high school. We became very close. We referred to ourselves as "sisters." She came to us through A.F.S., American Field Service, a foreign exchange student program.

Maria stayed with us from August 1969 to June 1970. In 1972, I went to Brazil to be her bridesmaid. The year before, I had celebrated Christmas with her and her family in her hometown of Belo Horizonte.

Neither of us were very good letter writers. We promised to keep in touch. Somehow, we never did. Nevertheless, I always thought about her. Whenever anyone asked me what wishes I had, my first answer was always "to see Maria." The thought of her often made things a little more tolerable. Unfortunately, the only access I had to her was in my thoughts.

Dr. Schatz gave me two passes during my stay so that I could leave the hospital. He seemed to understand how much I needed a change of scenery. One pass was for Thanksgiving Day. The other for a regular Saturday.

My father was supposed to pick me up that morning. The plan was that I would spend the day at my parents' home.

I was sitting on my bed waiting for him to arrive when the phone rang. "I'm not feeling good," he said. "I have a cold." He was not going to come and get me.

Despite the fact that I had now been in the hospital for three weeks, he told me, "You have to take the train. I'll pick you up, and we're going to Cathy's house." I did not want to go there. Cathy had made no effort to visit, call, or even send a card. He knew that. "Well, your mother is in the hospital, so it is either Cathy's or you'll have to stay at the hospital." I had to get out, even if it meant going somewhere where I knew I would not be made to feel welcome.

If there was going to be a problem, I thought it would come from either Cathy or me. I was worried that I might not be able to keep my anger, about being so ignored, in check. Instead of Cathy snubbing me in her own home or my losing control, the trouble came from someone whom I barely knew and who barely knew me.

We were sitting in the living room. Suddenly, Miriam, her mother-in-law, turned to me. "If you would just get a job," she pronounced, "you would not have this problem."

I was dumbfounded. Neither my father nor Cathy came to my defense. I was on a pass from the hospital. I might end up having brain surgery. Instead of compassion, I received armchair (cruel) psychology. Dr. Schatz had given me the pass because he was hoping to raise my spirits. Instead, I came back to the hospital a wreck. Karen, one of the nurses, stopped in my room. "Did you have a nice time?" she asked. Before the question had left her mouth, I broke into sobs.

Karen, other nurses, and the doctors had become my main sources of support. Dr. Schatz saw me six days out of every week, including Thanksgiving morning. My main doctor, in terms of treatment and follow-up, was really my resident, Dr. Roeschman. He was young, not much older than I, with reddish-brown hair, wearing a beard and an easy smile. He came to my room more than once a day, when possible. Many evenings, if he had time to spare, he also came by. We would talk about anything. It made me feel that he defined me as a person as well as a patient. Talking about the weather, clothes, or nothing in particular, reminded me that there was a life beyond the pain and the hospital.

Because I did not look sick or need assistance, the nurses did not hover. I was in long enough that some confidences were shared. I even considered some of the staff "friends." I seemed healthy and, except for the pain, I was. I did not want to talk about the pain. I did not want to look like I had pain.

Dr. Schatz brought me into the hospital because I had pain. Everyone knew I had pain. I said it once. Why should I have to say it again? Because I did not remind the nurses that I had pain, they seemed to feel I was all right. Once, when one nurse commented, "I know you are in pain because of the way your eye looks." I was annoyed. I only wanted my initial words to speak for me. That attitude must have played into the minds of the people who doubted whether I really had pain.

I did not realize it at the time, but I was not guiltless in the questions that were raised about the intensity of my pain. I needed the act to maintain my emotional stability. I enjoyed being treated like I was not sick. I suppose I hoped thinking would make it so. But, of course, it did not.

CHAPTER FIVE

I was no more able to do things in the hospital than I had been outside. In fact, some of my problems were increased.

Reading and anything that required me to use my eyes were out. My father brought me a latch hook rug kit. I tried to do it, but my eye refused to cooperate. The only thing that I thought would be pain free was watching television.

In 1976, at Jefferson Hospital, the sets were attached to the ceiling, one to a room. I was able to watch as long as I laid flat on the bed and looked up, approximating the normal resting placement of my eyes. The colors and movements on the screen made the pain worse. The normal environments and involvements of the hospital added to the pain. At home, I used a sixty-watt bulb. I do not know what normal hospital wattage is. It was definitely greater than what my eye could comfortably tolerate.

I had trouble talking with more than one person at a time. I like to look at people when I talk with them. That means using my eyes. Each additional person required me to move my eyes more.

Explaining my situation and answering the questions of up to fourteen people at a time provoked the pain. The examinations were often greater harbingers of pain. The hospital-imposed necessity of a wheelchair and litter arrival to some tests meant eye movement and breeze—another equation of pain.

My conscious decision to allow tests and therapies that would exacerbate the pain was no different than at St. Vincent's. I agreed to many, even though I knew how high the level of pain would be, either from the start or by the time we were finished. I could never know which ordeal would provide the answer. The pain forced me to agree to them all.

After the arteriogram came an electroencephalogram. This is a test to measure brain waves in the same way an electrocardiogram measures heart waves. It requires the technician to place electrodes on and in the scalp. I knew in advance that it would increase my pain. Who was I to say the brain's electrical system did not cause it? It was too bad, too disabling. I had to let them go ahead.

I sat up on the litter. I literally put my head in the technician's hands. As she rubbed gook all over my scalp, she explained, "This helps with the conduction of the signals from the leads to the machine." Information usually helps to put a person at ease. Nothing could do that for me now.

My insides twisted with fear. Lucy*, the technician, tried to be nice. She did her best to assure that her touch was gentle. That made it worse. Gentle touch was always worse than harsh. If I could wait it out long enough, the stronger touch would make stronger pain. Then, hopefully sooner rather than later, it would reach a plateau, and I knew it could get no worse.

When there is a break in the touch, the pain ebbs back a little. Which should help. Unless another touch is coming.

Lucy was trying so hard. It was not her fault that she was hurting me. There was no way to protect me or not set off the pain. The wires had to be put in place. A couple of codeine pills and my willpower allowed me to remain in control.

The test itself is a matter of simplicity. "Lie down and relax" is the only instruction. I could try to do that. The second part of the test turned the suggestion into little more than a bad joke.

Some forms of seizures are triggered by the flashing of light at a specific interval. Lucy directed me to "keep looking at the light." I knew it would not trigger a seizure. I was right. It did not. It only affected the pain. With each flash of light, the pain whipped me anew. Every flicker was a reassault. I had to fight so hard not to cry, not to scream. It was to no one's surprise that the test results gave us no new information.

Chronic pain is a strange disorder. It is totally subjective. As such, it can be a problem of the mind as well as the body. Another way to approach it, especially when the answer is so elusive, is psychiatrically.

Before Dr. Lanes, the psychiatrist, arrived, I was angry. I had just learned that my father, without my permission or knowledge, had informed Dr. Schatz that I had a psychiatric history. I had made two suicide attempts, one at age seventeen and one at eighteen. No one had asked me about it. It was not something I saw a reason to volunteer. My father, in his effort to deny the medical basis of my pain, decided not only that it was relevant; he decided that it was his information to divulge.

Dr. Lanes saw me the day after I learned about this. I began to believe once again that Dr. Schatz felt my problem was psychosomatic. When I asked him if one thing had to do with the other, the discussion with my father followed by the almost-immediate consult with Dr. Lanes, he denied it. His denial did not matter. My suspicions were aroused.

I spoke with Dr. Lanes a few times. There was no benefit. The pain remained the same.

Dr. Schatz suggested that I talk with the staff psychoanalyst. I was not happy about it but, of course, I agreed. After all, this person might have some good ideas.

Dr. Schatz consulted me on the choice. "Would you be willing to talk with a woman?" "Sure." Why not? What difference did it make?

When he told me her name, it was one with which I was familiar. When I worked as a volunteer in my local hospital, years before, Dr. Kenig was an intern. I liked her then. I could think of no reason to object to her now. When she finished her internship, she told me, "If there's anything I can ever help you with, I'll be glad to do it." She said this during a conversation about my future plans. I had mentioned that I had hopes of going to medical school. When she walked into my hospital room, I reminded her of it. "I don't think this is what you meant," I concluded.

The moment she walked into the room, I knew I would not be able to talk with her. It had nothing to do with the fact that I had known her in another context. It was related to her size. She was so pregnant she looked like she could go into labor at any moment. If she had asked me what my fantasies were, I would have been embarrassed to tell her. I was certain anything unpleasant I might say could begin her contractions. The interview did not go well. It was obvious to us both that we could not work together.

The next day, the nurse told me an appointment had been arranged with a male analyst. "I should have realized how difficult it would have been for you to talk with someone you knew," Dr. Schatz told me later when he came to my room. It had nothing to do with that or her being female. I did not tell him my real reason for being unable to talk with her. It sounded ridiculous. I merely nodded my head in agreement.

The analyst conducted the session in neutral territory. He arranged to meet me in a room down the hall from my room. Getting to him was interesting. Not because I was afraid of the interview. It was how I was escorted to it. Joanne, one of the nurses, walked down with me. She kept pace with me, one arm draped around my shoulders. It gave me the feeling that I might have something to worry about.

Dr. Armstrong* turned out to be a nice, pleasant person. The interview itself was fairly innocuous. "Tell me about your pain." I repeated, for the umpteenth time, how it had started and what it felt like. I answered his standard therapist question: "How does that make you feel?"

"How was it for you growing up?" he asked me. No one in my family has clear memories of their childhood. I was completely unaware of having been a child. That made it difficult for me to give him any idea of what my life had been like. He reached the same conclusion that I had already known was foregone. "I do not think you should try analytic psychotherapy." He had no suggestions about what to do for or about the pain. There had been nothing to fear nor was hope obtained. I left the meeting with both my mind, and pain, intact.

That was not the end of the attempts to appeal to my psyche. Dr. Goodman and Dr. Ericson's were still to come.

Dr. Goodman, a psychologist, specialized in hypnosis. Often, chronic pain is the result of, or made worse, by stress. When it is, relaxation and learning new ways to handle life's pressures can be very helpful. Hypnosis is one way to do that. I had no reason to believe that my own pain would be helped by it. At least I knew the therapy would not make the pain worse. At best, it might even prove to be enjoyable.

Dr. Goodman arrived at my room after 11:00 P.M. He pointed to Dr. Roeschman and Dr. Tigar*, another resident. Both followed behind him as he came into my room. "Would you mind if they observed?" he asked me. I did not mind at all. In fact, I was happy to see them. They were two people I knew, and I had become friendly with one of them. I felt slightly more secure having someone I knew in the room. Even though I was aware of the medical uses of hypnosis, somewhere in the back of my mind I still harbored the picture of the lady standing on a stage and acting like a chicken.

Dr. Goodman instructed me to lie back. "Make yourself as comfortable as possible. I'm going to talk to you for a while. The only thing you need to do is lie back, listen, and relax." These were instructions I had no problem following.

I heard him tell me about a forest, some bushes, and little animals. As he spoke, I could feel myself become more and more calm, more and more peaceful. His talk then turned to the pain. "The right side of your face does not hurt. It will not bother you anymore." *Oh no!* I thought. He was telling me the right side should not hurt. I was afraid my mind would take that as an instruction to start having pain on that side. Before I could become too agitated, I heard a voice from the end of the bed. Dr. Roeschman was whispering. "Dr. Goodman, the pain is on her left side." Dr. Goodman spoke again. "The left side of your face does not hurt." Inwardly, I breathed a sigh of relief. *It's okay,* I thought. *When this works, it will be for the left side.* That was the word I always used on myself. "When" it works, never "if." He continued to speak for a few more minutes. As he got to the end of the session, he said, "I am going to count to five. On five, you will awake, feeling refreshed and alert. One . . . two . . . three . . . four . . . five." And awake I was. I felt great. There were smiles all around. Then the resident asked Dr. Goodman how long a session usually takes.

He turned to me. "Carol, tell us how long you think this took." I did not want to seem foolish. It seemed so short a time. I added a few minutes to my answer. "Maybe fifteen minutes?" With a look of satisfaction, he replied, "You're wrong. It was forty-five." I laughed. "Come on, that's not true." "Yes, it is," he said. "It was forty-five minutes." He turned his arm towards me. I looked at his wristwatch. It had been forty-five minutes.

It had been hard to gauge the actual time. It really had felt as though only a few minutes had passed. I did not remember much of what he had said. I recalled something about a bunny and that the story had been sweet. To my mind—short and sweet. The only other thing in my memory was the suggestion that my face would not hurt (right and left) and Dr. Roeshman's correction.

I had enjoyed it. I was definitely "under," but I was totally aware of everything happening around me. I heard the conversations of the residents. I listened to the nurse taking the blood pressure of the lady in the bed next to me. The sensation was essentially one of floating.

Dr. Goodman's instructions did not take about the pain. They did about how I would feel upon coming out of the trance. It was midnight, but I felt as though I had just awakened from a great night's sleep. It took over an hour before I came down, enough to stop walking the halls and chattering to the nurses. There was also an interesting sidelight. For days, the rumor persisted that Dr. Goodman had asked me for a date. If he had, it must have been while I was "under."

I wish the relationship between Dr. Ericson and me had been as simple and pain free.

An anaesthesiologist, Dr. Ericson also practiced acupuncture. After he tried it on me, I was not totally convinced his education had been successful. Acupuncture is one of those peripheral medical treatments that I always believed to be more placebo than probable. As with the tests, though, I felt I had to give it a try.

He arrived at my room in the afternoon. We talked about the specific location of my pain. The areas of my body that corresponded to the pained area, according to acupuncture theory, were the webs of both hands and both ear lobes. He placed needles in all four. At specific intervals, he twirled them. The needles themselves did not hurt. The pain from his rotation of them was excruciating. I knew from the sensation that they had been placed directly in a nerve. Each time I complained about the severity, he answered, "That is the way it's supposed to feel. It means that the needles are placed correctly." In all that I heard or read about acupuncture, I found one constant—it was not supposed to be painful.

I liked him less and less. As he rotated and waited, he asked me how my face pain was. "Is it better yet? Is it any different?" The needles hurt so much I was of two minds: I wanted him to stop, I wanted the acupuncture to work. I was certainly willing to make a trade, face pain for hand pain, knowing that hand pain was a therapy that I could ultimately stop. I had to answer truthfully: "No. The pain is no better." I found myself continually adding a rationalization to each response. "The television's on. The light and flickering from the screen is probably why I still have the pain." Another answer, "The light in this room is very bright. That's probably why the pain is still there." I kept trying to come up with any answer that would make him stop. Finally, the right reason arrived. The treatment prescription is for twenty minutes. He had never told me the clock was the ultimate arbiter. Thankfully, on the dot, he wrapped up his tools of torment and left. When Dr. Schatz arrived that evening, I told him I did not want Dr. Ericson to touch me again. The neurosurgeon had already made one visit. If there was to be any chance of anaesthesia, I would not trust Dr. Ericson to put me to sleep.

The first time I saw a neurosurgeon was a week before Dr. Ericson started his treatments. No one broached the idea of surgery. Nevertheless, long before he arrived, I had a feeling I would be seeing him. A definite diagnosis had not been reached, so there was no reason to consider any operation. Still, I had been admitted so quickly. I was on a floor that shared neurology and neurosurgery patients. It seemed to me that a surgeon had to be waiting somewhere.

Dr. Osterholm was not eager to operate. Surgery was the last thing he wanted to do on me.

I had seen him a few times when I worked in my local hospital, years before, in the emergency room. On the rare occasions we had to call in a neurosurgeon, he was one of the ones on the list. I vaguely remembered him as a tall, very attractive man.

My memory had not failed me. Still tall, his hair was a distinguished shade of gray. His face was very handsome and calm. We talked about the pain. To my surprise he said, "I have a few ideas." My reaction was anything but calm. "What are you going to do to me?" I asked in a voice shrill with apprehension. It took a long time before I really understood and appreciated the form of his answer. "Not *to* you, *for* you."

But before he did anything for me, there was more to go through besides the debacle with Dr. Ericson.

CHAPTER SIX

The next test was done to see if deadening the trigeminal nerve would be of any benefit. By injecting a local anaesthetic into the pain area, they could see if loss of sensation would result in a cessation of my pain. A number of shots were required to affect the entire area. If a mere touch could trigger the pain, I did not need much imagination to know what a shot in my face would do. Keeping my pain words to myself not only keeps me from speaking my pain. It stops me from doing what I most often feel I need to do when the pain comes.

I do not scream. I grit my teeth, grimace, and tighten my body. It is a rare time that a sound escapes me. They were escaping now. I could not help the moans and crying. The neurosurgical resident injected the drug under my left eye. He also gave me shots in two or three places in the left forehead. The pain was enormous. It did not stop as the Novocain hit its mark. The resident seemed oblivious to my sounds and pain motions. He was not unaware of the reaction of the nurse.

Ignoring the sounds I was making, I imagine that the sight of someone being shot in the face, particularly so close to the eye, is unsettling. How unsettling became obvious when the doctor looked over at the nurse. "Are you always that white?" he asked her. He told her to sit down. He freed himself from his gloves and called on my telephone for another nurse. A nurse's aide arrived. She stood by my side for about three minutes and then asked, "Is it getting warm in here?" She, too, was told to sit until another nurse could come. Suzanne, another RN, arrived next.

She was strong enough for anything. She gripped my hand and refused to let go until the session ended. I had very minimal relief, but it was enough to put me on the surgical schedule.

There was another problem with the injections besides the shots themselves. The trouble was the two doctors performing the procedure. I did not like either of them. Dr. Martinez was a tall man of average weight. His dark brown hair, eyes, and accent gave away his Latin background. I found him to be a nasty man. I tried to keep away from him as much as I could.

The other doctor was also of foreign background. I did not know which one. A shorter, slightly stout man, he gave the injections. Dr. Martinez stayed in the background and observed. This other doctor, Dr. Markson*, gave me my first lesson in the way doctors stick together when one of them behaves badly.

One afternoon, he came into my room. He told me he had heard the hypnosis had not worked. "I can also do hypnosis," he said. "If you would like to try it again, we can do it now." My inability to say no surfaced. So did my hope. On the one hand, it seemed very odd that a neurosurgery resident would come in and offer to hypnotize me. On the other, it could not hurt to try it again. "If you think you can do it and it might help, all right."

He told me to lie back and get comfortable. He started to talk to me in the prototypically soft cadence of induction. I do not remember what he said. I only know he did not succeed in hypnotizing me. Even though I got nothing out of it, he did. As I waited to go into trance, I felt a hand on my thigh. For a minute or so, he massaged me. Up and down. Up and down.

I did not know what to do. I sat up and told him it was not working. "I'm not going into trance," I stammered. "I don't want to continue." I was so overwhelmed that he would be touching me, much less in the guise of hypnotizing me, that I said nothing. When I later told Dr. Schatz and Dr. Roeschman, they laughed. They were going to make no effort whatsoever to investigate or chastise him. I was only a patient. If a member of the staff made a sexual contact, under the guise of therapy no less, it was no big deal. Since Dr. Osterholm was my surgeon, I would probably not have to see this resident again unless he accompanied Dr. Osterholm. It seemed it would only be to my detriment to pursue it.

A few days later, I overheard Dr. Schatz and Dr. Osterholm talking as they stood outside my room. The idea of surgery was not very popular. Normally, it would be the non-surgeon who objected. This time it was not. Dr. Schatz began by saying, "I want you to discuss the possibility of surgery with her." Dr. Osterholm, to my surprise, replied, "I will not. I don't think she should have surgery." The conversation we had at our first meeting underscored his reservations. I could agree to an operation if he decided to offer one, he said. But, he added, he did not know what he would find, and he was not sure there was anything to find. The main object would be to explore.

Dr. Schatz won. A few days before the surgery, Dr. Osterholm came to my room with the consent form. He handed it to me for my signature. Then he turned to the three residents he had brought along. He murmured something to them. Then he turned back to me and said, "You need to sign this."

"Wait a minute. What did you say to them?"

He shook his head. "Nothing. Now sign the form."

It was my turn to shake my head. "I know you whispered something to them. What was it?"

Finally, he gave in. "I told them I didn't think we could help you."

I knew he was unsure of what might result from the surgery, but the directness of his doubt scared me. I refused to sign. I told him I wanted to speak with the psychiatrist first. I wanted Dr. Lanes to ease my fear by telling me surgery was appropriate. I met with him and repeated to him the conversation I had had with Dr. Osterholm. He worked non-directively. "It's up to you." I thought about it and came to the conclusion, again, that, "If it's offered, I have to try." Two days later, I signed.

Fate seemed not to want me to have surgery. I was all set to go on December 13, one and a half months after I had arrived. On the evening of the twelfth, Dr. Osterholm came to my room.

"We had an emergency surgery tonight on a man with a cardiac problem. He has B-negative blood type also and used the entire supply. Your operation has to be cancelled." "I know I won't need any blood," I assured him, "so there's no problem." He refused to accept my word that nothing would go wrong in the OR. "The hospital rules require blood on hand. We'll have to wait until the supply is adequate," he told me. "Do you want to go home and return after the Christmas holiday?"

Of course not.

"I've been here this long. I don't want to have to wait for a readmission date." More importantly, the pain took precedence. With a possible answer in reach, Christmas was the least important time on my mind.

Surgery was the most important. A few evenings before the operation, the hospital had a Christmas party for those of us able to go. A more motley bunch could not be imagined. The staff decorated the walls and a tree, but nothing could hide the various physical disasters many in attendance had experienced.

Both my parents visited that evening. They went down with me to the basement, where the party was being held. I had not wanted to go, anticipating the scene that I now found before me. As much as I had thought about the operation, I had not considered the specifics of it. One of the things I had not thought about was how much hair I would lose. Dr. Osterholm had told me my entire head would have to be shaved, but I only thought about the possibility of losing the pain. At the party, I saw my first bald patient. I did not realize how bad it would look. I can still remember turning to my mother and saying, "Oh my God! Look at that."

That was the only thing I ever said about my hair. I did not spend much time thinking about having my head shaved. Unlike most neurosurgical patients, I did not have to worry about how it would be done. Normally, the hair is taken while the patient is still awake. The only benefit of being unable to have my left head and face touched was that I would have to be asleep before the barber could come near me.

I thought I felt emotionally fine about the surgery. The falsity of that idea was demonstrated the next morning, for my parents and the staff. I did not find out how upset, and upsetting, I had been until three months after the surgery. That was when my father finally agreed to tell me what had happened.

Both my parents arrived early the morning of the surgery. I told the nurse who escorted them that I wanted to take a shower before she gave me the pre-op shots and the orderly came to take me to the OR. "I want to wash my hair one last time." She, smiling, agreed and went to get some fresh towels. I got up from the bed and headed towards the bathroom. I took a step or two. I was not aware of anything else that happened after that except for an incident in the elevator.

The orderly and I had a disagreement about my lying down and being strapped to the stretcher. I insisted on sitting up. "You can't sit up. You have to lie down. You'll fall off," he scolded me. I responded, very logically, "If you put the seatbelt on me, I will be caught if I start to fall." That was all I remembered. I suppose he won the argument.

After I came back to the floor and I was lucid, the nurses kept telling me I had them laughing for days. I thought they meant the incident in the elevator. It did not seem that funny to me, but if it kept them happy, I was pleased to oblige.

It seems their mirth was related to a much more vociferous argument. Evidently, I never made it to the shower.

The nurse and orderly got me out into the hall and put me on the gurney. It seemed I was not sure I wanted to go through with the operation. "For two cents," I kept repeating, "I'd call this whole thing off."

The residents kept saying, "It is still not too late to change your mind." I was so agitated that they called downstairs to tell Dr. Osterholm I would be arriving late. While I was loudly letting everyone know how I felt, the orderly kept telling everyone how much trouble he would be in if he did not get me down to the OR on time. Resident after resident tried to calm me. My father seriously considered revoking my permission for the surgery. Evidently, everyone who could possibly be involved with getting me to the operating room was there. Everyone, that is, except me. I was there in body but not in mind.

Finally, I arrived downstairs. Eight hours later, I returned to my floor—bald and pain free. In a surprise to all of us, including Dr. Osterholm, he found the reason for the pain. Even though my X-rays were all negative, he found some erroneous vascular connections (known as arteriovenous malformations). He relieved the pressure the vessels were causing along the trigeminal nerve. Except for an area near my temple, smaller than a dime, the pain vanished.

The surgery was on December 19. By the twenty-third, I felt well enough to ask Dr. Osterholm if I could have a pass for Christmas to go to my parents' house. I was tired of being in the hospital. I wanted to be finished with all of this. My mother had entered a psychiatric hospital a few days before, and I rarely even saw my father. I needed a break. He refused my request. It was too soon after the surgery, he said, for me to leave the hospital.

Christmas afternoon in the hospital turned out to be better than I expected. That afternoon, I heard a knock on my door and turned to find a wonderful surprise. The nurses let my father bring my sister Leslie's children up to see me. Scott was nine and Todd five. It was not only the best Christmas gift but the best day of my stay at Jefferson, except when I realized the pain was gone.

Two days later, December 27, I was discharged. I returned to my parents' home outside of Philadelphia to start my recuperation. I had a very slight fever when I left the hospital. By the next morning it was 103 degrees Fahrenheit. Back I went to Jefferson for another three days. It was only the flu. Upon my discharge, I went back to my parents' house. I stayed a few days before deciding I wanted to be home.

I returned to New York and waited the six weeks Dr. Osterholm told me to wait before I could consider my recovery over. At the end of that time, I bought a new dress and a wig and went looking for a job. A week and two interviews later, I was hired at

House Beautiful magazine as a clerical worker. It was a good job, and it paid well. Best of all, I quickly became friendly with two of my colleagues.

Blanche was an older woman who had worked at the magazine for years. After I found the job, I started to audit a graduate psychology course at the New School for Social Research. I mentioned it to Blanche and, a few days later, she introduced me to Jan, a young woman in another department of the magazine. She was also taking courses there. Our friendships worked out better than my classes. I only attended a few because I really did not want psychology.

I went mainly because I knew bald was not the way to win an audition. My relationship with Blanche, and Jan, lasted much longer than the three or four classes I attended.

Best of all, I knew I had time. The pain was over, and I had finished with Dr. Schatz. I had last seen him when I was in the hospital with the flu. He told me I should see him in his office in a few weeks. I kept the appointment, and we both marveled over the success of the surgery. As I rose to leave he said, "I want to see you for one more appointment in two months." Quickly, I said, "No. I just want this to be over with. Thank you, but I don't want to come back for another visit." "Well, I'll be here if you need me," he replied.

Such a nice man, I thought. It was a kind way to end our relationship.

Things were finally where they should be except for my acting. That was on the back burner (until my hair grew back). I did not mind my job, and I had made some very nice friends. Jan, Blanche, and I spent the majority of our weekends together. They introduced me to areas of New York I had not known about. They also reintroduced me to the world of friendship.

I had to practically promise my boss's boss that I would not become ill again. He was understandably reluctant to hire someone who had been so recently disabled. I told him the surgery was completely successful. I had no reason to believe I could not fulfill the demands of a job. I assured him that they would not be wasting their time training me.

My immediate boss, Lillian, a tall red-haired woman, first appeared to be very intimidating. In fact, she was an extremely nice person who did everything she could to assist me in learning my job.

Everything felt just right. I knew my life was back on track. In fact, I could no longer even remember how the pain had felt.

One afternoon, I was furiously typing away to meet a deadline for a report that I had to distribute the next day. It was about three in the afternoon. The paper needed to be finished in time to be copied, but I would make it. With no distractions, I knew I would be finished in about half an hour.

But then I became distracted. Suddenly I was seized by a lightning-sharp pain in my left temple.

CHAPTER SEVEN

"You knew this was going to happen!" I shouted at Dr. Schatz.
Two days after the pain attacked, I was sitting in his office.
My emotions ran rampant. I was angry, upset, afraid—very, very
afraid.

Now I understood why he had said he would be there if I
ever needed him. He had to have known that the success of the
operation might be temporary. Not that it mattered. Even if he
had told me, I would not have believed him.

I saw him twice before he suggested that I find a neurologist
closer to home. I trusted Dr. Schatz. I wanted to continue as his
patient, but he had a point. It was way too expensive, in time and
money, to continue seeing a doctor whose office was two states
away.

He did not have a recommendation. I resorted to the old
standby. My mother got the name of a doctor from a woman whose
daughter had attended my high school and now lived in Manhattan.

Linda suffered from severe headaches. After seeing several
doctors who could not help her, she found Dr. Barrett, a neurologist. A few appointments with him, Linda's mother told mine, and
her headaches were gone.

I called Linda. I explained to her who I was and how I got her
name. She told me the same story that my mother had gotten
from her mother. "Dr. Barrett stopped my headaches; I recommend him very highly." We talked for a few more minutes about

what she had been through. We also discussed how my pain differed from hers. Before ending the conversation, she reminded me of what I already knew—her success might not be mine.

Armed with her reminders, I went ahead and made an appointment. My initial reaction to him was the exact opposite of my first impression of Dr. Schatz. That should have been a clue.

I had seriously considered not going back to Dr. Schatz for a second appointment. I left our first meeting feeling that he thought the pain was psychosomatic. That had made me dislike him, at least at first. I liked Dr. Barrett.

Before doing an examination he, like Dr. Schatz, spent about twenty minutes with me in his office. After that, he escorted me to an exam room. He did a complete neurological check and seemed to know what he was doing. I felt that I was in good hands. He told me he had some ideas; we should start by my trying some drugs. My good feeling quickly turned to disappointment. I read the two prescriptions he handed me. Both were for drugs that had already been tried, at St. Vincent's and with Dr. Schatz.

Of course, a new doctor does not necessarily mean a new regimen. Because I liked him, I kept the second appointment.

I was having side effects from both of the drugs. The Dilantin, an anticonvulsant, made me feel as logy as it had the first time I tried it. The other, Triavil, a psychotropic, gave me a urinary problem.

He did not seem bothered. "Don't take them then." I had not been on them very long, about two weeks. As they had not helped before, it was not a big thing. I really had not expected that they would work this time either.

"Has there been any change in the pain?"

"No."

His response was off the wall. "If thy eye offends thee, pluck it out."

What? I thought. It seemed to be a statement made to minimize my complaint, at the least. I felt like I had returned to Dr. Lanning and his remark—"It isn't really *that* bad." Then, he said he wanted to redo the blood studies that had been done twice before. "Come back in four days. Amy [his nurse] will draw the blood then. Once I have the results, I'll bring you to the hospital for more advanced tests."

I did not know what to do. I did not want to have the tests repeated. I definitely did not want to go to the hospital.

It did not occur to me to call Dr. Schatz and ask what he thought. Dr. Barrett was not inspiring a lot of confidence in me towards him. But what else was there to do? What else could I do? He was my doctor.

If I had someone to talk to. If I had family that cared. But I had no one. The choices and decisions were mine and mine alone. The pain was the only other voice. And it outshouted my inner voice. It blocked out all common sense.

I returned to his office as instructed. Amy took me into an exam area. She had me roll up my sleeve. We talked about nothing. I do not think she noticed how much effort I was putting into not crying. She wiped down the inside of my elbow. She picked up a tube and put it on the end of the needle. Just as the needle pricked my skin, I could not contain myself any longer. "Please don't tell Dr. Barrett," I said, in a voice shaking from the effort not to cry, "but at this point, I think it might be worth it to go into the hospital rather than wait for the results."

Amy rose from her chair. "I'll be right back." As soon as she left the room, the tears started to flow.

I heard Dr. Barrett's footsteps as he neared the room. I forced myself to swallow back the tears.

"I'm going to arrange for you to come into Columbia Presbyterian Hospital. They can do the tests there."

The battle to fight the pain was becoming too hard. Every aspect of it had returned. The last thing I wanted to do was go back to the hospital. Yet, maybe, it was also the only thing I could do. I was unhappy that Amy had ignored my request that she not tell Dr. Barrett. But I was also greatly relieved.

Dr. Barrett did not have as much pull as Dr. Schatz. I would have to wait for the admissions office to call me when they had a room available. That could be in a day. It might take weeks.

The only way to wait it out without going crazy was to continue working.

Leaving the house to get to work was awful. It was May. The breezes were light. Perfect weather unless you had trigeminal neuralgia. The eye pain was made worse every time I filed a paper or typed a report. I jumped each time my desk phone rang. It took all the strength I could muster not to cry from the pain. It took all the effort I had not to break down each time the person on the other end of the phone was not a hospital admissions clerk.

Finally, after what felt like forever but was only a week, they called. As I waited for the clerk to tell me what I desperately wanted to hear, Lillian, my boss, approached my desk.

"Please come into my office as soon as you're off the phone." I had mistyped an extremely important report.

I knew that was why she had summoned me. I was annoyed with myself for having made the mistakes. I was angry with myself and the pain, that was the reason I had made the errors. I was happy that I finally had a confirmed date for the hospital. I was sad, and furious, that the pain was forcing me to go back to the hospital. She was unaware of all of this. I entered her office, unable to hold back my tears any longer. "Are you all right? Sit down." She pointed to the chair at the side of her desk. "What's going on?" *Oh boy. The last thing I needed. Someone being nice to me.*

I tried to keep my mind on work. That might force the tears and feelings into retreating. I continued standing. "I'm sorry. I know I made a number of mistakes on the report. I'll go fix it right now." Then I apologized for taking a personal call. She was not concerned about that. "I know you don't use the phone that often. Please. Sit down. What's wrong?"

That did it. Her kindness and concern zapped my last ounce

of resistance.

"It's nothing." Pain, emotional or physical, is a private matter. I wanted to keep quiet, but my mouth refused to cooperate.
"I'm afraid of going back into the hospital." I fought the effort of
my lips to turn down. "That was them on the phone. They have a
bed for me tomorrow. I have to be there at two o'clock. But," I
quickly added, "I'll be in tomorrow morning. I'll leave from here."
It was important to me that I minimize any time I would be losing.
I hoped that would help to keep her from firing me.

Mr. Baker, the executive who had hired me, had practically
made me swear on a Bible that I would not become sick again.
Given that I had only just recovered from the pain, it was not
unreasonable for him to be concerned. Would they be wasting
their time by training me?

The pain was gone. I could wash my face. I was fine. "I won't
get sick again. It's over." Dr. Osterholm had worked magic—at
least that was what I believed at the time. It never occurred to me
that, unknowingly, I might be telling a lie.

Instead of being angry, Mr. Baker was as concerned as Lillian.
"Don't worry about coming in tomorrow morning," he told me.
"And we'll hold your job for you as long as possible."

At the end of my first week in the hospital, the job was still
mine. At the end of the second week, Lillian sounded a little less
convincing. At the end of the third week, I felt guilty and practically offered the job back. At the end of the fourth week, I was
fired.

I had worked for them for only three months before the pain
returned. To allow me one week for each month worked was certainly above and beyond the call of employership.

Four weeks can seem like a day or a year. The behavior of
Dr. Barrett and his residents made the time in the hospital seem
like decades.

Dr. Barrett was an impressive-looking man. In his forties, his
black hair was conservatively cut. He carried his few extra pounds

well on a tall, seemingly fit body. He did not walk; he strode; long steps accompanied by the authoritative carriage of a doctor.

Whenever I saw him, in the office or the hospital, he was dressed in nice slacks, an attractive shirt, and most often, a suit jacket. He always wore a knee-length white coat, the doctor's uniform, over his outfit. The day he arrived in my room, dressed in a light blue striped suit, without the doctors' uniform, I had to smile.

"That's a nice suit," I said. "You look good."

"You mean I don't look professional?"

Huh? I thought. That idea had never entered my mind. Dr. Barrett seemed to believe the old saying, "Clothes make the man." Unless clothed in the definitional robe of medicine, I guessed, he felt less important. As it turned out, I would have preferred that he look less professional and act it more.

The day he told me, "If you jump out the window, you will only break your ankle," it seemed merely (merely?) eccentric and inappropriate. We had never discussed depression, suicide, or how I felt about my circumstances. I had to assume he was referring to the possibility of a suicide attempt. Since the issue had never come up between us, I could not understand why he made the comment.

It was a weird experience. Strange, but not dangerous. The next incident could have been.

Lithium is used in the treatment of manic depression. After doing my own research, I was able to accept that psychotropic medications were often prescribed for chronic pain. The research showed that the actions of the medications were on the part of the brain involved with pain sensation and interpretation. My paranoia about the pain being called psychological was assuaged by this knowledge. That was the reason for some of the drugs Dr. Schatz had tried.

Lithium had not been one of them.

Dr. Barrett told me about the potential risks and side effects.

If I became toxic from the drug, my hands would sweat. A few times a day, Dr. Barrett or one of the residents would come by and shake my hand. No sweat. No problem.

Unfortunately, I did have a problem—a big one. I was "blacking out" for a few seconds at a time. It happened so fast that I was not aware of them. I did not fall or lose control. I only lost a few seconds of time. After it was over, I would forget it had happened.

One morning, I awakened not feeling well. For some reason, thermometers were not kept in the rooms. When the nurse came in, I asked her to take my temperature. One minute, the thermometer was in my mouth. The next, it was in pieces, scattered about the floor.

The nurse was mad. "Why did you *do* that?" I had no idea what she was talking about. I had no memory of the thermometer having been in my mouth. Since I had no memory, I said nothing to anyone about it. She had apparently not charted it. My hands continued to stay dry.

One afternoon, Dr. Barrett and I were talking. All of a sudden, I noticed him giving me a very strange look.

"And?" he asked expectantly.

"And what?"

"You were telling me about your mother."

I had no idea what he was talking about. I had no idea we had been talking. The next thing I knew, a technician was drawing blood for a lithium toxicity level. It was very positive. I was being poisoned by the lithium. Dr. Barrett immediately gave the order to stop it.

I was very upset. It should not have taken my "blacking out" in front of the doctor before anyone realized I was having a bad reaction. It was a sign of an uncaring and unobservant staff.

The second incident was worse. Especially because I felt that Dr. Barrett enjoyed my discomfort.

A cocaine-and-sterile-water solution seems to help some people who have chronic pain. Dr. Barrett had me lie down on my bed. He took a cotton swab and wetted it with the solution. To reach the area needed, a cluster of nerves known as the spheno-palatine ganglion, the swab needed to be pressed up against the inside top of my left nostril. This is done with alacrity.

It hurt horribly. As always, I worked hard not to make any pain sounds. My body refused to cooperate with my will. It spoke for me as my hands turned to fists, my knuckles turning white from the effort.

Dr. Barrett smiled down at me. "You would really like to hit me, wouldn't you?"

Probably.

He told me the swab had to stay in place for twenty minutes. That was twenty minutes too many. It was awful. I wanted to sit up or move to a more comfortable position. I could not. My body had no energy. A black cloud settled in my mind. I knew people who used cocaine "recreationally." I had never understood the lure of it. If I had any doubts about it being fun, they were all gone. Nothing about it could even remotely be called pleasant.

Dr. Barrett came to the room twice before the twenty minutes was up. "Are you high yet?" he asked. The third time, thankfully, he removed the swab.

It was a terrible experience. It hurt so much when he put the swab up my nose. It made my mind and body feel awful. And it did nothing for the pain.

"It doesn't always work on the first try." He wanted to do it again the next day. "This hurt so bad. I don't want to do it again!" I said in anguish. "I'll be back tomorrow," he replied. "We'll try it again." I wanted to refuse. I could not. After all, who was I to say "no"?

I was not in control. Whenever a question of treatment came up, no matter how awful, the part of me that needed to be rid of the pain was my spokesperson. I agreed to four more treatments before Dr. Barrett agreed with me that it was not helping.

I appreciate teaching hospitals. The residents are closer to their education than the attending doctors. They are eager to learn. The majority recognize that patients come to doctors for relief or, better yet, cure. They have not yet been jaded by too many years of hearing too many complaints, of seeing too many patients and too few cures.

Dr. Stein, one of Dr. Barrett's residents, was the first one I met who seemed to feel that my only reason for being in the hospital was to teach him.

CHAPTER EIGHT

Early one morning, Dr. Stein, a dark-haired, clean-shaven, youngish man, wearing eye glasses and a short white medical coat, walked into my room. Another equally coated young man followed.

Dr. Stein carried a tray on which sat a very, very large syringe. Next to it was a very, very large needle. I was not scared. They had nothing to do with me.

He stopped at the edge of my bed. "Lie on your side."

"Why should I get on my side?" I said, remaining upright.

"We have to do a spinal tap. Lie down."

Now I was afraid. "No. No one told me about a spinal tap. I won't do it."

He was annoyed. "Dr. Barrett told you about it last night. I have other patients to see. I don't have time for this. Now lie down."

The fact that I said "I won't" did not matter. The fact that Dr. Barrett never told me such a thing was not important. I was not a person to Dr. Stein. I was only a spinal column that he wanted to tap. He tried a few more times to force me to let him do the tap. Finally, he gave up. He turned to go. His partner never uttered a word. As the two walked out the door, Dr. Stein said, "I have other things to do. Then I'll be back."

A few minutes later, Dr. Barrett came into the room. "I'm sorry. I thought I had told you about the tap last night. You need to let Dr. Stein do it. It might give us some new information." I felt outmanned and outmaneuvered. Defeated. I said, "I'll let Dr.

Stein do the tap, but I don't want him back in this room again, ever, after that." Dr. Barrett said, "That's fine." Dr. Stein got his tap. I got the results: negative.

Dr. Barrett kept his word. For two days, Dr. Stein did not come into my room. On the third day, he was back.

He acted as if nothing happened. He offered no explanation, excuse, or apology. If I had family that cared, I could have turned to them. They would have fought for me. Instead, the childhood lesson remained into adulthood: Standing up for yourself can be dangerous. It is safer to keep your mouth shut. I was stuck with Dr. Stein.

Dr. Barrett ordered repeats of many of the painful/pain-inducing tests. Another electroencephalogram. Another negative. More eye studies. More negatives. And then I met a doctor who scared me in a completely new and terrifying way.

The first few eye studies were done by a resident. After three days and negative results, I was seen by the attending doctor.

Dr. Minor* knew my diagnosis was trigeminal neuralgia. I knew he would have to touch the pain area to do his exam. I reminded him that I could not tolerate touch on my forehead, temple, and left eye. "Please warn me before you touch me, so I can prepare for the pain, okay?" He nodded his agreement. But, he did not mean it. He never warned me. Instead, for some reason, he seemed to take more touches than absolutely necessary. When he looked over at the ophthalmology aide and began to speak, I understood why.

In an accent that sounded Germanic or Austrian, he said, "This is the way you should do torture. You reduce the level of tolerance, so all you have to do is touch them." The aide and I sat there stupefied. Learning to keep quiet was not an issue. With my Jewish last name and the word Jewish written on my wristband, I was not going to open my mouth.

I returned to my room, wondering how much worse things could get.

When the neurosurgeon arrived in my room, I was afraid he would want to operate, but my main feeling was relief. This man seemed normal.

Dr. Brisman, a bespectacled man, soft spoken and slender, spoke with me for a while. After going over my history with me, he said he had a few suggestions.

One was the use of a machine called a transneural stimulator. Like the machine I had seen on the TV program so many years before. The TENS, as it is called, would be tried in the rehabilitation department. A doctor was not necessary. A therapist would explain how it worked. She would show me how to use it.

Jennie* held the unit in one hand. It was rectangular, about five inches by three inches by one inch. In the other, she held a black oval pad. This would have to be adhesive taped to my forehead.

The attaching of the pad to my face made the pain immediately increase tenfold. The pad was attached by wires to the box. The box would have to be hung to the waistband of my pants or I would have to wear a belt, something I never did. Once it was in place, she told me she would turn it on. "Only to the lowest setting. You'll barely feel it." She turned the dial. And I rocketed out of my chair.

The connections were wrong. Instead of a small dose of electricity, I felt as though I had put my hand into an electrical outlet. Despite the intensity, I only had a small red mark where the pad had been. Since it was obviously a mistake, I agreed to try it a few more times. She and I came to the same conclusion. It was not for me.

The one thing that made the pain and the waiting somewhat more bearable were the friends I had made at *House Beautiful*.

Jan and Blanche visited a few times each week. They always came with smiles and treats. One day, they brought a plant from Lillian, my boss. Another day, Monica*, another employee from

the magazine, visited. She brought with her a box of Godiva chocolates.

Dr. Barrett played the bad guy. He arrived a few minutes
after Monica left.

"I'm going to start you on a new drug today. It is what's called
a MAO inhibitor." He handed me a paper. "This is a list of foods
that you can't eat while you are on this kind of drug. The interac-
tion between the food and the drug can raise your blood pressure.
It can potentially be fatal."

Staying away from the first food on the list would not be a
problem. I hated liver. Cheese and nuts were foods I liked but
not favorites. Not eating them for a while would not be a bother.
But the next food, oh dear, was chocolate.

I pointed to the beautifully packaged box of candy. "I just
got these," I whined. "Can't we wait a while?"

"You can have one. No more. I want to start the drug tomorrow, and your system needs to be clear of all of the foods on the
list." As he turned to go, he stretched out his hand. "You don't
mind if I have one, do you?" he asked as he took a handful.

What could I say? The pain took precedence, even over
chocolate. The rest of the candy went to the nurses.

Starting the drug did not interfere with another visit from Dr.
Brisman. "I have a procedure I think might help you."

I did not want another surgery. I did not want any surgery.
Only people with something really bad, like a tumor, have brain
surgery. Not someone healthy. Not me. After all, as I continually
told myself, I was not sick. I just had pain. Despite my stomach
somersaulting in fear, I had to ask: "What?"

"I'd inject an anaesthetic directly into your trigeminal nerve.
I do this by going through your cheek. The needle is then maneuvered through a natural hole in your skull. Then, the Marcaine
is injected into the nerve." *Oh God,* I thought. *How can I do this?*
I was so afraid. Afraid of the pain, afraid of the surgery, afraid the
pain wouldn't go away.

"You'll be awake, and we'll be taking a number of X-rays

throughout to verify that the needle is being placed correctly.

"There are risks. You could lose the sensation in that side of your face. A chance also exists that you could lose feeling in your eye. There is also a chance that your pain could be made worse."

It sounded awful. It sounded workable. What else could I do? I had to say, *Yes.*

The morning of the procedure arrived. Within minutes of being wheeled into the X-ray suite, I regretted that answer.

Janine*, a nurse from the floor, came to the OR with me. She began doing all the things I was used to having done to me before an operation started. She assisted me onto the litter. She put a sheet over me. She pulled a strap over my abdomen. She picked up my hands. She placed them at my sides. (Wait a minute. This is not normal.) She put each one in a wrist restraint. She attached it to its respective litter rail.

"What are you doing?" I asked, my voice rising in fear.

"We don't want you to hurt yourself by reaching up and grabbing the doctor's hands or the needle." That did not make much sense to me. Why would I do such a thing? I assumed she knew what she was doing. She did, but she kept the real reason for the binding to herself. The procedure is so painful that restraints are the only way to keep someone from jumping off the litter with the needle still in their cheek.

Dr. Brisman determined the correct placement in two ways. X-rays seemed to be taken constantly. Intermittently, he asked me, "Do you feel the pain? Tell me where it is."

It was the pain that was so awful. He knew the needle was in the right place when it touched the trigeminal nerve. When my temple exploded in lightning.

"Please . . . ," I pleaded. I had no other words. The pain was too awful. I wanted him to stop. I had to let him keep going. Maybe, just maybe, this would be the magical procedure. They say you have to get worse before you can get better. If that was so, well, maybe this would do the trick.

Finally it was over. He removed the needle, but there was one more touch to go. "I have to touch your forehead to see if you still have feeling there." He was standing behind me. I could not see to know when he put out his hand. I did not know where exactly he was going to touch. At the moment his finger made contact, I grimaced and let out a meek groan. Both the sensation and pain were intact. He sounded truly sad when he said, "I'm sorry."

So was I. Sorry that it had not worked. Sorry that I had agreed to it in the first place. But there had not been a choice. Not to my mind. And at least I had not been made worse.

Nothing else could be thought of or offered. My discharge was scheduled. In four days, I could go home.

Two days before that, Edna, my college friend and former apartment mate, and her husband, Stan, arrived in New York. They had driven from their home in Wichita Falls, Texas, to visit with Edna's father and other relatives in New Jersey. They had planned to visit me on their way back home. It was supposed to be at my apartment, not in the hospital.

It was the first time Stan and I met. We did not exactly like each other.

Our backgrounds are very different. We had little in common. Stan was also one of those people who seemed to need to see physical evidence before believing that someone really has pain. Not unlike many of my doctors.

The first thing I do when someone visits me in the hospital is to offer them soda, and food, if I have it. It is my way of saying, "I may be in the hospital, but I am still in charge. I am in control of me. I am in control of my surroundings." Stan's interpretation was the opposite.

"It's obvious you enjoy being in the hospital," he said to me later. "You were smiling and having a good time." I *liked* being in the hospital? Not in the least.

CHAPTER NINE

I hate being in the hospital. One way of trying to make it seem a little less intimidating and frightening is to appear to have as much power, no matter how illusory, as possible. That includes setting up housekeeping.

I tried explaining this to Stan.

He is a very healthy man. He had not had a lot of experience with hospitals or what it feels like to be a patient, especially when the patient does not have something easily defined and explained. All he saw was someone not complaining. I worked very hard at not appearing ill or in pain. Pain is only visible if you express it through body positions or sounds. I did neither. He could not see it. I could not, and would not, verbalize it. It was an unwinnable argument.

A good man, Stan accepted me because I was his wife's buddy. Edna asked if I wanted to go back with them to Texas. I jumped at the chance. I needed to get away from what I was letting the doctors do to me.

Hope has no logic. Maybe if I could get away, the pain would stop. Logically, I knew it was real. I knew a change of location would not be the magic bullet. That knowing did nothing to negate the dream that some change, any change, might make it stop.

I went home for a day so that I could pack. We arrived in Texas six days later. Along with the things in my suitcase, I brought the pain, narcotics, two other drugs, one being the MAO inhibitor, and the diet restrictions. In spite of that, I intended for us to have a nice time together.

Stan had a new motorcycle. He wanted to take me on a ride with him. That meant the wind in my face and wearing a helmet. The same problems I had when Jamshyd wanted me to ride with him. I felt the same way I had with Jamshyd. If I continued to say "no," Stan would see it as my making a big deal out of nothing. It always seemed easier to agree, despite knowing what would happen.

Riding on a motorcycle was an extraordinary thing. Of course, it would make the pain worse. Which it did, in spades. The idea that merely being a visitor could make the pain worse was a concept far beyond my grasp.

Going out at night, taking a walk, visiting local sites of interest, choosing groceries—all required too much eye movement. Talking requires eye movement. Talking to two people is double the movement, double the pain.

I felt caught. It had been two years since Edna and I had seen each other. It was so important for me to be there with her. It was of paramount need to stop the pain. I was unable to stay in the moment and enjoy our time together. Instead, I spent most of my time counting down the minutes until I could go home.

I did not have the money for plane fare. I had to take a bus. The ride down had been hard enough. Each curve, pothole, and stop made the pain worse. As the car lurched, so did my eye. I thought it would be different on a bus. Because they are so large, you should not be able to feel every movement. I was wrong.

I was so miserable. I had to leave Edna's without enjoying more than a moment or two of the visit. The pain had not been affected, even a little, by the drugs, not even by the extra codeines I was taking. No matter what happened, no matter what I did or what I tried, the pain was always in control.

I spent the rest of the summer going back and forth to Dr. Barrett's office and trying new medications. He spent the summer shifting between two philosophies. One day, he accepted my description of the pain. The next, he did not. "If I can tolerate my indigestion, you can tolerate your face pain."

Had I not been seeing my therapist, Carolyn, listening to him might have driven me crazy. As a psychologist, she could not make medical diagnoses, but Dr. Ravitch, the psychiatrist who shared office space with her, could. He and I spoke on a number of occasions. He read my medical records. He agreed with me, Dr. Schatz, and Dr. Osterholm. My medical problem was just that—medical.

There were times when I tried to convince myself that Dr. Barrett was right. I often found myself thinking back to that day at my sister Cathy's house when her mother-in-law told me all I needed was a job.

Bob, one of the actors from *Hello, Dolly*, was also living in Manhattan. Between auditions, he managed a Thom McAn shoe store. I called him. I did not like having to tell him about the pain, but I did. I told him what I could and could not do. Then I asked him for a job.

He had always been a nice guy. It did not bother him. And he offered me work hours at the store. I was now a saleswoman! At least for a few hours each week.

I knew my eye would never be able to tolerate working the cash register. Bob assured me that would not be part of my job.

The store only sold men's shoes. My job was to fit them and bring out the shoes they wanted. Looking for the shoes in the backroom required that I use my eyes. That was a problem. Luckily, most of the men who came into the store knew exactly what they wanted. That spared me from having to search in the stacks. The pace was slow. That gave my eye enough time to recuperate between the infrequent hunts for the right pair and size. It was the perfect job. Unfortunately, what made it perfect for me made it ripe for change.

One day, the regional manager came into the store. "This store can't carry two employees. There isn't enough traffic. We're going to have to transfer you to another store." Oh no. Now I had to explain the situation, especially why I could not work a cash register. He, too, was a nice man. "I'll try to get them to assign you to the floor."

I was assigned to the cash register. I worked the floor on occasion. I hate to perpetuate a stereotype, but this store catered to women and children. It was the rare customer who knew what she wanted or the size she wore. This one was too tight, this one too big, this one too . . . "I don't know." I was constantly using my eye to look for another pair. Then, before I could have a chance to rest it, I would have to ring up the purchase. It was only for two days a week, half a day. But it was agony.

Quitting was a bad option. I needed the money.

After the first operation stopped working, Blanche, my friend from *House Beautiful*, told me about the social security disability program. The idea that the pain might not go away slowly seemed more real. I did not want to think of myself as disabled, appearances to the contrary, as they say, notwithstanding. I convinced myself that applying for disability benefits did not negate the chances to become able. It only made sense to put in an application.

I was again receiving public assistance. After being fired from the magazine, I had no other way to make money. Social security required that I be disabled for eighteen months before I could qualify to receive benefits. That could only happen if they determined that under their rules, I was disabled

I made $50.00 or so from the store. That helped a little. The public assistance check was small. I hated accepting it. The normal level of pain was becoming intolerable. Anticipating the increase from walking outside my door, getting to the store, using my eye in ways that I knew would make the pain worse, was a horror. Financially, physically, emotionally . . . something had to give.

One night I was sitting in the bathroom. I was getting ready to take my nightly pills. The two adolescent suicide attempts I made had been carefully thought out. When, how, where were not impulsive decisions.

I held the bottle in my hand. *The pain is so bad.* Tears formed behind my eyes. The thoughts started to come quickly. *What am I going to do?* Almost unconsciously, I poured the contents of the bottle into my hand. *I don't think I can take another operation.* I stared at the little circles of white dotting my palm. *Take them.* I sat immobilized by the voice in my head. *TAKE THEM!* The next thing I knew—they were so tiny, it was so easy—they were in my mouth and down my throat.

I shook myself aware. There had been eighteen pills in the bottle. That would not be enough. *I need to take the codeine, too.* I stood, starting to shake. I found the codeine bottle. I poured the pills out into my hand. The sight of them was mesmerizing.

They were not like the ones I had just taken. These were big and round. They tasted like aspirin, only more bitter. *I can't. It'll make me sick.* I was beginning to panic. *What if I have not taken enough? What if it is enough to hurt but not kill?*

I found the phone number of poison control in the Yellow Pages. My fingers shook as I dialed. A man answered the phone, and I told him what I had done. "I took pills, and I'm afraid I didn't take enough, and I don't have any more. Please, tell me what I should do." He asked me my age. "Twenty-six," I said. His voice sounded annoyed as he repeated the number. "Twenty-six."

"You have to make yourself vomit." He told me how to do it. I did as he instructed, and the pills came up. Even so, that did nothing to stop my fear that I might have merely injured myself. The idea of living with the pain was petrifying. The idea that my aborted attempt to die might leave me in an even worse position was untenable.

I stayed awake all night, afraid to sleep. If I fell asleep, I was afraid of a coma or brain damage. The thought was irrational. Any damage would have happened already but, "You never know." I was fine when morning came. I went to work. Pupils the size of pennies were the only evidence of what I had done.

Carolyn and I spent most of our sessions talking about the pain. I did not tell her about the pills. I certainly did not intend to tell Dr. Barrett. It was my secret; no one's business but my own.

The rest of the summer and the beginning of fall were un-eventful. I tried to concentrate on hope and a future. I knew, when the pain stopped—and I had to believe in that certainty—I would start auditioning again. I decided I had to do something to help make it a reality. I would find a voice teacher. The problem, as usual, was money.

I asked the Thom McAn store manager to relieve me of work-ing the cash register. He refused. I had no choice but to quit. I tried waitressing for a night. Looking at customers, writing or-ders, dealing plates, scanning the room to check that my customers needed nothing—my eye rebelled in pain.

I always swore there were three things I would never do: sell shoes, be a waitress, be a maid. As a struggling singer/actress, waitressing was part of the fantasy and the reality, if you wanted to eat and live. The other two were not. In the life I had now, they became the only possibilities.

I was not totally surprised when waitressing proved to make the pain worse. Could cleaning do the same? *Nah.*

My voice teacher charged $20.00 for a half-an-hour lesson. Carolyn knew someone who was looking for a cleaning lady. Mrs. Jackson* asked me how much I would charge to clean her apart-ment. I was not thinking about my circumstances. I did not think past the voice lesson. "Twenty dollars."

I should have charged more. Not that it mattered.

My apartment was very small. It did not require much work. Had I thought about it, I would have realized I always cleaned it in piecemeal fashion. Even cleaning requires eye movement. The sweep of a cloth across a bookcase, the movement of the vacuum across a long carpet . . . I had to look, and move my eyes, to do this. Even when working as a maid, the pain intruded. Something had to be done to stop the pain. To my astonishment, it was my father who initiated the next round of medical intervention.

Charlie, as I called him, agreed to see Dr. Ravitch with me. He was the psychiatrist who shared the office with Carolyn. One day, he suggested that my father and I see the play *Whose Life Is It Anyway?* He thought it would give my father a chance to see that the pain was mine. Only I could decide how to handle it.

It was a lesson he needed. He was paying for my medical care, since I was no longer at the clinic. I was very appreciative, but each bill payment came with a precondition. The first was that I see a dentist.

Dr. Gelb specialized in temporomandibular joint dysfunction. In 1978, this was a new diagnosis for some forms of facial pain. Some patients with trigeminal neuralgia get relief through dental procedures. Usually, the cause of their pain, unlike mine, is not a verifiable brain disorder.

My father decided the cause of my pain was dental.

I knew my pain was not dental. Dr. Schatz said it was not dental. Dr. Osterholm proved it was not dental. Dr. Ravitch agreed it was not dental. Dr. Gelb examined me. He took X-rays. He diagnosed it as not dental. My father still insisted it was dental.

Dr. Gelb had a suggestion. He thought I should see a nutritionist. One just happened to be on his staff.

I met with Jim*, and we talked about my eating habits. I never ate well. Sugar and junk food were the mainstays of my diet. I also found that junk food seemed to cost less than fresh produce and proteins. Twenty-five cents was easier to pay for a Twinkie than a dollar for bananas. A Twinkie did not go bad. Fresh food did. It was not as though I did not know what I should be eating versus what I did. He wrote out a list anyway, and I agreed to give it a try. He admitted that he did not think it would have any effect on the pain. It should, however, help me generally because I would be eating healthy food.

My father told me he would give me $10.00 a week. The money was to pay for the fresh fruits and vegetables. He was happy to spend $40.00, each and every month, on food. Paying for anything was fine—as long as it allowed him to deny the truth of my pain.

He agreed to go to the play. Only someone in total denial could mistake the point of the work; each person has to make his own decisions. Each chooses his own consequences. My father was in total denial. I was not aware of the depth of it until I answered the ringing phone that greeted us when we came back to my apartment.

"This is Dr. Barrett." He was returning a call my father had made to him that morning. My father took the phone. The play had had no impact. "I want you to tell her it is psychological." He listened for a minute or two then handed me the receiver.

"Hello, you wanted to talk to me?" No, he did not want to talk. "Your pain is psychosomatic," he declared. "You just need a good psychotherapist." Then he hung up.

My mouth hung open. My doctor, the person who I thought was my doctor, had joined forces with my father. A non-physician, with an agenda of his own, was directing my medical care. I could not believe the lengths to which he would go to keep me from getting the medical care I needed. That's why I was so amazed when he called me a few weeks later.

"I just talked to Dr. Osterholm. He wants you to call him. He thinks he can do something for the pain." I shook my head, checking to make sure I was not imagining things.

I did not know what had changed my father's mind. I was very curious, but I kept my curiosity in check. I did not want to say something that might jinx the change.

Dr. Osterholm only accepted calls on Fridays, between 9:00 A.M. and 12:00 P.M. It seemed that the line was always busy. I was becoming convinced that I would never succeed in reaching him. Finally, four Fridays later, I got through.

"I was in there. I know what you have. I think I can fix it." *Oh my God. Hope.*

I had to wait until January (1979), two months later, for him to try and "fix it." My nerves started to get the best of me, hope started to falter. I needed to have him reaffirm that surgery could help. This time, I got through, but he was on vacation. I was unhappy about not being able to speak to him, but it was okay. Any doctor in his practice would do. Dr. Northrup, one of the other surgeons, came to the phone. "I know about you and your problem. I've talked with Dr. Osterholm. I think you should have the surgery." That was exactly what I wanted to hear. I was afraid, but I was ready, indeed eager, to go into the hospital again.

CHAPTER TEN

It was the perfect way to start the new year. On January 15, 1979, I checked back into Thomas Jefferson Hospital in Phila-delphia. God was in his Heaven. All was right with the world. How could it be otherwise? Dr. Osterholm fixed me the first time. I knew he could do it again.

As I understood it, one of two things would happen. He would remove all the extra vessels, if possible. If not, he would com-pletely sever the fifth nerve. Either was fine with me.

The thought of having my head cut open again was not a happy thought. Brain surgery always carries bad risks.

The possibility of side effects was worrisome. The feeling of knowing that Dr. Osterholm had stopped the pain before was elating. I imagined all the things I would do once the pain was over. I visualized all the eventualities opening before me. All but one.

It never occurred to me that Dr. Osterholm might change his mind.

"I want you to try the needle procedure again." The one that had been tried a few months before by Dr. Brisman. The one that could easily be classified as torture. Worse, still, he would not be doing it. Dr. Martinez would. I pleaded with him, trying to get him to agree to do the operation. If he would not, and he really believed the other procedure might work this time, he had to do it himself.

"I already tried it. It didn't work. It was the most painful thing I've ever had done to me," I whined. I begged, "Why won't you just cut the nerve? I know that's what needs to be done." He would have none of it. "Surgery is more dangerous for someone of your age. I won't do it."

Unfortunately, his reasoning made sense. "The change in plan is strictly for your protection. And it won't be as bad as the last one. You still have to participate, but you'll be getting anaesthesia. Instead of a general the anaesthetist will give you a short-acting drug. Except for the times we need you to respond, you'll be asleep." I repeated my question. "Please, won't you operate? Like we talked about?" He repeated his answer. "No."

Oh boy, I thought. *I guess I don't have a choice.*

Something had to be done. The pain had to go.

"I'll agree," I said, "but only if you'll do it." I did not like Dr. Martinez. I had no trust in him. Dr. Osterholm refused. "I don't know how to turn on the machine."

Dr. Martinez walked into my room. "I like you better this time" were the first words out of his mouth. I did not know he had not liked me. I only knew that my feelings of distaste towards him had not diminished.

Some of the nursing staff confirmed my fears. They told me about mistakes he had allegedly made. According to them, more than one malpractice lawsuit was pending. I had no way to confirm it. I could see it being in the realm of possibility.

No alternatives were offered. I was consumed with the need to be rid of the pain. I would have to let Dr. Martinez, a doctor I did not like, do the procedure I did not want. Dr. Osterholm would not agree to anything else. He repeated, "Dr. Martinez is the only one who knows how to do it."

No one thought to suggest another hospital or another surgeon. I did not think to ask. Once again, not having a family with whom I could consult meant there was no one to remind me that other options might be available. Others can see what you cannot.

It was hurtful to have no family for support. It was also harm-

ful. When there are people who care about your welfare and love
you, they want you to have the best. They may be able to ask the
questions that need to be asked. The ones that the pain blinds
you from seeing. I trusted Jefferson. I trusted Dr. Osterholm. He
fixed me before. He fixed me there. Hope. Expectation. Absence
of pain. The influencers of choice.

Dr. Osterholm and I (and Dr. Northrup and Dr. Martinez)
agreed that the pain was from a brain defect. Nevertheless, again,
I was required to talk with a hospital psychologist. Dr. Marquette
and I met on three occasions. We never talked about my "problems." Instead, on the first visit, he told me he would be giving
me a Minnesota Multiphasic Personality Inventory. The test is
used to determine a person's emotional state. It can also address
questions as to whether a person's pain is physical or psychosomatic. I thought the issue had been cleared up, once and for all,
with the findings at surgery.

Dr. Marquette, a tall man who hid his kind smile behind a
well-trimmed short beard, spent the second meeting explaining
the test to me. The MMPI (as it is called) is a very long test. "I'll
give it to you at our next meeting. There are five hundred sixty-
seven questions. The answers will be true or false. It usually
takes about an hour and a half."

"You'll be reading the questions to me?" I asked. "No. But
I'll be here if you have any difficulty with any part of it."

I did not need to wait until next time. The problem was immediate. There was no way I could take the test. Not if I had to
read it.

"I can't tolerate using my eyes for something like that. It
involves way too much eye movement. I won't be able to do it.

"I would do the test," I said, "but . . . only if you read it to
me."

"Some of the questions will be asking you about your private
thoughts. It could be very uncomfortable for you if I were to read
them for you and fill out the answers." I would be telling my very

personal, very private, thoughts and feelings to someone I neither knew nor had reason to trust.

What the heck. To get to the surgery and the end of the pain,
I really had no choice. I had to take it. If it was too hard, we
would stop.

Some statements seemed to have no obvious point. "I enjoy
detective or mystery stories, I enjoy children, I love to go to
dances, and, I like tall women" were easy for me. The questions
to determine mental status were easy to find: "Evil spirits pos-
sess me at times, I am a special agent of God, I believe I am
being followed, I have strange and peculiar thoughts." The answers to those came easily as well.

I found it embarrassing to admit "I am easily embarrassed."
"I am likely not to speak to people until they speak to me" and
"Even when I am with people, I feel lonely much of the time"
forced me to admit out loud what I normally tried to keep private.

Some questions seemed to be inappropriate for a trigeminal
neuralgia patient living on narcotics.

"At times my mind seems to work more slowly than usual,"
and "I often feel as if things were not real" defined my reaction
to the codeine. "I can read a long time without tiring my eyes,"
"The top of my head sometimes feels tender," and "My skin seems
to be unusually sensitive to touch" defined my pain.

Only one question stumped me. "I think life is worth living."
With my face pain and long history of depression, I was not so
sure. I played mind volleyball with the answer. True or false?
True or false? Two or three minutes passed. I looked at Dr.
Marquette. He looked back at me. I could hear the ticking of the
clock in my mind. I was on the verge of false. Then hope, once
again, raised its head. In a soft voice, I answered, "True."

A few days later, Dr. Marquette had the results. He told me
what I already knew. "You're depressed. You should consider
staying in therapy." And what I thought everyone else understood. "There's no evidence to indicate that your pain is
psychogenic." The rhizolysis had already been scheduled. Would

the procedure have been canceled if the findings had gone the other way? It did not occur to me to ask.

The night before it was to be done, a resident told me I was scheduled to go to the radiology suite at 1:00 P.M. There was a lot of discussion about what type of medications Dr. Martinez would be using. The main drug would be Brevitol, a short-acting anaesthetic. That would permit them to awaken me as necessary. Before I went downstairs, I would be given another drug. This one would facilitate the anaesthesia.

The floor nurses ordered the drug from the pharmacy. The pharmacist refused to give it to them. It was too dangerous. Resuscitation machines had to be immediately available, which were not, on patient floors. Discussions were held. It was decided that the anaesthesia could be safely given without giving me the drug. That made me even more nervous than I already was.

"Relax," they told me. "Everything's arranged." I was definitely on the schedule for the next morning. I did not need to fast. I could eat breakfast. Being informed about which drugs would be used and being allowed to eat made me feel a little better. It had been torturous the first time around. These amenities made me feel the second time might not be as bad.

Morning came. Dr. Martinez walked into my room. "How are you?" he asked. "I still don't want to do this, but I'm ready to go." "You've had nothing to eat or drink since last night?" he queried. "No, I had breakfast this morning. The resident told me I was allowed to eat."

The resident was wrong. Even though the anaesthetic was not a general one, I was not supposed to have anything in my stomach. The procedure had to be put off for two days. I was angry and upset. I did not want to go through with it in the first place. Now I had two additional days to fret about it.

The second time, there was no cancellation.

An orderly took me downstairs. Dr. Martinez was there. I was there. The nurse and the X-ray technician were there. The anaesthetist was not there. Dr. Martinez was livid. We waited over half an hour before she arrived. With each passing moment, Dr. Martinez became more and more angry. I believed this time the procedure would be more tolerable since I would be asleep for much of it. I still worried about the pain he would trigger. To that, I added a worse fear—that someone in the grips of a rage was going to stick a needle into my head.

I was positioned on the gurney. I tried to see the faces, especially Dr. Martinez's. Before I could decide how mad he might be, the anaesthetist bent down to my face level. "You're going to go to sleep now." The next thing I knew, Dr. Martinez was yelling my name. "CAROL! CAROL! Wake up. Tell me where you feel the pain!" *Oh God! The pain. The pain!* I was being stabbed by a lightning-hot poker. "In my temple. Please stop," I begged. "Please." Then, they sent me back to sleep.

Asleep, awake. Asleep, awake. Dr. Martinez bellowed my name. Each time his call waked me, the agony assaulted. "Where is the pain now?" he kept repeating. "Where is it now?" I could not get away from it. Each time they brought me up to consciousness, I cried. "Please stop. Please." No one listened. On and on it went. I thought he would never stop. The anaesthetist leaned over me again. "It's over. You're going to go back to sleep." Finally. Blessed oblivion.

When I finally struggled up to consciousness on my own, I was sorry I had. Dr. Martinez had lived down to my expectations.

Before the procedure, he listed the same potential risks as had Dr. Brisman: I might lose sensation in the painful area of my face. There was a lesser chance that my cornea might become anaesthetic. If my face became numb, it might turn out to be a painful numbness. If my eye became numb, there was a chance it would become infected. If it did, or if I got something in it, I would not be able to tell something was wrong. There was a chance I could lose the eye. All were in the part of my face which was already pained from the tic.

The good news was that I still had feeling in my eye. The bad news was that I had none in my face. The pain remained. Yet the entire left half of my face, forehead to jawline, was numb. It felt as though a dentist had injected me with Novocain. If I touched that side of my face, the only way I knew it was there was when my hand felt the physical resistance of skin. The area of numbness included my left tongue. Numb, too, was the inside of the left half of my mouth. I no longer had taste in that half of my mouth or tongue. I also had trouble swallowing, so much so that my pillowcase had to be changed every few hours.

The pain had not changed at all. Except that, now, I could not feel the touch. I could not tell where or when someone touched me. I only knew I was touched because the pain was triggered. In addition, I had sharp pains in the lower third of the left side of my face, an area that had always been pain free.

Two days passed. Dr. Martinez did not come by. Dr. Osterholm did. His major concern was the status of my left eye. For the first two days, it was fine. "If you were going to lose the feeling in the eye, it would have happened immediately," one of the residents told me. I was very happy to hear that. Unfortunately, it was not true. On the third day, my eye turned bright red.

Dr. Osterholm came to my room later that day. He put a cotton swab against my cornea. I did not feel it.

Two more days passed before I was seen by the ophthalmologist. He told me my eye was no longer tearing. "It has to be covered if it's to be protected from drying out." The pain ruled out wearing a patch or any type of covering. Anything used would touch the upper two-thirds of my face and scalp. Impossible. The nurses decided to use Saran Wrap. They taped it to the right side of my face, along my forehead, over to the back of my scalp, then bloused it out over the left side of my face. I looked and felt ridiculous.

I worried constantly about why this had happened. It seemed to matter more to me than to Dr. Martinez. It was eight days before he made a visit to my room.

I was beside myself. Everything seemed to have gone wrong. No one seemed to want to talk to me about it. The resident would come by each day to ask how I was. He would listen for a minute and then leave. He did not want to know about my problems or the complications. There was only one person left to whom I felt I could turn.

I had not seen Dr. Schatz since the last appointment eleven months before. In the interim, he had changed hospitals and had a severe heart attack. I did not know if he still practiced. I called his office. I was in luck. It was his first week back at work. We arranged that I would get a pass from Jefferson. I walked over to Wills Eye Hospital, about five minutes away, my body in street clothes, my face still partially swathed in plastic wrap.

I was happy to see Dr. Schatz looking so well. He examined me, but he said, "I want you to come back and see Dr. Savino," another neuroophthalmologist with whom he practiced, "before we make any decisions."

Dr. Savino laughed when he first saw me. He pointed to the plastic wrap. "Why do you have that on your face?" I explained that it was the only way to protect my eye. After a few more chuckles, he suggested that it might not be necessary.

He proceeded with the examination. A look through the slit lamp showed no big problems. My eye did appear red and dry. A Schirmer test, holding a special paper to the eye and seeing the amount of liquid shed, showed that I did have tearing. He flicked a wisp of cotton into my eye. This was a problem. It did not know it had been touched. The numbness meant it could not defend itself. As to the Saran Wrap, "You can take it off and keep it off." He gave me an ointment for dry eye. "Put this in when your eye gets red. That will keep it moist." I spent a few more minutes talking with Dr. Schatz. Then I walked back to Jefferson, this time without the Saran Wrap.

Eight days later, Dr. Martinez appeared in my room. "Your eye is red," he diagnosed, "have you been crying?" I could not believe what I was hearing. "Didn't you see the chart?" I asked incredulously. "The feeling is gone in the left eye." "I don't have to see the chart before I come to see a patient," he told me huffily. It seemed obvious the last thing he wanted to do was find out how I was. Nonetheless, I proceeded to catalog my complaints.

He did not respond to anything I said. Except when I told him that I could not feel on the left side of my mouth, inside and out. "Everything I drink spills." Suddenly, he became interested. "Let me see you drink," he demanded. I picked up the glass. I held it to what I thought was my mouth. I promptly spilled it all over myself. "Of course, it spilled. You're not holding it to your mouth. And your mouth is closed." He did not give me a chance to respond. Without sensation, there was no way I could tell if the glass was directly against my lips. I was unable to know if the left side of my mouth was open or not.

Dr. Martinez's only response to my statement that I could not taste was to tell me, "That's not possible." He did not think to test it. After having spent so much time in the past being told that my pain was psychological, I found it easy to believe that the loss was only my imagination. To counter that, my roommate, Rebecca, agreed to help me do a blind test. I had a box of candies at my bedside. With my eyes closed, she picked out a couple of filled chocolates. I tasted them using only the left side of my mouth. Even with an inside filling as tart as lemon, I could not identify the candy. It was not my imagination. It was me.

Finally, the point came where Dr. Martinez and I could only argue with each other. Things came to a head the day I asked him, "Why didn't you tell me this could happen?" His answer floored me. "The roof could have caved in. The machine could have exploded. I did not have to tell you about that either." Talking to him had become impossible. Worse, I had become the culprit instead of the victim.

Other patients of Dr. Martinez would ask me how I felt about him. I decided to answer the same way I had about other surgeons who had operated on me. I never felt it my place to say anything. I knew my results might not be another's. I did not want him to hurt anyone else. I also did not want to interfere in another person's medical care. I gave non-responses such as, "Yes, he was my surgeon" and did not elaborate.

One afternoon, the nursing supervisor came to my room. She told me that she had heard I was saying bad things about Dr.

Martinez. I was to cease and desist. "Since you are not able to talk to him [Dr. Martinez] without arguing, a nurse will have to be present every time he sees you." They were very concerned about Dr. Martinez. No one, it seemed, was interested in me.

Dr. Osterholm and I did have one conversation about the side effects. He and a resident came into my room. My anger was enormous. "What about the numbness, what about the loss of taste, what about the fact that I cannot drink from a glass without it spilling all over me?" I snapped. "I'm only twenty-eight. I intend to date again. Would you want to take me out to dinner when I can't even drink from a glass!?"

The resident tried to calm me down. "Dr. Osterholm is too old for you," he said with a smile. I was not laughing.

Dr. Osterholm did not answer. Instead, he asked, "Have you reached the end of the line? Is this the end of your rope?" I assumed he meant suicide. I had never discussed the issue with him. I did not intend to start now. The truth is, my mind was so consumed with anger about what Dr. Martinez had done that any murderous thoughts I had were not directed towards myself.

Two days later, I was discharged from the hospital. Two weeks later, I saw Dr. Osterholm in his office. He did the follow-up for Dr. Martinez.

Dr. Osterholm told me there was nothing else he was willing to do. "I think you should make an appointment with Peter Jannetta, up in Pittsburgh." He wrote out the name for me. "This man," he said, "is one of the best trigeminal neuralgia surgeons around."

CHAPTER ELEVEN

Dr. Schatz agreed with Dr. Osterholm.

I trusted Dr. Osterholm. I had total faith in Dr. Schatz. He and I sat in his office. I was telling him about all the problems I was having. The new ones that were a result of Dr. Martinez's rhizolysis procedure.

When I first started with Dr. Schatz, we both made an effort to adapt to each other. My biggest problem was his vocabulary. Not quite a woman of the seventies, I blushed every time someone cursed. Even the mildest of oaths turned me red.

Dr. Schatz sprinkled his conversation with "four-letter words." Each time he used one I flinched. I thought my automatic reaction was inward. He was not an easy man from whom I could hide my feelings. He caught on to them early in our first meeting. "I'll try not to use those words around you." He worked hard at it. He was usually successful. "I know how you feel about my using these words. That's why I'm using them." I could not imagine what he was going to say.

"He [referring to Dr. Martinez] really f—ed you up." I felt as though I needed to shake my head clear. Was I really hearing what I was hearing? It is one thing for a doctor to suggest another physician had made a mistake. For Dr. Schatz to put it in those words! . . . Doctors are like police are alleged to be. They have their own "code of silence." There was no discussion or follow-up. He just put the sentence out there and let it hang.

My file folder lay on the desk in front of him. He opened it up. A letter from Dr. Osterholm was on the top. He took a quick look at it. "I agree with Dr. Osterholm. I think it might be a good idea for you to see Dr. Jannetta."

I didn't know what to think. I knew Dr. Osterholm had only wanted to help me. It was never his intention to inflict harm. And yet Dr. Martinez had done nothing but harm.

I never anticipated that a surgeon could make my pain worse. I never thought that a doctor would not be totally truthful about what might possibly happen to me. I felt incredible anger towards him. But that anger did not extend to Dr. Schatz and Dr. Osterholm. I continued to trust them. Since the referral came from them, I had to try.

Dr. Peter J. Jannetta had refined an operation specific for trigeminal neuralgia. The surgery was considered to be one of the best for tic. He was considered the best practitioner. In fact, the operation is called the "Jannetta Procedure."

His reputation preceding him, I harbored the hope that, if he offered to operate, he would be able to stop the pain. I also thought he might be able to repair some of the damage from Dr. Martinez's procedure.

The first appointment available was in February (1979), a month after Dr. Martinez's procedure. Regardless of Dr. Jannetta's namesake operation, I knew what needed to be done. I needed to have the nerve cut. That was what I wanted Dr. Osterholm to do. I planned to ask the same of Dr. Jannetta.

I knew the operation for which he was famous involved decompressing (reducing the pressure on) the fifth nerve. It is essentially a form of the operation Dr. Osterholm did in 1977. He had relieved the pressure that had been caused by the extra blood vessels.

Dr. Jannetta based his surgery on the theory that tic is caused by a vessel lying directly on the nerve. If one was found, it was moved away. A Gelfoam sponge was then placed on the nerve; in between the two. This, theoretically, relieved the pressure. Without the pressure, there should no longer be pain.

I did not want to participate in theory. I wanted the nerve cut. If the nerve was severed, my thinking went, it would be the last possible procedure they could do. Once they killed the nerve, it could no longer carry the pain. Once dead, there should no longer be a way to have pain.

I took a train up to Pittsburgh. My appointment was for 10:30 A.M. the next morning. I spent the first few minutes answering questions printed out on a "Trigeminal Neuralgia Protocol Form." Then I sat and paced in my mind, alternating between hope and fear.

An hour or so later a nurse called my name. She came over to me and walked with me to an examining room. After a bit, Dr. Howard Gendell, one of Dr. Jannetta's residents, came into the room. A young man with a shock of dark hair, matching moustache, and nice eyes, he introduced himself and shook my hand.

The completed information form sat on a desk. Dr. Gendell picked it up. After looking it over, he asked me the exact same questions: Where is the pain? How long have you had it? What drugs have you taken for it? Have they worked?, etc. He asked me to elaborate on some of my answers. "Okay. Sit on the table, please. I'm going to do a neurological exam now."

Every exam was difficult. I had to gird myself to withstand the pain. I never questioned if they would touch my face. I only worried when.

Dr. Gendell could not consider his neurological exam complete if he did not verify the pain. The area defines the diagnosis. He had to touch. I was very unhappy about having to allow two people, Dr. Gendell now and Dr. Jannetta later, to touch my face. No doctor would consider operating if he did not have a totally clear picture of the area. There was nothing I could do. I prepared myself for the first onslaught.

He finished his general neurological examination. Then he touched my upper left face. And set off the pain.

His eyes looked sad, or so it seemed to me. He excused

himself from the room which allowed me a few minutes in which to recover. He returned sometime later accompanied by a youngish-looking man, around forty-five years old, dressed in a light gray suit. Dark haired, and apparently fit, this man, who somehow reminded me of a teddy bear, turned out to be Dr. Jannetta. We spoke for a few minutes. To my surprise, he made no attempt to do any examination. A part of me was pleased that he did not touch my face. Another part wondered what determinations he could make when he did not check for himself.

Evidently, Dr. Gendell's word was sufficient for his deciding on a course of action. I would come into the hospital. They would do some tests. Only then would a decision be made as to the next step.

As I walked out to the anteroom, I saw Dr. Gendell. I called out his name. "Will you be doing the surgery? Which one will it be?"

His response was measured. "Until we have tests results I can't tell you what, if any, will be done."

I hated to think that I was coming back into the hospital without the guarantee of surgery. It was not that I wanted to be operated on. I did not want to get my hopes raised again. I did not want to agree to the same studies for the second, third and fourth times. I did not want to come in to be told, "Sorry, nothing we can do." Nevertheless, I could understand his reluctance. It had only been one meeting. He had only the other doctor's reports on which to rely.

"What choice is there?" said the pain.

It confused me that Dr. Jannetta did not make any attempt to examine me. As someone who may be cutting into my brain, he seemed a little uninvolved. That, in my experience, was not unusual for neurosurgeons. Their distance was usually personal, though, not professional. The others had always performed their own exams.

I came into the hospital on March 11, 1979. The residents— Dr. Gendell; Dr. Lester, a thin, quiet man with light brown hair;

Dr. Jordan, an attractive, tall, dark-haired southerner; and less frequently, Dr. Allbrink, a heavy-set man with a full head, full beard and full moustache of lively red hair—were my main sources of care. At least one of them saw me every day. Dr. Jannetta came by rarely.

I arrived in the same condition I was in as when I had left Jefferson Hospital, three months earlier. The pain was the same, the area of numbness the same, the eye was the same. The cornea numbness had not resolved. The ointment suggested by Dr. Savino was helping. I applied it several times a day. It was sufficient to keep the eye moistened. It was also tearing, sometimes erratically, on its own.

I saw Dr. Richard Jordan first. I liked Dr. Gendell, but it was to Dr. Jordan that I really took. I am a sucker for southern accents. The first word out of his mouth, and I was hooked. I found him to be as kind and caring as he appeared at first glance.

I was not overjoyed when the first thing he did was schedule me for a CAT scan. Obviously we would be starting from scratch. Again. This would be the fourth CAT scan, as it was the fourth hospital. And the fourth negative.

The results of the arteriogram followed suit. The taking of the arteriogram did not. Unlike the adversarial radiologist at Jefferson, Dr. Rosenbaum had showed that he had a human side.

Soon after we started, I felt an agonizing pain. Unlike the first time, it did not strike my face. Instead, it went down the center of my back. "Oh my God!" I screamed. The pain was incredible.

"Don't move!" he ordered me. "Where is the pain?"

Between gasps, I was able to say, "Down my back." As with the first arteriogram, my sobbing became uncontrollable.

Dr. Rosenbaum did not yell at me. Instead he explained, "The catheter is too large. It's causing your arteries to go into spasm. I'm going to take it out and replace it with a smaller one." He did not ignore my obvious distress. "If you want me to stop at any time, you let me know."

His assurance that I controlled the test was the best pain

medication he could have given me. My arteries continued to go into occasional spasms. Because I knew I could trust him to stop, I felt confident that the pain would remain this side of bearable. Together we got through it.

My crying continued throughout the procedure. As I lay on the litter, waiting to be taken back to my room, another resident came to my side. He looked down at me. "Why are you still crying? The test is over."

I learned early on in my life that crying was not a good thing. It never got you what you wanted. Also, there was hitting in my house.

At age nine or so, I came to the conclusion that my father liked it when I cried. I often felt that the reason for the hitting was to see the tears and hear the sounds. I was not old enough to make any guess as to why. I just knew that if making me cry gave him satisfaction, I would not cry. He could hit me as hard as he wanted, yell, scream, and do horribly terrible things. It did not matter what he did. I would not cry.

The difficulty is that you cannot control when and if you will do something like cry. If you actively block off that ability, you have to, by necessity, deny yourself access to your feelings. Certain emotions trigger the crying reflex. You cannot pick and choose.

The many years I had spent not doing so (despite so many reasons why I should have) had taken their toll. The only times I had no control were when I was severely ill or physically exhausted.

I never forgot an office visit to my family doctor. It was many years ago, when I was in my early teens. I felt awful; I had a very red, sore throat and was exhausted. I was running a fever of 104 degrees Fahrenheit. Dr. Berkowitz asked me how I was feeling. My answer was to break into sobs. It was not because I felt so awful. It was strictly a physiological reaction.

On my next visit, I felt much better. The fever and strep throat were gone. I did not cry.

"Oh, I see you are feeling much better this time," he said with a smile. I said nothing. It had nothing to do with how I felt. Weakness had made me weak. The strength that allowed me to reinforce my emotional fortress had returned.

It took the combined force of severe and unexpected pain, and fear, before the invisible moat between my conscious mind and my feelings could be crossed. Once I started to cry, it was very difficult to stop. A faucet had been opened. It required a wrenching of my will to close it off.

After all of the pain that the doctor and I endured, the results were the same as before—negative.

Next came a visit by a neurologist. This one, like all the others, had nothing to add. He did have something to question. "Why are you smiling?"

There were many lessons taught in my childhood. This was another that taught me how to control my emotions. How to hide what I felt.

As a child, I learned that no matter what you feel, you smile. Being sent to my room for an infraction was the punishment. The lesson, spoken outright, was: "I don't care what you feel. You do not come out of that room until you are smiling!" Unfortunately, I never unlearned it. In fact, as I got older, I seemed to smile more. The worse things got, the harder I grinned. The more I grinned, the more convinced this doctor became that a large portion, if not all, of my pain was psychological.

I did not report having pain while we talked. That most probably added to his perception.

I had the background aching-type pain. It was always there. So accustomed to it was I that when asked if I had pain, I would usually shrug my shoulders or say "no." I assumed the question meant increased pain.

My pattern of thought had not changed since my admission to Jefferson Hospital. I came into the hospital because I had pain. I saw no reason to constantly reaffirm that. When the doctor brought his hand close to my face to see where the pain was, the pain started. He said the pain resulted from my suggestibility. "Because you're expecting the pain to come from touch, then touch makes you think you have pain." I knew he was wrong. My expectations did not cause the pain. I believed that when the lag-in-pain change came in 1977. When it did not come immediately it must have been because I needed to remember it was supposed to start. I had come far enough to know that explanation was bogus. My pain was real.

I had no better explanation. I could not explain what made the pain begin. So I responded with my old standby. I smiled. Apologetically, I added, "I don't know why I feel the pain before you touch me. I just know that I do."

The ophthalmologist suggested the same treatment ideas that had/were already being attempted. He found nothing in his eye exams to explain the pain.

Finally, some new things.

I was sent downstairs to see an audiologist. Since I had no complaint about my hearing, it seemed a little silly. But then, so did the consistent repetition of the other tests. Besides, I did not think these tests could hurt me. It was the putting on of the earphones that did. I tried to put the left side of the headset against my left ear. It was very hard and large. It touched against the left side of my face. And it triggered the pain. Sue*, a young dark-haired woman with a kind smile, was only too happy to accommodate me. "You don't have to do anything that you think will make the pain worse." I held the left speaker away from my head but within hearing distance. The results were the same as always. Nothing wrong with my hearing either.

The second test was an electromyogram of my face. It would test how well my facial muscles, on the left side, worked.

The trigeminal nerve has two functions. One is sensory, the other motor. Dr. Martinez had left me with injuries to the former. That was why I no longer had feeling in my left eye, face, and mouth.

I did not know for which movement functions the fifth nerve was responsible. I looked fine. My face moved well.

I supposed that the test was ordered to check for non-visible motor damage to the trigeminal nerve. Neither Dr. Jannetta nor the tester told me the results. I assumed they were negative.

On March 15, three days after my admission, Dr. Jordan came to my room to discuss the proposed operation. "We have scheduled you for tomorrow morning." The procedure would be a repeat of Dr. Osterholm's surgery. Dr. Jannetta would be doing a Jannetta Procedure.

I learned my lesson from Dr. Martinez. I did not intend to take anything for granted. I had written out a list of questions.

I began by asking the usual: Where would the surgery be on my skull? What exactly would Dr. Jannetta do? How long is the recuperation period? What are the chances this will stop the pain? I had to trust that Dr. Jordan, as the designated spokesman, would tell me the truth. He answered them all. Then he added the usual risks. "There is always the potential of stroke, coma, or death from any operative procedure." I knew that. That was not where my concern lay. The next question was the most important.

"Can my face be hurt in any way?"

I wanted to be certain that I could not be disfigured. Before Dr. Martinez, it had never occurred to me that my appearance could be at risk. I had learned from him that I could not assume anything. I thought the motor function of the fifth nerve was solely responsible for facial movement. This was why I asked Dr. Jordan specifically about the chances of damage to my appearance. It was the hope of going back on a stage that kept me going. I could not afford an injury to my face. "Your face can't be hurt."

The next morning I woke early. I waited for the orderly to come fetch me. Instead, Dr. Jordan came to the room. "We've decided to cancel the surgery. Dr. Jannetta wants to try some other things."

CHAPTER TWELVE

The first "other thing" was a psychiatric consult. Again. Given that surgery had already been scheduled, it made no sense. Dr. Jannetta had not sat and talked with me. Nor had anyone else. There was neither reason nor explanation. What could I do? I had no option. If they decided no surgery, go psychiatric, I had no say in the matter. Unless I went home. That was not a choice. As long as the surgery was still being touted as a possibility, I had to stay.

Two days passed. The only medical person I saw was a medical student doing his psychiatric rotation. I did not see an attending psychiatrist. I did not see Dr. Jannetta. I received no new drugs or tests. It did not matter. They rescheduled the surgery. Once again, for the next day. Morning came. I waited for the orderly. Instead, Dr. Jordan came to the room. "You won't be going to the OR today." No reason was forthcoming.

An internist visited me that afternoon. Dr. Miller* sat on the edge of my bed. He was a nice man, gray haired, probably in his fifties. He gave me time to repeat my medical "resume." He resurrected the idea of a body-wide vascular disorder. He was the first who did not insist I repeat all the blood studies that had been ordered during every other hospital stay I had had since the spontaneous blood clot in my leg in 1971. His only suggestion was that Dr. Jannetta collect all my old medical records. He thought it was important that they be evaluated. Other than that, he had no ideas.

The other visitor was Dr. Millward, the psychiatric resident.

He was in his twenties, had light brown hair and wore glasses. He wore a short white medical coat over his tan trousers and blue-and-red, lightly striped, white shirt.

He seemed to be a nice person. He spent about twenty minutes with me. "I don't know. Maybe hypnosis could help you."

Dr. Goodman's efforts at Jefferson Hospital had not helped. In addition, sometime after the pain returned, I had seen a psychiatrist in New York City who specialized in hypnosis.

I had been very nervous about seeing him. I was afraid he would tell me I had psychosomatic pain and that he could not help me. I knew that was not the truth, but I feared it just the same.

Dr. Herbert Spiegel is one of the premier pain hypnotists. One test he does to determine a person's hypnotizability is an eye-roll test. The ability to roll one's eyes up into one's head has something to do with trance potential. I knew any attempt to roll my eyes would trigger the eye movement pain. I knew that even this visit, to a doctor who would not touch my face, would be pain provoking. And it was. What it wasn't was helpful. Except to my psychological state. "Your problem *is* organic. I don't think what you have is amenable to hypnosis." I had no reason to believe that a third try at hypnosis would be any more beneficial. I did not want to seem disagreeable. I told Dr. Millward I would think about it.

A day later, an attending psychiatrist came to see me. A little older than Dr. Millward, Dr. Horn had Janis Ian–type hair, unruly and, in his case, short. Over his brown eyes, he wore a pair of wire-rimmed glasses. The shirt he had chosen was yellow with brown stripes. He was not wearing a doctor's uniform.

We talked about whether I should or should not have another surgery. "I believe surgery should be done only when there are objective indicators," he said. I shrugged my shoulders. "I agree." It made no sense to me that a debate still lingered over whether the pain was real or not.

Dr. Schatz showed me the texts. Dr. Osterholm described finding a lot of vessels that did not belong. Both had proved to me, beyond any doubt, that my pain had an anatomical cause. Unfortunately, it never took much to convince me that my pain could be psychosomatic. If a doctor told me it was subjective and a result of my psychological makeup, I was easily swayed.

The medical team seemed to be of two minds.

Dr. Allbrink, the resident, became actively involved in my care. That was because he subscribed to a theory.

There is a brain chemical, serotonin, that is involved in pain perception. When the level is low, pain perception may be increased. Dr. Allbrink wanted to try a medicational and nutritional regimen. If they could increase my serotonin level, maybe they could reduce the pain. If it worked, it would be great. No surgery would be necessary. Only a better diet.

He ordered a blood test that evaluated my nutritional state. It came back normal. He decided to go ahead anyway. One part of his therapy did not please me. In addition to the codeine that I continued to take, he started me back on Elavil, the psychotropic drug that I had been given in every other hospitalization, which was always of no avail. Added to that was another drug, Clonidine. This, too, has, among its many uses, an action on the psyche.

I had to drink a can of Sustacal with each meal. This is a chalky, thick, unpleasant-tasting drink that contains large amounts of various nutrients. It would, hopefully, increase my blood levels of serotonin, as well as other pain mechanism chemicals.

I choked down the drink; I swallowed the pills. Neither had the desired effect. The Sustacal might have increased my nutrition. It may have made my body healthier. I suppose that in itself was a benefit.

The pills only made me tired. The tyranny of the pain persisted. Added to it was the emotional trauma. Only eight days had passed, but the twice-canceled surgery made it seem longer. They kept dangling in front of me what seemed an answer— surgery to cut the nerve. Like the donkey and the carrot, each time I thought the hope for relief was within reach, they yanked it away.

I spent the next few days taking the drink and the drugs. No other therapies were tried nor other tests attempted. I saw Dr. Millward again. He did not come to try therapy. He asked me for a favor. "Would you be willing to let me present you at the weekly psychiatric conference?"

The boredom of being in the hospital was getting to me. At home, I knew there would be a break in the day when I could go out. I controlled my own medication. I alone decided when and where I would take it. That allowed me to get out, read, and do other things that I knew would make the pain worse. Doing these things, even though it meant drugging myself and suffering more physically, helped me to make it through each day. If a psychiatric conference would give me something, anything, to do, then I was amenable.

The meeting was scheduled for the next afternoon. It lasted about an hour. I sat in front of a circle of fifteen psychiatric residents and medical students. I did not notice any notebooks or recorders. Men and women, mostly young, sat around attentively. Dr. Millward gave them a synopsis of my history. "Do any of you have a question to ask Ms. Levy?" Some did. Most were about the pain itself. They did not ask me about anything embarrassing or terribly personal. They were respectful of both my feelings and my privacy. I assumed it proved interesting to them. In any event, they had nothing to offer. To me, it was of benefit. It gave me one hour less sitting in my room, waiting.

Dr. Jordan came to see me every day. Unlike some of the medical people, my ability to speak medicalese did not intimidate him. Instead, his actions showed he appreciated it. He came into my room one afternoon, carrying a copy of an article he had found. "I think you'll want to read this," he said, handing the papers to me. "This is what you have." The article gave me the reason why I kept hearing, "I have never seen this before." The article had been published in the journal *BRAIN*. In 1942.

The article described a brain syndrome called Bonnet-

DeChaume-Blanc. Trigeminal neuralgia is one of the possible symptoms of this vascular disorder. The authors discussed the type of aberrant blood vessels that had been seen in my eye. They mentioned, too, the vascularized birthmark I had that delineated the area of pain.

The fact that it could change was an interesting finding. Dr. Schatz had always pointed it out to the medical students and residents he brought to my bedside. His threat to "expose himself" had a long-term effect. Like Pavlov's dogs, all he needed to do was mention the fact that a blush would change the mark. I automatically blushed in anticipation of his joking threat. No joking matter was the fact that the article suggested that such a birthmark was diagnostic. It mentioned other signs and symptoms that I did not have, such as seizures and mental retardation. Although I did not fit the picture completely, thank God, I felt I was finally holding something in my hand that said I had a legitimate reason for the pain. The article made me wonder why I was having so much trouble getting people (doctors) to believe my pain.

After the second thing Dr. Jordan offered me, I realized I bore some of the blame.

I asked for a pass to leave the hospital, but I had nowhere to go. I just needed to be out of there. Dr. Jordan asked me if I wanted to go with him to the medical library. "It's just a few blocks away. If you'd like to come with me, you're welcome." I happily took him up on it.

I felt that once we were out of the hospital, we were two people, not doctor and patient. I would not say or do anything to make the trip medical. When the wind started blowing, it embarrassed me that I had to put my hand up in front of my face to try and protect it. I felt foolish. I commented that I hoped he was not uncomfortable with the way I looked as I walked. He said, "No." Then we went on to talk about the weather and the library.

"Why don't you just look around?" he suggested when we got there. "I have to get some books. I'll be finished in a while."

While we talked, I had one of the spontaneous tic pains. The last thing I wanted was for Dr. Jordan to know. "I think I'll just look around," I said. I quickly walked away. I found a little alcove where I felt I could not be seen. I stayed there until the pain stopped. The lightning lasted for less than half a minute, as always. As I started to come out from my hiding place, another stab started. It was not common for the pain to repeat, but sometimes it did. This was one of those times. I had three or four attacks. I waited for a few minutes to make sure they were finally over. I went back out on the floor. A while later, I met up with Dr. Jordan, and we returned to the hospital.

Later that evening, he came by the room to talk. This was his last night. He was going to continue his residency at another hospital in the South. He commented that I seemed to do fine that afternoon. "Maybe the pain is not that debilitating," he said. I finally had an opportunity to find out why some doctors' perceptions of me contradicted my reports of pain.

"Did you notice that I walked away from you today?"

"Yes," he answered. "I thought you went to look at the books."

There was no reason he should not have thought that. After all, that was what I said I was going to do.

"No. The pain was terrible," I said. "I kept having the spontaneous ones. I went over to the corner where I could have them in private."

"Why didn't you say anything?"

"You were doing something nice for me by letting me accompany you. I didn't want to make it a medical situation."

"Oh." We chatted for a few more minutes. Then he said goodbye.

Dr. Gendell took over the brunt of my care. I had been on the Elavil for only three days when he told me they were going to take me off of it. I had not seen nor talked with Dr. Jannetta about the drugs or anything else. I knew the drug usually took two or three weeks to work. It made no sense.

The date was March 24. His next statement explained it all. "We've put you on the OR schedule for the twenty-seventh." I gave him a questioning look. "Is this going to be canceled, too?" He said, "No. Dr. Jannetta is leaving for Germany that day for a lecture tour."

I was no longer sure if I was ready for surgery. It seemed that they would start a new treatment or suggest a therapy only to stop it before getting the results. I would ask, "Why am I being .put on the OR. list only to be taken off?" And they would say, "We're still trying other things."

This time surgery would happen. The reason was simple. "There's no choice. If you want the operation, you have to have it then or you can't have it. Dr. Jannetta won't be here after the twenty-seventh."

I telephoned my parents. They had been calling me. They said that they both wanted to come up for the surgery. Even though it always ended badly, I asked them to come. I needed to have someone there for me. We had spoken after the first and second scheduling. Both times, there had not been time for them to get to Pittsburgh. This time, they had three days.

Both parents were in my room. My father stood to the side. My mother sat on the edge of my bed. Dr. Jannetta and Dr. Gendell entered the room. They remained standing at the end of the bed.

Dr. Jannetta explained the procedure. He asked me if I had any questions. I had already asked Dr. Jordan about the possibility of injury to my face. He had said, "No." I asked Dr. Gendell when he told me the surgery was scheduled. He told me that it could not happen. In a separate conversation with my mother, she told me he said, "The trigeminal nerve is an inch away from the facial nerve. There is no way we can injure it." My father also reported to me a similar conversation he had with Dr. Jannetta. After Dr. Martinez, all three of us worried about my face. I felt I had to ask Dr. Jannetta directly. The question was so important I asked it three ways. "Can my eye droop? Can my face be hurt? Can it be injured in any way?" I asked in a rhythmic cadence.

He gave me the same answer he had given my father. "I PROMISE you your face cannot be injured."

I prepared for the surgery. I felt confident that it would work. After the second time it had been scheduled, they allowed me another day off. That time, I went shopping. I was so sure it would work. He had not made a pledge as to the pain being fixed, but I hoped.

I wanted to be ready. I went to a drugstore. I took my time picking out just the right color and brand of mascara. I took my time at the bookrack. It hurt me to look through their offerings. That was okay. I wanted to get exactly the right book. The kind that I had been waiting to read through, cover to cover, without having to stop because of pain. I picked a mystery.

Once I awakened from the anaesthesia, I would be able to touch my face again. I would be able to wear makeup. I was certain I would be able to read as long as I wanted. No assurances had been offered that it would work, but with Dr. Jannetta's reputation preceding him, I felt I had a very good chance.

On March 27, I finally went to the operating room. It had been explained to me beforehand that it was standard to spend a day or two in the neurosurgical ICU after the procedure. I awakened there a few hours later. My parents were at my bedside. As I moved my mouth to say, "Hello," they watched in horror. Dr. Jannetta had been wrong. The left side of my face was paralyzed.

CHAPTER THIRTEEN

I knew something was wrong by the look on their faces. "Nurse!" they yelled in unison. One ambled over to the bed. She glanced at me and then quickly glanced away. She said nothing. Rapidly, she walked back to the desk. I saw her pick up a phone.

A few minutes later, Dr. Jannetta walked into the unit. I was very surprised to see him. Dr. Gendell had said he would be leaving directly after my surgery for his trip to Germany. I had also been told that while he was operating on me, his son was having an emergency appendectomy at the Children's Hospital on the opposite side of town.

He stood at the side of my bed. He looked down at me. He seemed preoccupied. I assumed it was because of concern about his son. "How is your son doing?" I asked him. "Fine," he said as he put his fingers together by my left ear. He rubbed them together. "Can you hear that?"

"Yes."

"Okay."

The scene was repeated four times that evening. Each time, he said nothing. Except to ask if I could hear the rubbing together of his fingers. He did not explain why he kept asking about my hearing. He said nothing about the surgery. He never asked if the pain was gone. Each time, he walked away as soon as I said I could hear the finger scratching. I tried to call after him, to no avail.

The nurses and residents were also acting strange.

Pam was a pretty dark-haired nurse. She was one of my nurses before the surgery. She shared some stories with me about her boyfriend and other things going on in her life. She liked coming into my room and chatting. In the NICU, her attitude changed. I could not even get her to give me pain medication. Each time I asked her, she gave me a weird look, one I could not interpret. She would not respond to me. It was hard work even getting her to respond to my bell. "What do you want?" she would ask in a harsh voice.

Dr. Gendell and I had had a friendly relationship. I knew nothing of his personal life, but we chatted at times. About nothing in particular, but he laughed at my jokes. He responded to my chatter. Now, he could barely look at me.

He came into the NICU the next morning. He nodded at me. "Do you still have the pain?" "Yes."

He nodded again.

"How long am I going to have to stay in here?" I asked. He did not answer. He turned away instead. I tried to get his attention, but he ignored me. He was walking over to the next cubicle. I got out of bed and followed him. "Can you tell me how long I will have to stay in the unit?" I asked him again. He wheeled around. "You are not supposed to come after me! You're supposed to stay in that bed," he snapped. He was obviously angry with me. I had no idea why.

No one had yet to tell me what was wrong. Or even that something had gone wrong. It was truly bizarre. I had absolutely no clue as to what I must have done to make people so mad.

I developed a urinary infection. I could not use a bedpan. I convinced the nurses to let me walk the few steps to the bathroom. There was a mirror in there. I know I must have looked at myself. I must have seen the paralysis. How could I have not? And yet, I do not know when I finally learned about it.

My mind has a very effective way of dealing with the intolerable. It blocks out the awful.

I had no memory at all of my childhood. Through analysis, many years later, I learned that there had been sexual abuse. I

tried very hard to make it not true, but the circumstantial cor-
roborative evidence, as well as long-term behavioral symptoms,
gave truth to the returned memories.

One specific incident of unawareness happened when I was
driving in a severe blizzard. Carol, my friend, and I were on our
way to visit a college in upstate Pennsylvania. The weather was
fine when we left Ambler, but within less than an hour, we were
caught in a blinding snowstorm. All of a sudden, the car started
to skid. I remember the first second of it, during which I was still
aware of what was happening. Then nothing.. When I "came to,"
the car was stopped. It was turned around, about fifty yards in
the other direction from where we had started. I had steered beautifully, hitting neither the medial strip nor the grassy area next to
the shoulder. I was not aware of any of it, and yet I had kept us
both safe.

There had been two other incidents where this happened. In
both instances, my safety was severely threatened. I think the
same thing may have happened when I looked into a mirror for
the first time. I cannot remember looking in the mirror. I do not
recall seeing, or acknowledging, what must have been there.

After two days, an orderly brought me back to the regular
floor. I wanted to be back there. It was noisy and nerve-wracking
in the NICU. I could not get anyone to talk to me. The nurses on
the floor had been nice. I assumed that once I was back where
things were not always hectic, things would go back to the way
they were before the surgery.

I was wrong. Everyone treated me like a pariah. I must have
done something wrong to make people so mad at me. I just had
no idea what it might be.

Before the surgery, some of the nurses would come into my
room just to chat or watch the soap operas. Since the surgery,
they would rarely enter the room. They no longer came by to see
if I needed anything. If I wanted medication, I had to ring my
bell. They would come in the room just long enough to give me
the pill. The rest of the time, they stood at the door almost as

though it was a room of contagion. If I had something to say, they cut me short. Being ignored was infuriating, but they never came into the room long enough to give me a chance to express my rage. There was only one explanation I could think of. As long as they did not spend time with me, they could pretend nothing had gone wrong. Maybe that was understandable. After all, that was what I wanted to do, too.

The paralysis was complete. I could not move any part of the left side of my face. Most importantly, I could not close my left eye. I had to go back to using plastic wrap, as I had been forced to do after the Martinez surgery. Something had obviously gone wrong.

Dr. Jannetta had promised me nothing would happen to my face. *What happened!* I repeatedly asked myself. "What is this? Why is this?" I repeatedly asked anyone who would listen. No one would or could tell me. It was a question no one wanted to hear. Despite what had happened to me (and the fact that his son was recovering from surgery), Dr. Jannetta, too, escaped. He went to Germany. The only people responsible for my care now were the residents.

Dr. Gendell came to my room every morning. He could not, or would not, talk to me. I literally could not get him to meet my face.

I was furious. The pain was still there. There was no change in it, not even a little. Dr. Jannetta had disfigured me. I knew that now.

Dr. Gendell would only talk about the need for eye care. The eye had turned a bloody red. There was no way to keep it closed. "You have to keep the plastic wrap on. There's no other way for it to be kept safe. Otherwise, it'll dry out." I tried to ask him all the questions that overwhelmed my thoughts and emotions. "How come?" "What happened?" "What will happen?" "Will the pain go away?" "When can I leave?" He turned from me each time.

No matter what my level of fear, volume, or supplication was, he would not reply. He either got angry—"I have other things to do today besides spend all my time here"—or walked out the door.

I did not know what to do. I had no one to talk to. My parents were never nets of safety for me, but almost anyone would have been better than nothing. My father left the hospital after I went back to the regular floor. It was decided my mother would stay with me.

For the first three days, she acted the same as she had the other times. She sat in a chair in the corner of my room. She kept her sunglasses on throughout the day. She almost never raised her head. She said nothing. On the fourth day, she talked. She still could not look at me. But at this point, someone, even someone who could not be the kind of person I needed, was better than no one.

I was consumed with an overwhelming rage. My mind felt like a pressure cooker perched above a high flame. I could feel the bubbling of the rage. It roiled and boiled under a thin veneer of control. I had reason to be upset. It had happened to me, and no one would tell me why.

The anger that the staff directed at me made no sense. It was as though they blamed me for what had happened. For the way I looked. For the thing that they could not ignore. I asked to see a psychiatrist. I could not get anyone to listen to me. This way, someone would be forced to. Except that he never came.

I was essentially responsible for my own care. How on my own I was was brought home to me during an exam by Dr. Allbrink.

One morning, Pam, the nurse, came into my room to give me my pills. She put them down on the breakfast tray. Without a word, she turned to leave. "Could you wait a minute, please?" I asked her as I pulled the neckline of my gown away from my neck. It was damp at the area of the incision. "I think something might be wrong." She took a cursory look. "You must have washed your hair and gotten it wet." I had not. I told her so. She shrugged with her mouth and shoulders and left the room. Ten hours later, Dr. Allbrink came by. I mentioned that my neck was wet. "It started this morning."

"Why didn't you tell anyone?"

"I did. I told a nurse."

He was very upset. "Who did you tell?" he demanded. "I should have known about it then."

For some completely irrational and unknown reason I wanted to protect Pam. "I'd rather not say. I don't want to get anyone in trouble."

He let it go. But I did not get off as easily as Pam. He insisted on doing a spinal tap. Drainage from the site can be a sign of infection, even meningitis. For once, luck was with me. It was a signal of nothing.

After a few days, Dr. Mark May came to my room. A tall, somewhat large man, he was an ENT specialist who subspecialized in the facial nerve. The small world that neurology and neurosurgery inhabits gave us a pleasant social footing. We talked about Dr. Schatz, someone for whom we both had affection. He looked at the records he had brought with him. He studied my face. After repeated requests that I make various expressions, with no success or even tiny movement on the left side, I asked him, "Is this going to go away? When will I get the movement back?" He did not feel he could tell me anything about what recovery, if any, I could expect. At least not until another EMG was done.

I returned to the same testing area and the same doctor who had done the pre-surgical test. After he completed it, he told me he would compare today's test results of the facial nerve with the original graph.

"What do you mean? I didn't have any tests on my facial nerve?"

"Yes, you did. That was the nerve we tested the last time."

I had not known that. His statement made me aware, for the first time, that there were questions about my facial nerve even before the surgery. He had not told me, after the original test, what it showed. This time, he made no effort to keep the results from me.

"It doesn't work," he said, as he removed the leads from my face.

"What doesn't work?" I asked. "The machine?"

"No. Your face."

His words hit me like a sucker punch to the stomach. It took my breath away. My mind went blank.

When I got back to the floor, the nurses advised me that plans were being made for my discharge. The post-hospital plans were for me to be detoxified from the codeine. That made no sense. They had kept me on it throughout my stay. There had never been any suggestion that I might be addicted to it.

Donna, another floor nurse, told me the "doctor," she never said who, told her to tell me that I should consider giving hypnosis another try. "Don't forget, you need to keep that eye covered." No doctor came to talk with me. Nobody mentioned the paralysis. Nothing was said about what I should do about the pain.

No one was on my side. Surgery had been performed instead of the psychological approach that had been repeatedly procured and discussed. The operation had not helped the pain. I was disfigured. "I don't get it. How can they discharge me without any kind of plan?" Donna had no answer for that question.

I doubted that they had operated because it was Dr. Jannetta's last day in town. They must have agreed on the physical basis of the pain. Somehow, though, they felt it acceptable to discharge me with nothing more than a repeat suggestion that I try hypnosis.

After telling me the plan, they sent me downstairs to see Dr. Folk, the ophthalmologist. He was a large, affable man. "Your eye is in trouble," he said. He told me there was good reason to have concerns about it. "I want to see you every day until your discharge," he said. "It's of utmost importance that you continue to keep that eye covered. You must continue to wear the Saran Wrap." The paralysis included my ability to blink, or even close the eye. Unable to do either, it was left open to catch any infections or foreign bodies that happened to float by.

My discharge did not take place immediately. For three days, I stayed in my room. There were no attempts at any therapy, for mind or body. Dr. Folk was the only doctor I saw. Each day, he reaffirmed the danger for my eye.

My feelings ran the gamut. It was hard to stay with one for any period of time. All of them were negative or painful.

I was discouraged, worried, and frustrated. *Why couldn't he have stopped the pain?* I hated Dr. Jannetta and Dr. Gendell for having done this to me, for having taken away my face, my identity. For stealing my dreams. I could not bear to look at myself in a mirror. How was I going to face the world? Depression, loneliness, bitterness all raised their specter. Why don't I have a family? Why do I have to go through this alone? The reality ate at me. The truth of what they had done was almost too large a burden to bear.

The staff behaved as though it was my fault. They kept away from me as often and as far as they could. The emotional pain of dealing with the paralysis almost overwhelmed the physical pain of the trigeminal neuralgia. Dr. Gendell and I could only fight. I kept asking, "Why?" "How?" He never answered. He would get mad instead. Always over nothing, but then, that was the point—to talk about anything but what had happened to me. With no one willing to talk to me, I again asked to see the psychiatrist. It was obvious that everyone involved in my care agreed on one thing. Anything was better than directly confronting the issue.

I asked more than one nurse to call psychiatry. Everyone was upset. It seemed that getting someone to talk with me, or at least listen to me, would benefit us all. They said they would, and then never followed through. Finally, I made the call myself.

Dr. Millward, the resident who had seen me earlier in my stay, came to my room during his lunch break. He gave me twenty minutes of his time. He deflected all my attempts to express my anger and frustration. He could not, or would not, deal with either what they had done to me or my rage over it. I did not see anyone else from that department. Technically, I did not even see him. At least, according to the official record. When I obtained a copy of it, I found he had made no notation in the chart. I was totally on my own.

Finally, Dr. Gendell and I had it out.

"I'm leaving, even if it has to be AMA [against medical advice]."

"Don't you want to wait until Dr. Jannetta returns?"

Huh?! I said in my mind. Dr. Jannetta had left the night of my surgery. No one wanted to talk to me about that, the pain, or anything else. Why would I want to wait to see him? For that matter, why would I want to see him?

"Will it make any difference?"

He said what I expected, "No."

I felt like screaming. I wanted to scream all along, but this was worse. We were playing some kind of game. Maybe if we ignore everything that had happened and invoke Dr. Jannetta's name, it will all go away.

The *coup de grace* came when I went back to see Dr. Folk. Even though it was a Saturday, he told me he would be coming in. He did not. Instead, I was greeted by a first-year resident.

I exploded inside myself . . . The anger swelled, roaring thoughts at me. *Even Dr. Folk doesn't care. The one guy I thought I could trust! He said he would be here. He was the only one who treated me like a human being.* Now, I could not even trust him. Then, to make matters worse, which should have been an impossibility, I could not trust his resident.

I knew the condition of my eye. I knew I needed to continue the treatment Dr. Folk had started.

Dr. Folk had given me a lubricating ointment, the same as Dr. Savino had recommended after the procedure by Dr. Martinez. It helped, in conjunction with the plastic wrap, to keep the eye wet and covered. I knew that the worse thing I could do was use an antibiotic. With an infection, you need one to kill off the bad bacteria. Specific formulations kill off specific germs. Using the wrong one can remove good bacteria that are of benefit. If there is no infection, this opens up the environment for one. I was not surprised when the resident told me his plan. He prescribed an antibiotic.

I was beside myself by the time I returned to the floor. Not only had they taken my face, as I had come to think of it, but a first-year resident was telling me to do something I knew could hurt me. I didn't know what to do. I told the floor nurse that I was leaving. "I'm getting out of here as soon as I can!" Then I went back to my room. I packed while I tried to calm down.

My poor roommate had been very kind through all of this. She indulged my moods without intruding on me. That morning, I had to do something physical. I went for the first thing I could find. Something that would not hurt anyone or anything. I kicked my night table.

I had not thought of, or even noticed, the large paper cup of Coca-Cola sitting on the end of it. The table moved slightly. The Coke was another matter. It went sailing. Soda spewed through the air. It splashed everywhere, discoloring the bed, walls, and floor. It did not help to release my anger. Instead, embarrassment and shame were added to my emotional stew. I stormed off to the bathroom. I took a deep breath, or two. Then I got a handful of paper towels and mopped up the mess.

No one was concerned or interested in why I had taken the action I had. Not one person asked me about it. Instead, Marge*, another nurse, told the doctors that I had purposely thrown the Coke.

"She's in a rage. She can't be trusted."

Contrary to her statement, I was not out of control. That is why I intentionally picked an inert object. No one cared about the truth. It was important that I should remain the bad guy. Maybe that was how they relieved themselves of feelings of guilt. Of the knowledge that is usually kept under lock and key—that sometimes people are badly hurt instead of helped.

"You're going to have to go to another room," Marge said. "Linda's* [my roommate] expecting company. Who knows what you might do!" I had immediately apologized to Linda. She was sick. The last thing she needed was my fury. But she understood. "I don't blame you. I can only imagine how you must be feeling." She knew I did not throw the soda.

I could not take it another minute. I phoned the hospital manager. "I have got to get out of here!" I told him. "People are yelling at me and on top of that I am being given dangerous treatment by the ophthalmology resident. This is not a place of health or help. It's a place of torment."

After a while, he came to my room. I assume he spoke with the staff first. He agreed that my discharge was a good idea. There was a problem though. Only one train a day went to New York. It had already left. I had no choice. I had to stay in Pittsburgh.

I had no money. I could not afford to buy a plane ticket or pay a taxi driver. Luckily, everyone's eagerness for me to leave spurred them on. My sole purpose in staying would be to remind them of the horrors they could perpetrate. No one wanted that. The manager arranged for the hospital to pay for one hotel night and the taxi. Donna, one of the nurses, lent me $10.00, so I could afford to eat.

As I waited for the papers to be processed, Dr. Folk revived a bit of my trust. He called me on my room phone.

"I'm sorry," he said. "I'd forgotten, until now, that I was supposed to come see you." He listened as I spun out my tale of horrible diagnosis. "He gave me a script for an antibiotic even! I can't use that in this eye!" He agreed with me. "Absolutely not," he said. "You can't put antibiotic in that eye. It can make it worse."

More important than the right treatment was the fact that he continued to treat me as a person. And a person who knew what she was talking about. We talked for a few more minutes. Then he repeated his reminder that I needed to have good supervision of the eye. "I'll do that, really," I said. I listened, but my attention was elsewhere. My mind was concentrated on getting out of Pittsburgh.

A taxi picked me up and deposited me at the Hilton. I was exhausted, but I finally felt safe. The next day, I felt even safer as the train pulled away from the station. I wanted to leave Dr. Jannetta and Pittsburgh far behind. Because of the damage that had been done, it was a wish that would remain unfulfilled.

CHAPTER FOURTEEN

My parents and I decided I would stay at their house for a few days. That was not where I wanted to go. But I knew I could not go back to my apartment. Looking into a mirror or watching someone else's face react to mine were constant reminders of what Dr. Jannetta and his residents had done to me. On my own, I did not know how I would have reacted.

The problems that resulted from the loss of sensation after the rhizolysis procedure at Jefferson Hospital had been bad enough. The numbness in the left side of my mouth meant using a straw every time I wanted to drink. Eating was also a problem.

I was in the hospital cafeteria with my mother. She had visited a couple of days after the procedure. She bought me a plate of spaghetti. As I ate it, the sauce dripped down my chin. My inability to feel if my mouth was closed or not resulted in the food not always staying in my mouth. After that, I never went anywhere without a mirror in my pocket. I never finished a meal without checking to see if my face was clean.

I did not think of it all the time. If I had a snack, for instance, I did not always remember to look. Shortly before I left for Pittsburgh I was comfortable enough to drink without the straw. If I held my lower lip up to meet the rim of the glass, I was okay. Either that or I would take one little swallow at a time. I even stopped checking my face every time I ate.

Because of the paralysis, my mouth no longer closed properly. I had to use a straw again. I always checked in my mirror now. Food continued to drip down my chin. But it also fell out of my mouth. I could no longer chew with my mouth closed. My chewing manners went the way of my facial movement. Out of the question.

Discomfort, vanity, and embarrassment turned out to be the least of it.

At the end of the week, I learned the hard way what Dr. Folk had meant when he talked about supervision of the left eye. No one had spelled it out to me, specifically. I had not been told what horrors might have to be done to it in the name of protection.

I was in jeopardy of losing my eye. It had turned bright red. I continued wearing the plastic wrap. But it was no longer helping.

I had been out of the hospital for four days. I wanted only to recoup my physical and mental strength. Instead, I had to see a doctor.

Dr. Juan Arentsen, a corneal specialist at Wills Eye Hospital, seemed like a very aloof person. Tall and large, he spoke with a South American accent. I did not have time to think, one way or the other, if I liked him. I was just worried about my eye. He examined it using the slit lamp machine. "This is not good. I want you to come back tomorrow, so I can look at it again."

I returned home and went back to see him the next morning. Dr. Morrison, one of the residents, saw me first. He indicated that I should be seated again at the slit lamp machine. "I think it might have gotten whiter." I said to him with a smile. Unsmiling, he answered. "It's not going to get any whiter."

I sat in the examining chair and waited for Dr. Arentsen. My thoughts were spinning. *Of course it'll get whiter. Nothing's going to happen to this eye. I know it.* I used my thoughts to reassure myself.

As Dr. Arentsen entered the room, so did Dr. Laibson, the senior partner. He looked at me as he walked towards my chair. Three to four feet away from me, he stopped. He turned to Dr.

Arentsen. In an almost-angry voice, one I don't think I was sup-
posed to hear, he said, "Why wasn't it done yesterday?" Dr.
Arentsen's answer was beyond my imagination. It was brutal.
"It's too ugly. I didn't want to do it unless I had to."

"It" is a tarsorrharphy. Dr. Arentsen told me I would have to
have the eye sewn shut. It was unable to protect itself any other
way. If I did not have it closed surgically, there was a very distinct chance I would lose it to an ulceration or infection. He told
me I had to have the surgery. I felt numb and far from my body.
Yet, from some unknown place inside me, I was still able to hear
and answer. I nodded my head, "Yes, I agree." As I sat in the
office, Dr. Arentsen told one of the residents to call the operating
room. "Tell them we want the next room that's available." It was
10:00 A.M. I was scheduled for 1:00 P.M.

I could not speak. There was nothing to say. Dr. Jannetta had
already done the worst that someone could do. When he took my
appearance away, he also took my hopes and dreams. If I could
not stand looking at myself in a mirror, certainly, no one else
would want to look at such a face on a stage. Surgically closing
my eye was merely one more insult.

My mind could only take so much.

Dr. Morrison seemed to be concerned that I showed no reaction. He stopped me in the hall as I walked to the admissions
office. "Do you understand what is happening?" he asked me
gently. I nodded and continued on. I felt like I was in a dream.
Or, more aptly, a nightmare. Part of the feeling had to do with the
pace. This was not a time to dawdle. There was no time to make
decisions. I was a marionette. The doctors and my eye pulled the
strings. I had no say in what was happening.

My father met me at the hospital and went with me to the
admissions office. I knew, or assumed, he meant to be a comfort.
He would not listen to me though. Over and over, he kept repeating, "This is hell. This is hell." It was. It was my hell. But it was

obvious it was his, too. How could I say anything? Anything I said would have made matters even worse. Although that hardly seemed possible.

Finally, I was sent upstairs to a room. My father decided, at my urging, that he would return to work. I sat on the bed counting the minutes.

I was so tired. I was less than a week out of the hospital, recovering not only from major surgery but from an emotional beating. Now they were hitting me in the psyche again. My mind was aswirl. I wanted so badly to sleep. Fear kept me awake. *If this was a dream and it felt so bad, what might happen if I slept and had a dream within the dream?* The fright was too real. I forced myself to stay awake until the orderly came with the litter two hours later.

I was still asleep from the anaesthesia when I was taken back to my room.

The next morning, Dr. Arentsen came to see me. It was early. I had not yet been in the bathroom. I had not yet seen the horror he had wrought. There was no indication on his face as to how bad I looked. After all, he was used to it. "Go ahead and do what you need to. I'll be waiting in the exam room at the end of the hall."

I changed out of my dirty hospital gown. I put on the clean one a nurse had left on my bed. I thought about what I might look like as I put on a robe over the gown.

There had been neither phone calls nor visits. No one seemed to be interested in what had been done or how I was doing. As always I was alone. There was no hand to hold or shoulder on which to cry.

I steadied myself and walked into the bathroom. I braced myself to look into the mirror.

I wore no bandage. There was no buffer between me and "it" when I came face to face with myself in the bathroom. *Oh my God. What did they do to me? Oh no. NO!* It looked disgusting.

For my first look, it did not help that blood had encrusted itself around both lids and the eye. In addition, it was not closed completely. Maybe if it had been, it wouldn't have looked so bad. It would have been just a closed eye. This was something else. This was monstrous.

I looked in the mirror. The lids on both sides of the eye were sutured shut. A small area in the middle lay unsewn. I stared at it. I wanted to look away, to pretend it was not there. Just like the onlookers at an accident. My eyes sought the wreckage that used to be my open left eye. The left pupil stared back at me.

Feelings and thoughts assaulted me. Rage, anger, disgust, horror. Emotions that had no names. I wanted to smash the mirror. I spoke out loud. "This cannot be right. People don't have things like this done to them." I tried to convince myself of that. *Oh God*, I pleaded. *What happened?*

Dr. Arentsen was waiting. I had to calm myself. I did not want anyone to see me feeling like this—that I could work at changing. I did not want anyone to see me looking like this. That was something about which I could do nothing.

When I had the blood clot so many years before, I lost the pulses in my foot. I was very afraid they were considering amputation.

I was taken into a room with seven vascular surgeons. They looked at the X-rays. They discussed the options. I was so frightened. To not give in to my fear, I decided I would look at this as an opportunity to learn. As long as I could make it impersonal, I could close myself off from my feelings. It was me about whom they were talking. That knowledge had to be ignored. Only then would I be safe from the emotions breaking through. I worked the same thought magic on myself now.

Thinking of it as a thing, rather than a part of me, I understood why he had left the opening. There had to be access. Otherwise, he could not examine the eye. I even knew why he had done this to me in the first place. It was of no consolation. I knew how it looked. I knew how I felt. Dr. Arentsen may not have shown any sensitivity when he said how ugly it would be. He had, however, spoken the truth.

The one thing, the only thing that kept me going was the notion that this would all be over.

I kept telling myself it was temporary. Dr. Jannetta had said, "I promise you your face cannot be injured." Surely, this was a mistake. It would go away. No one said anything, but it had to be the truth. It was the only way I could keep hope. I think the thought that it would end, at some point, was what kept me sane. Certainly, it was not Dr. Jannetta.

I returned to his office for my six-week follow-up visit. I was first seen by Mr. Bissonette, a non-M.D. surgical assistant. He asked me about the pain.

"I'm going to examine you. Close your eyes."

"Are you going to touch my face?" I asked in fear.

"No. I'm not going to touch you there. Close your eyes."

I had not learned from my experience with Dr. Jannetta. I closed my eyes. And he touched the left side of my forehead. And set off the pain. Not an apology or a word did he express. He turned toward the door and said, "Dr. Jannetta will be in, in a few minutes," and left. Speechless, from the pain and his lie, I sat on the litter, fighting off tears.

A short time later, Dr. Jannetta strode into the room. He was trailed by a resident. The resident stood near me. Dr. Jannetta took a stool over in the corner. He did not come close enough to me to see the amount of paralysis. He did no neurological testing. "How is the pain?" was his only question.

He left it up to me to mention the paralysis. I had thought about what he might say when I asked him why he had not told me it could happen. *What might be his excuse? Maybe, he would say, "I did tell you. You must have forgotten." Maybe, he would blame my intelligence. "I told you, but you must not have understood." Maybe, he would apologize.*

"Why didn't you tell me this could happen?" I asked.

His answer was one that had never occurred to me.

"I have done four hundred of these, and it never happened to me before."

It still had not happened to him. It happened to me! I was astounded. He was not saying that the paralysis was not a possibly known side effect. He was saying it was not a possibility because he had been the surgeon.

The rest of the appointment went by in a blur. He told me he wanted to write to a neurosurgeon in Argentina about another procedure for my pain. He rose from the stool. I stood. We walked towards the door. He opened it and gestured for me to walk through. "Well, good luck to you then."

I was numb. He gave me no explanation for what had happened. He did not test to see what level of paralysis there was. He made no suggestions for testing or therapy.

I did not know where to turn. No one accepted responsibility. No one made any attempt to fix what had happened. I had nowhere to turn. So I turned in the same direction others turned when the medical profession turned on them. I looked for a lawyer.

I did not immediately think about seeing one. The thought first came to me after Dr. Martinez equated not telling me about the loss of taste, etc., with not having to tell me, "The machine could explode, the roof could cave in."

I had no time to pursue the thought. I was in Pittsburgh three months later. I also believed that Dr. Jannetta might be able to fix the things Dr. Martinez had "broken." No one said that, but I thought that was one reason why I had been sent to him so quickly. If he could undo it, then there would be no reason to go after Dr. Martinez. Instead, both of them injured me and injured me severely. I would have to sue both of them.

The decision grew out of my anger—my anger about the lies, the loss of taste, the addition of pain where there had been none before, the disfigurement, the additional injury to my eye. If those were not enough, it also came from the world.

CHAPTER FIFTEEN

I knew I looked disgusting. When medical people see people who are physically damaged, they act normal. They are accustomed to seeing the worst that can happen to the body. The people in the street and in my family were not.

Actually, that is not quite accurate. My sister, Leslie, who had worked as an X-ray technician prior to having children, acted the most repelled.

Often, she was one of the first people to see accident victims after they arrived in the emergency room. Broken, bloody bodies were not unknown to her. When I had the first surgery, she would not come into my room without knocking. She told me she wanted to give me time to put on my turban. It was not that she thought I was uncomfortable being seen without hair. She could not accept the way the baldness looked. Given her disgust at my hairlessness, maybe I should not have been so unprepared for her response to me now.

"I do not want you to see Scott and Todd [her children, my nephews] unless you have your sunglasses on," she ordered me. "They are not to know or see what is wrong with you."

That was a hard order to follow. Scott, age eleven, was not very interested. Todd, age seven, was much more curious. Every time we talked, he did not look at me. He looked at my left eye. The sunglasses that I now wore, both indoors and out, were not opaque. Anyone standing close to me could see through the lens. It was obvious Todd wanted to know exactly what it hid.

I know how a child's imagination can work. I knew that, often, the things dreamt of are worse than any reality. Finally, I could stand it no longer. I asked him if he wanted to know about my eye. He said, "Yes." Before I took off the glasses, I explained to him that I had had surgery.

"My eye does not look very pretty. The doctor had to sew it closed. There's a little hole in the middle. It's pretty bad looking." He still wanted to see.

"Are you ready?" He nodded. I took off the glasses. "Oh," he said. Now he knew. He seemed fine about it. As Todd and I talked, me sunglass-less, Leslie walked into the room. She gave me a murderous look. She ordered Todd out of the room.

"How could you do that?" she yelled. "I told you, you are not to take off your glasses in front of them!" I tried to explain that Todd needed to know. "He's always staring into my left lens. He wants to know what's under there. He needs to know. Then he doesn't have to imagine even worse things." My reasons did not matter to her. "If you take them off again, I won't let you see either of them, ever."

This was not my first problem with her. She had often expressed her distaste for my predicament. My financial situation seemed particularly disagreeable to her.

Leslie seemed offended that I was on welfare. I was offended that I was on welfare, but I was not going to let myself be humiliated into living off my father. That was the choice.

I prided myself for not becoming dependent on my family. Leslie complained to me that I talked too much about being on assistance. I was not aware that I did. Maybe it was true. I thought I was handling a very hard situation fairly well. If I talked about it too much, I suppose the reason was hope. Hope that someone in the family would say they were proud of me. Many people would choose to go back to their family. Even though we did not get along, it was still an option. I chose, instead, to fight. I was very hurt by the fact that no one was recognizing the effort it took to stay independent, to not give in to the pain. My comeuppance came during a conversation with Scott, Leslie's oldest son.

I was visiting at his house. We were standing in the family room. I was dressed casually. As always, I was wearing penny loafers with a penny in each shoe.

Scott looked down at my shoes. Then he looked up at me. He pointed to the pennies. "Are you wearing them to let people know how poor you are?" An eleven-year-old does not come up with a thought like that on his own. I suspected he must have heard it from his parents. No matter where I went, I seemed to get slapped in the face.

I could find no source of comfort. I felt that most keenly when I returned to New York. I was always aware of how many incredibly attractive people lived there. Often, I would see famous models and actors. Everyone was gorgeous.

No one said anything about possible surgeries or exercises. I was stuck with my immobile left face. Dr. Schatz and I had not discussed any other treatment for the pain. After the duo of Dr. Jannetta and Dr. Martinez, I did not want to be cut again. I now had to consider how I was going to deal with my time. I did not want to think about my appearance.

But I found I had to. My anger over my face was not going to disappear. I thought I controlled it. It turned out there was at least one situation where it controlled me.

To get to Carolyn's (my psychotherapist) office, I had to walk past Lenox Hill Hospital. After a while, I noticed something strange. People dressed in white gave me questioning looks when they caught my eye. I could not figure out why. Not until I started to become aware of my behavior. Unbidden, each time I saw someone dressed in what looked like medical clothes, I would give them a dirty look. Anyone, whether in a butcher's outfit, white cotton pants, or a nurse's uniform, caused my eyes to get small. My jaw clenched. It took a very conscious effort to stop myself. Strangers should not get the daggers that were meant for Dr. Jannetta.

The other thing I had to deal with was my life.

Every day, I would find something that needed to be done. I would compute the amount of time it would take to complete what I thought of as "the task of the day." Then I would wait.

As I had realized shortly after the pain started, 2:00 P.M. was the warmest part of the day. I continued to arrange my day around 2:00 P.M.

The mornings were not so bad. I had the afternoon to look forward to. The evenings were the hardest. Every night, my thoughts were the same: *Is it going to be the same tomorrow? How am I going to get through another day with the pain?*

I hated the pain. I hated the drugs. I hated how they made me feel.

Dr. Schatz and I were still trying different pills. None of them helped. I was still taking codeine. It continued to make me feel awful. When I started them, one-half grain made me feel like I was walking in a fog. I now took half a grain every two hours. The fog never lifted. I could not understand people who took drugs for fun. I never found any enjoyment from them. My greatest joy would be to not have to take them.

I could not believe that the next day would be the same as the last. I often found myself thinking, again, that this was all a dream. When I woke up, it would be over. Ultimately, of course, I knew it was reality. It would be impossible for so many people to populate one dream.

My waking dream was that I would go back to acting and singing. The dream was an intermittent help, but every time I tried to hang on to it, my face would come screaming into my memory. I tried to reduce my awareness of it by not looking into mirrors. I tried never to eat anything in public. Then I would not have to use the mirror to check my chin and cheek.

I hung on one day at a time. If I made it to the night, I could stave off the emotional agony. At least until the next morning.

The night gave me two benefits. If I was asleep, I could not think about the pain or my face.

The other was that I never had pain while I slept. Each time a doctor asked if the pain awakened me, I always felt suspect when I told them, "No." It seemed that if the pain was really bad, it should keep me awake.

When I developed the occlusion in my leg, one of the first symptoms was cramping. It would awaken me at night. With tic, not being waked by pain is a diagnostic sign. No one knows why, but trigeminal pain is not triggered during sleep. I had been unable to lie on my left side in my usual sleep position. I could not take the chance of my face hitting the pillow. Once I turned on my right side and fell asleep, I was unaware of the pain until I awakened the next morning.

Summer became fall, and fall, winter.

I had to increase my codeine. When I started taking it in 1977, I took half a grain every four hours. I was now taking up to fourteen grains a day. I had to reduce my time outside. By January, I could not take more than a half an hour out-of-doors. Some days, I had no choice but to remain inside. Between the wind, the cold, and my inability to wear a hat, winter was mostly intolerable.

In November, I found enough courage to stop wearing my sunglasses indoors. I would do this when I was around people I knew. I was tired of everything having a red cast to it.

In December, I decided I would no longer wear my sunglasses except outside. It was circumstance that forced my hand.

I was coming back from the *Nutcracker Ballet*, at the Academy of Music, in Philadelphia. This was my personal tradition every Christmas. Although it hurt my eye terribly to watch the movement of the dancers, I refused to give it up. It was worth the extra pain and increased drugging. The audience was mostly made up of families. Being there and watching and hearing the children let me pretend that I was part of one.

Leaving the theater was difficult. There were so many people. Many of them behaved as though they had to get out of the building as quickly as possible. To the left and right of me, people were using their arms to push others out of the way. The less anxious swung coats and hats and gloves around as they worked their way into them. Wending my way through the crowd was an exercise in fear. Fear that someone or something would touch the left side of my face. Horror that the tic might be set off by the inadvertent touch of an arm, coat, or glove.

Once out on the street, I assumed I was safe. I had to watch where I walked. I needed to take care that I kept a good distance between me and others. Just in case. I was in control of the proximity. It would be my fault if touch happened.

As I reached the door of the train station, I breathed a sigh of relief. No wind, no leaves, and fewer people. I felt much more secure.

To get to the main floor, I had to go down a long flight of stairs. I was wearing my sunglasses. The station was poorly lit. I stepped down on what I thought was the first step. I went flying through the air. Over and over I went, tumbling down half the stairway before coming to a stop. What looked like the first step had been the second. If I had not been wearing dark-lensed glasses, I probably would not have missed it.

My left wrist took the brunt of the fall. I felt nauseated and like I was going to pass out. I heard that was how you would feel if you broke a bone. I went to a policeman. "I think I broke my wrist." I did not want to go to the hospital they suggested. He asked me to move my fingers. I could. "If you can do that, then you didn't break anything." I took the train back to my parents' house. I waited for them to come home from a party. It seemed to take hours. Finally, I heard their car in the driveway. I met my father at the door. "I think I broke my wrist."

Both wrist bones were broken. We went to Chestnut Hill Hospital, where I had volunteered. Not only was I disfigured, I had also gained weight. Dr. Habboush was on duty. We had been friendly when I worked there. I was embarrassed by how I looked now.

He and the nurses kept asking me about the pain in my wrist. I barely noticed it. I had to keep my eyes moving to answer all of them. The hospital lights were unbearably bright. I kept taking codeine tablets. No matter how many I took, I could not get the pain under control.

The pain in my wrist barely registered. Not even when Dr. Habboush pulled hard on it to get the bones back in alignment. All I cared about was getting out of there as soon as possible, so my eye could calm down.

My arm and hand were in a cast for six weeks.

I always had one medical pride: No matter what else I had, I had never broken a bone. My embarrassment was not worth it. The glasses came off.

My emotional pride was tied up with my perception of myself as a healthy and able person. To maintain it, I tried to hide more than just my eyes. I tried not to admit to the pain. I would find any excuse to leave a room rather than say I needed to rest my eye. People probably wondered why I had to go to the bathroom so often. And why it always took me half an hour. I preferred they think I had a weak bladder rather than know I could not take the pain for one more minute.

Sometimes, my friend Jay, or others, would comment that the pain must not be too bad. I stayed even in pain-producing situations. No one ever saw me take a pill. This was another trick at which I had become very adept.

I never left my apartment without a bottle of codeine in my purse. I always made sure I had three pills in my pocket as well. I knew how many I had taken by counting the amount of times I refilled the pocket. I made sure no one was watching as I took a pill. If they were, I would cough and cover my mouth. No one was the wiser that a pill had slipped between my lips.

The charades, the weather, the pain—a triad that made the winter physically and emotionally difficult.

Dr. Schatz and I went back to discussing various surgeries. Neither he nor Dr. Jannetta was aware of my intention to sue. He had written to Dr. Jannetta, asking if he had any other ideas. Dr.

Jannetta wrote back that he would write to the surgeon in Buenos Aires.

Dr. Schatz and I had our first argument. He told me about the letter. I was not interested in going to South America. "Is there anything else I need to do medically with Dr. Jannetta?" I asked him. I wanted to make sure there was no need for any further follow-up.

"No. Why?"

I trusted Dr. Schatz. It never occurred to me he would want to protect someone who had injured me. Especially after his candid statement about what Dr. Martinez had done to me.

"I'm going to sue Dr. Jannetta because of what he did to my face. He promised me this couldn't happen."

He sounded angry. "Well," he said, "I don't want to have anything to do with this."

The call ended with both of us feeling wronged. I was afraid that his feelings about the suit would make him abandon me as a patient. He disagreed with what I was doing, but I had not misplaced my trust. He did not cut me loose. Instead, he began a correspondence with a neurosurgeon in California.

Television, again, informed me first. While in the hotel, in Pittsburgh, I had seen a program called *Lifeline.*

The program showcased a different doctor each week. They were shown in the operating room, on rounds, and in their private lives. One of the surgeons was a Dr. Charles Wilson. Dr. Schatz had not told me the name of the doctor to whom he had been writing. *Wouldn't it be funny if this is the guy?* I thought as I watched the show.

Dr. Wilson wrote back to Dr. Schatz in the middle of January (1980). He did have a surgery in mind for me. He would wait to hear from either Dr. Schatz or me.

The show filmed him performing two operations. One involved a woman with a hemifacial spasm, a movement tic (or spasm) in the face. It was caused by vascular compression on her facial nerve. Dr. Wilson relieved the spasms by removing the cause of the compression. Mine might be the fifth nerve instead of the seventh. But if he fixed her, it seemed to me, he could fix me.

The second surgery was on a man with vascular tortuosities in his back. The procedure was extremely complicated. Dr. Wilson had to move various vessels. Some of them had to be relocated to a very sensitive area. In the middle of the operation, he left the room. He wanted to take a breather to decide whether he should continue or not. Vessels were where they should not be. Normal landmarks were obliterated. He needed time to evaluate whether or not he should continue. He decided he should not.

Both operations were decompression procedures. That was what I needed. The operation for the facial tic was much easier than the one on the man. I could not afford to think about that second operation. I focused on the first. After all, if he could so easily cure her tic, I knew my success would not be far behind.

CHAPTER SIXTEEN

The first thing I had to do was figure out a way to get to San Francisco. There was no way I could afford to buy a plane ticket. Not on the $352.60 per month I was receiving from public assistance.

The only possible way would be to ask my father to lend me the money. His answer did not surprise me. "I'm not going to give you any money. Not if it's to have another operation."

He feared what might happen if I got cut again. I was afraid of that, too. My fear was tempered with hope and necessity. His made him deaf.

Dr. Ravitch and Dr. Schatz both spoke with him. "Carol has no other non-surgical options left. She's exhausted them all." He did not want to hear that. He acted as though it had never been said.

The scope of his denial made him blind to the truth as well. Even when it was placed directly in front of him.

Dr. Schatz knew what I had. He knew what I needed. He was also aware that my father was refusing to help me get it. He called me on the phone. "Do you think that your parents could come with you to an appointment? Maybe if I explain the situation to them directly, it might help."

The three of us went into his conference office. "Mr. Levy, I asked you to come in today so that we can talk about the disorder Carol has. I want to show you what the books have to say."

His nurse helped him get three very large multi-paged textbooks from the top of his bookcase. The first he opened to a large map of the brain. It was like being shown a map of Pennsylvania.

"If you look here [and here, and here]," he said, using his finger as a pointer. "These are the areas where Carol's anatomy is unusual." He found a small line. "This is the trigeminal nerve." His finger began circling more generally. "I want you to notice the way the blood vessels look in this picture."

He opened the second book. The diagram was equivalent to a township map. It zoomed in on the fifth nerve as a local map zooms in on a hometown.

"The trigeminal nerve looks like this. As you can see, it is not enrobed in blood vessels." He looked up to see if either parent was following what he was saying.

My mother remained silent. My father nodded his head as though he understood.

Dr. Schatz thumbed through the third book. Finally, he found the page he wanted. "Mr. and Mrs. Levy, this is a description of the syndrome Carol has. It is the reason she has the pain. It talks about the exact kind of extra vessels that she has. These vessels are what is causing the pain."

With his finger, he marked the specific paragraph that summarized the difficulty. He turned the book around so that they could read and see the diagrams for themselves. They both bent slightly forward. They appeared to be reading. When they were done, they turned the book back around to Dr. Schatz.

He looked my father squarely in the eye. "Do you have any questions about this?"

My father had only one. "Don't you think she just needs a good psychotherapist?"

Dr. Schatz stood throughout the meeting. He remained standing. He looked at them both. He moved his eyes so that they met mine. His face showed sadness and anger. He looked back over at my father. "I have other patients to see," he said. Then he turned and left the room.

My father's refusal to acknowledge the reality was not only

from a fear of what else might go wrong. There was also accusa-
tion. I never blamed him for my medical problems. I did not
consider him responsible for what Dr. Martinez and Dr. Jannetta
had done to me. He, alone, judged himself guilty.

My parents are first cousins. That can cause birth defects.
Even though the pain did not start until age twenty-three, the
disorder (in this case, literally) began at gestation. The birthmark on my left forehead was visible proof of the errant blood
vessels that lay underneath my skin and in my brain.

The article Dr. Jordan had given me in Pittsburgh gave cre-
dence to a hereditary link. Often, when my father ate, he would
leave food on his lip/chin. He never seemed to feel it. One of us
always needed to point it out. In appearance, his face was asym-
metrical. Everyone has an unevenness to their features. His was
slightly more pronounced. The article mentioned both asymme-
try and numbness as two of the features that could be found in
related family members. If the cause of my trigeminal neuralgia
was hereditary, there had been no reason for anyone to suspect it
before I was born. If the problem resulted from their intermar-
riage, I bore no grudge. Once they got married, whatever was
going to happen was going to happen.

As far as the operations were concerned, his guilt worked
like a Rube Goldberg contraption. If he had not called Dr.
Osterholm, Dr. Martinez might not have operated. If Dr. Martinez
had not performed his procedure, then the initial injury would
not have happened. Had there been no damage, then I might not
have felt compelled to see Dr. Jannetta. Had Dr. Jannetta not
operated, my face would not have been paralyzed. Therefore:
Had he not called Dr. Osterholm in the first place, I would have
been fine. I often told him that I did not hold him responsible for
either the pain or the disfigurement. It made no difference. He
continued to feel responsible.

He refused to address the issue directly. Each time I tried to
talk with him about it, he would either change the subject or
walk away. Both reactions were often accompanied by rage. It
was not that he was ignorant about the information. He admitted

that they were first cousins. He merely refused to talk about it any further than that.

He could not deny the article from Dr. Jordan. In fact, he insisted on making a copy of it for himself. Always a man who needed to be in control, he knew there was only one thing he could do to manipulate the situation. That was to make sure, to the best of his ability, that I did not go ahead with anything more.

As before and always, I also preferred a non-surgical answer to the pain. I spent the summer of that year, 1979, doing two things: (1) I tried to find a way to get the money to fly to California and get to Dr. Wilson; (2) I encouraged my hope that I would not have need of him.

Dr. Schatz suggested I make an appointment with a New York hypnotherapist, Dr. Paul Sacerdote, a psychiatrist who specialized in chronic pain patients and hypnosis. I met with him for ten sessions. At the end of that time, as before, he and I came to the conclusion that hypnotherapy was not the answer for me.

No other alternatives were suggested by anyone medical. My father teased me with the promise of paying for my plane ticket. "I'll give you the money," he said in a tone I naively interpreted as sincerity.

In common sense and trust, I am as dumb as the proverbial bunny. I believed him. I did not foresee the second part of the offer. "I'll get you the ticket if you see another dentist."

This was the third time he held out a silver dollar only to change it into dust as my hand came within taking distance. *What could I do?* That was the question that always haunted me. If nothing else would help, I had to see Dr. Wilson. If the price of getting to California was to waste the time of another doctor and mine, well . . .

I saw Dr. Joseph Marbach in March. He was a very nice man. His gray-tinged hair, moustache and beard framed intelligent eyes and a smiling mouth. Although a dentist, he specialized in treating facial pain disorders.

I sat in a dental chair, for once not fearing the drill. He spent over an hour with me. He wanted to know everything about my pain. He asked what treatments I had tried. He nodded sporadically as I went through my list of drugs, surgeries, procedures, and alternative therapies. He was unimpressed with most of them.

His feeling was that nothing had been attempted in a systematic manner. He also did not believe I had trigeminal neuralgia. He felt my diagnosis should be atypical facial pain.

The difference between the two, facial versus trigeminal neuralgia, is primarily in the treatments. Every doctor I had seen spent time vacillating between the two names. I did not care which they chose. As long as they stopped the pain.

Dr. Marbach suggested I retry some of the drugs. He also wanted me to try some therapies about which he felt very strongly. One was an electrical stimulator, or the TENS machine, the one I had tried without success at Columbia Presbyterian Hospital. The other was the cocaine solution application to the sphenopalatine ganglion.

I shook my head. "No. I can't do either of those again. They were both awful and didn't help."

"You don't have to try the TENS again if you don't want. I would like you to reconsider the other." He walked me down the hall. "I want you to see something."

We stood outside a room. The door was open. "Take a look," he said.

There were a number of women sitting in a circle. All were engaged in some form of activity. Some knitted. Others read, wrote, or talked with one another.

It looked like any other group. Except for one thing. Every one of the women had a cotton swab sticking out of a nostril. No one appeared to be in pain or discomfort. None looked as though they were feeling the way I had when Dr. Barrett tried his soaked swab. It did not look like such a bad thing when viewed this way. But, once was enough. I refused to give it another try.

We returned to the exam room. We talked a while longer before Dr. Marbach stood to indicate the end of the appointment. "You know," I said as I walked to the door, "all I need is the right surgery. If someone would just cut the nerve . . ." He interrupted me. He was adamant. "Another operation is not the answer for you. You will only be courting danger if you have more surgery."

He was certain there was no possibility of relief. At least not in the near future. "It's not going to go away. I know this is very hard to hear and do, but, you are going to have to learn to live with it." He reached out and took my hand. "It'll take a lot of effort and patience. I hope that you will be able to find something that can make it a little more tolerable for you, at least."

I was no better off than before I had seen Dr. Sacerdote and Dr. Marbach. In fact, I was a little worse, because this was the first time someone had told me, "You have to learn to live with it." If you do not have it, then that is not an unreasonable suggestion to make. If you are the one living with it, it serves to further deflate any still-existing hope.

I had reached the end of my patience. My father could not insist I see another dentist. The three he hoped would help him say "no" to me about the surgery had said "no" instead to any other alternatives. It had been obvious to me and my doctors that my options were very limited. I thought maybe my father would come around if I fulfilled his condition.

"You know what Dr. Marbach said? He can't help me. You said you would help me get to California if I saw him and he couldn't help. I did and he couldn't. Can you lend me the money now, so I can buy my ticket?" Dumb, dumb bunny.

"I'll buy the ticket for you," he said. My heart leapt. "If you see another neurosurgeon." My heart plunged precipitously down into my stomach and ached.

What could I do? I called a hospital referral number and was given the name of Dr. Alan Rothman, a neurosurgeon. His office was in uptown Manhattan. It was a nice day, the kind where I did not have to be totally afraid of the breeze. I walked the hour it took, popping codeines as I went along.

It was a short appointment. A tall, big-boned man, dressed casually in slacks and a brown sweater vest over a dark red shirt, he was not casual in his attitude. As soon as I was seated in front of his desk, he asked why I had come to see him. "I've had trigeminal neuralgia since 1976." He also did not mince words.

"You would have killed yourself by now if you had that."

From the little bit of reading I had done, I knew that the number of suicide attempts and completed suicides among people with tic was high. He was the first doctor to say it out loud. I did not tell him that the subject was one with which I was intimately familiar. We talked a while longer. Then he examined me.

"You don't have many avenues left. Another rhizotomy might be an option. I definitely think you should not have another intracranial procedure." He repeated Dr. Marbach's sentiment. "No one should touch you with another surgery. It may only make you worse."

I knew I was not going to get to California with that opinion.

While I continued trying to find a way to save enough money on my own for the airfare, a strange thing happened. One afternoon, my phone rang. To my amazement, it was my brother, David.

I could not believe it. It had been more than four years since we had last had contact. "I just wanted to let you know, if you need anything, just give me a call." Almost tongue-tied from shock and surprise, I was able to gather my wits enough to say, "Thank you. It's really nice of you to offer." He said, "You're welcome," and ended the call.

My first thought, *Well, wasn't that odd?* was quickly replaced by a second. *Call him back, silly. Ask him if he'll lend you the money for a plane ticket.* I quickly picked up the phone, got his number from information and dialed it. I had to move quickly before I successfully talked myself out of making the call.

"Charlie [that is what I called my father] has refused to lend me money to go to California. There's a surgeon there who has an operation for me. It's the operation I need to have the pain gone. Dr. Wilson is the best one to do it."

"Oh no," he said. "I meant money for a psychiatrist."

It had been years since we had talked. As far as I knew, he

knew nothing about my situation and yet, on his own, he decided that the way to help me was to pay for psychotherapy? The only way he could have come to that conclusion was if he had talked with Charlie. He would have told him, as he did anyone who would listen, that I did not have a medical problem. "She just needs a good psychotherapist." I did not want to argue or debate with David. To direct the issue away from his possible collusion with my father, I did not reply directly to what he had said. Instead, I repeated Dr. Rothman's statement.

"I saw another surgeon in New York. It was at Charlie's insistence. He told me that suicide is an option. I need to try this operation."

I barely knew my brother. I did not want to talk about suicide with someone I barely knew. All I knew was that I needed the money. If it took repeating the words of Dr. Rothman, so be it.

It did not have the effect for which I had hoped.

"What's the name of this doctor? I want to call him. I want to hear him say that to me."

I refused to give him the name. I told him what the doctor had said. I was not a child whose word could only be accepted when verified by an adult.

"Since you won't tell me his name or phone number, I won't give you any money, not if it's for surgery." Before hanging up he wished me "good luck." So ended our one contact.

It was all up to me. I had to come up with a way to save a few hundred dollars.

CHAPTER SEVENTEEN

Since the time my father had decided he would not help me get to Dr. Wilson, my stomach had been perpetually on fire. I began living on Rolaids. Rarely did a week pass when I did not finish off a large, 150-tablet, full-sized bottle. Without them, my abdomen was a mass of burning, churning acid. There was no way I could stop taking them.

A semi-essential was the movies.

Each weekend, I tried to find one movie that might attract my interest. Even if I could not find one, I went anyway. Going meant I had somewhere specific to go. Something to do. Something that might help keep my mind off the absurdity and banality of my life. On weekdays, I would go to the bank, see Carolyn, or go shopping. As long as I did not browse too long, the eye pain would not get too bad. At home, I did not enjoy TV, but I did find a soap opera or two that could keep my attention. It gave me some semblance of a schedule. The weekends had nothing consistent to them around which I could build a pseudo-schedule. The movies were the way to do that.

Nonetheless, they were very painful. The brightness and constant movement on the screen worsened the pain. Most times, I would have to take two to three grains of codeine to get through an hour and a half of a film. I was often so drugged by the end of the feature that I could not remember much of what I had just seen. They were not only painful, something that I accepted as a cost of going to them. They were also very expensive. If I wanted to get to California, it was a price I could no longer afford. Once

I stopped going, it took only a few months before I had saved enough to make my reservations

A cross-country Greyhound bus ticket cost $99.00. It would take two nights and three days. I would not be able to read to while away the time. My eye would not permit it. The movement of other cars and scenery made the pain difficult, if not unbearable. I did not know how well the eye would tolerate the trip, in general. Riding in a bus was the last way I wanted to travel.

I hoped it would be easier going to California than the ride back from Texas two years prior. It was a nonsensical thought, but my thinking was the only thing over which I had control.

I could not change not having the money to fly. I could not change the unpleasant effects of the codeine. I could not change the pain. And I could not change the fact that I could only get to California if I took the bus.

The reason was very simple. I had to get to Dr. Wilson on the cheap because I would have to fly home. Meningitis is always a possible complication of brain surgery. After my discharge from the hospital, I did not want to chance a three-day trip on a bus, just in case.

I left from the Transit Authority bus station, in New York City. The ride was very hard on my eye, as I had feared. The pain ebbed and flowed, depending on what I was doing, just as it did at home. I turned my face away from the window. I shielded my eye from the sun. I took lots and lots of codeine. When the pain became bearable, I would talk with my seatmates.

The bus stopped often to pick up passengers. Sometimes, it was only for fifteen or twenty minutes. Other times, we had time to get off and look around.

The three-hour layover in Utah allowed another passenger and me to visit the Mormon Tabernacle. The trip, although difficult and very painful, turned out to be less unpleasant than I feared. With the exception of one moment of panic.

I never realized a cross-country bus ride would include the

stopping and taking on of passengers. Once I found a good seat, on the right side of the bus, in the inside seat, where my face could not be touched and the sun could not shine in my right eye, I felt safe.

The bus stopped. A number of people were waiting at the curb. I noticed the young woman coming up the stairs and entering the bus. She carried an infant in her arms. One of the few seats available was the one next to me. She would be sitting on my left side.

I moved over as far as I could to the right. I wanted to give her enough room to sit comfortably. She smiled at me. "Thank you," she said. And then, she did the unthinkable. She hoisted the baby up into the air. Then she slowly brought her down. The baby now lay with her head on her mother's right shoulder. Within touching distance of the left side of my face.

She was a sweet child, alert and awake. She was not ready to sleep. I held my breath. The possibility of her next move—what she would do; I was petrified. And then she did exactly what frightened me so. She started flailing her little arms. Her left arm. It could touch my face! What if she hit me? What if she set off the pain? I could not let her do that. I could also not explain to her mother that the mere touch of her child's arm against my face would set off severe pain. It would take too long. She could hit my face while I was trying to explain. Unless she had heard of trigeminal neuralgia, she would think I was a nut. Touch causing pain? Come on!

The fear took precedence. I was truly frightened that the child might trigger the tic. I did not want to scare the mother. I felt bad about lying. But what other choice was there?

"Excuse me," I said as I pointed to the upper left side of my face. Because of the dirt build-up, because I could not wash the area, it was an easy ruse to pull. "This is contagious."

Her face froze in fright.

"She didn't touch you, did she?"

"No," I reassured her. "I just wanted to let you know so that you can be sure she doesn't."

The woman jumped to her feet. She held her baby protectively. "We'll go sit somewhere else."

One other incident stood out in my mind.

We were stopped for a lunch break. All the passengers had exited the bus. We were all milling around the parking lot where we had been let off.

One of the other passengers came over to me. He looked friendly. "Where are you going?" he asked me.

"San Francisco," I replied.

His smile was cheerful. "Are you on vacation?"

"No. I'm not." I smiled back at him, but I did not want to continue the conversation. Not, at least, in the direction in which it was headed.

I attempted to make him the subject. "Are you traveling for pleasure?"

"No. It's a business trip for me." I smiled, happy to be talking about him. Not for long.

"So," he said again, "why are you going to California? What will you be doing there?" His voice remained lighthearted.

I tried to evade answering. He kept asking. Finally, I gave up.

"I'm going to the hospital to have brain surgery." I hoped that would end our game of twenty questions.

"Ha, ha, ha," he laughed. "No, really, why are you going to California?"

"I'm going for surgery," I repeated.

"Oh. Well. I wish you a lot of luck." His smile vanished. He turned and walked away.

Between the pain, the guilt about scaring my seatmate, and the fear that someone else would ask me if I was on vacation, I felt a great sense of relief when the bus pulled into the San Francisco Bus station. The date was May 5, 1980.

I collected my suitcase and went to the curb to hail a cab. Fifteen minutes later, I was talking to the admissions clerk at the Moffitt Hospital, UCSF (University of California, San Francisco).

I answered all her questions. The forms were filled out. She made copies of my insurance cards. She placed an orange plastic bracelet around my wrist, the one that said I now belonged to Moffitt Hospital. She secured it with a fastener. I sat in the waiting room, sorry that I was in the hospital, glad that the bus trip was over. An escort came and walked me to my room. All the things I had done so many times before in so many other hospitals. Familiarity breeds relief.

When we arrived at my room, relief turned to surprise. I had never known semi-private to mean four patients to a room.

Lois* was a dark-haired woman who appeared to be in her fifties. Her problem was chronic neck pain. I would soon find that she could also be a pain in the neck, to me. Her bed sat diagonally across mine.

Isabel*, a young girl from Peru, lay in the bed opposite mine. She was in her teens. She wore her long blond hair loose. The look in her large blue eyes was intelligent but questioning. It was a difficult time for her. Not only because of her severe chronic back pain. She was very alone because her family was home in Peru. In addition, she spoke almost no English.

Marthe* completed our quartet. She was a very pretty woman in her late thirties. Her olive-colored skin complemented her almost-black hair. She had been an advertising executive. She had come into the hospital for surgery, to have her benign brain tumor removed. The surgery had been successful, the tumor excised completely. Unfortunately, the side effects had been harsh. She was no longer able to interact, converse, or at times, even recall her name. It was to her that I was to become the most attached.

After the nursing preliminaries had been dispensed with, a tall redhead, wearing a plaid shirt and sports pants, strode into the room. He held out his hand to me. "I'm Dr. Wright," he said, smiling. "Why don't you tell me about why you are here?" He let me talk for a while. Then he did a neurological exam. After learning all he wanted to know, he offered his hand again for me to shake. As he turned to go, he said, "I have to talk with Dr. Wilson. I'll be back to see you in a little while."

I waited, expecting that he would be coming back with Dr. Wilson. Instead, a short time later, he returned alone. "I talked with Dr. Wilson. I told him what you told me. He no longer thinks you have what he thought you had. He's not going to operate."

I was dumbfounded. And angry. "I just took a three-day bus ride to get here. It took me months before I saved up enough money to pay the fare. Why? What made him change his mind?"

As upset as I was, I enjoyed the way he framed his answer. "Dr. Wilson says seeing Europe is different than reading about Europe. Now that we have seen you, he no longer thinks you have what he originally believed you did."

This seemed even worse than Dr. Jannetta. Even though he had never examined me personally, he and I had talked face to face. Dr. Wilson and I never met. He was making his decision based solely on someone else's exam.

After Dr. Wright left my room, I spent a few minutes fuming. Then I summoned a nurse. "I'm going home. I'm not going to stay here for nothing. I came for the surgery. Now they tell me it's not going to be done. There is absolutely no reason whatsoever for me to stay." She tried her best to calm me down. She saw it was not working. "Listen. Just try and calm down, please. Wait here for a few minutes, okay? I'm going to page Dr. Wright." I did not know what he could say, but I agreed to see him again.

"Here comes your friendly psychiatrist," he announced as he returned to my room.

Oh boy, I thought. *Here we go again.*

It turned out he did not intend to start the psychosomatic discussion that appeared to be the direction in which he was headed. He was merely trying to lighten the situation. Unknowingly, he had picked the one word which was sure to raise my hackles.

"We don't want you to leave. There are some things we want

to try. Dr. Wilson also wants you to talk with another surgeon who does a different form of pain surgery."

That did not sound unreasonable. Besides, in terms of pain and finances, I was in no position to turn around and go home, no matter what I said in anger.

Dr. Wilson came in to talk with me the next day. A gaunt man of average height, he looked just like he did on television. He repeated what Dr. Wright had said. "I don't intend to operate on you. I don't think my operation is the right one for you."

The other neurosurgeon they wanted me to see was Dr. John Adams. Very tall, maybe in his sixties, he had a specific surgery to offer. He specialized in implanted brain electrodes. They were akin to the type the model on *The Bold Ones*, the show I had remembered from so many years ago, had received. Before I had an opportunity to refuse it—I was no less adamant now than I had been when Jamshyd first diagnosed me and I recalled the TV show—Dr. Adams removed the choice from me.

"Which pain is the most important for you to try and stop?" he asked. "Is it the constant pain or the spontaneous and triggered pain?" That was a no-brainer. The worse of the two was the spontaneous pain. If I were a screamer, I could imagine screaming each time one hit. But they only lasted for half a minute or so. It was the other pain. Constant, and unremitting. The reason I could not work. With the tic, I could go to a job in a car. I did not have to be outside for more than a few minutes. I could wait for the spontaneous/triggered pain to stop.

Nothing stopped the eye movement pain. The background pain was always there.

It is often said that one of the hardest parts of dealing with trigeminal neuralgia is the fear of another attack. The possibility of a spontaneous pain scared me, a lot. There was nothing I could do to stop it. Nothing to stave it off.

I worked very hard at trying not to set off the pain by accident. I kept my head straight. Rather than moving my eyes, I moved my head from side to side if I needed to watch for cars or whatever. I ducked when there was even the slightest hint that something might touch my face. But once the pain was over, it was over. The constancy of the baseline pain was the more intolerable. Nothing stopped it.

"I want to stop the constant pain."

Wrong answer.

He shook his head. "Then I'm afraid my surgery can't help you." I knew it was the wrong answer even before it left my mouth. The problem was, there was no other. I wanted to work. I needed to work. I wanted to play. I needed to play. To do those things, I needed to be rid of the eye movement pain. I needed to not have pain all the time.

I hoped they would have something else to propose.

CHAPTER EIGHTEEN

Dr. Raskin, a tall, attractive and agreeably tanned man, with dark brown hair peppered with gray, came to see me. Dr. Wilson had asked for his opinion. He was a neurologist who specialized in treating headache and head pain.

With the exception of Dr. Schatz, it was a rare instance when a doctor would come into the room and pull up a chair. Most often, they stood at the foot of the bed, as most surgeons are wont to do. The non-surgical people tended to sit on the very edge of my bed, or a chair, ready to spring at the beginning of the last word of our conversation.

Whether sitting in a chair or standing at the side of my bed, Dr. Raskin always acted as though he had all the time in the world for me. Sometimes, he would see me more than once a day. Even though he was perhaps twenty years my senior, I felt we could have been friends had we met in a different context. He had the ability to make me feel I was still a person, not merely a patient or a problem to be solved.

We talked about movies, things of general interest, and chronic pain. He suggested I try, once again, some of the drugs attempted numerous times before. At least one of them, Dilantin, he tried in a new way.

Dilantin is an anticonvulsant. Although the exact mechanism is unclear, a number of different anti-seizure medications have been found to be effective in treating tic. I had tried the drug, in pill form, a number of times without success. Dr. Raskin asked me to give it one more chance to work. "I'll be giving it to you intravenously this time. That may make a difference." It did not. The pain was not changed. It did, however, give me the best and longest sleep I had had in a long time.

Because of the problem with my shoulder so many times before, Dr. Raskin wanted me to be seen by a thoracic surgeon. Scalenus anticus syndrome, also known as thoracic outlet syndrome, can cause facial pain despite the pain being felt in the shoulder. It is, very simply, a tightness in the shoulder area. It often causes an absence of the pulse in the affected arm. The theory, for facial pain, is that there may be a similar vascular reduction in the flow of blood coming into the neck and face.

Another Dr. Adams, the Philadelphia thoracic surgeon who had operated on me for the syndrome, had removed my first natural rib. Almost immediately, the blood flow returned to normal, and the pain was gone. Dr. Adams had found a juxtaposition of two of the scalenus vessels. The rib removal helped to untangle them.

Dr. Raskin felt that there was a small chance that the muscles had healed wrong. If so, there might be a vascular constriction of the vessels leading to my face. Conceivably, that could explain my pain.

Dr. Mirkin* thought it would not be a bad idea to go back in and "take a look." An orderly took me down to the OR at nine the following morning. The nurses got me ready, putting in an IV and generally settling me down. A nurse wheeled me into the operating suite. The anaesthesiologist took a syringe and, injecting the contents into the IV tubing, wished me well. "You're going to have sweet dreams now." The next second, I was asleep. A few seconds after that, or so it seemed, I was back in my room.

I awakened to the sight of Dr. Raskin standing at the foot of my bed. A nurse came walking into the room. She said nothing to me. She turned to Dr. Raskin. "They didn't do the surgery."

I started to cry. "I can't believe they didn't do it. How come? They put me out and . . ."

Dr. Raskin put up his hands. "Wait a minute. Don't get upset yet. Let me go find out what happened." He turned and walked out of the room.

I had feared the anaesthesia. It almost always made me sick. It usually took a couple of days before it completely wore off.

I had not wanted the operation. I truly doubted the problem lay in my shoulder. I could not accept the thought that I had gone through all the preparation, including being put "out," only to have the procedure canceled.

Dr. Raskin returned. He was smiling. "It wasn't canceled. Dr. Merkin found nothing to cut. Your first surgeon did a perfect job. The fact that they didn't do it just meant there was nothing there for them to do." Despite my feeling that it was going to be a fruitless procedure, my hope, outside the control of logic and intellect, raised itself. One more theory hitting the dust. One more unreasonable belief proving itself to be unreasonable.

After the non-surgery, Dr. Raskin wanted me to try another drug. Inderal is used for lowering blood pressure. Although mine was normally low, he thought that a decrease in pressure on the vessel walls that occurs with the use of this drug might reduce the pain. The action is similar to that of Reserpine, which Dr. Schatz had tried on me when he first hospitalized me in 1976. It had no effect on me then, other than lowering my pulse rate to forty-four beats per minute.

This time it would have a beneficial effect, even if it did not work on the pain.

Dr. Wilson and I had a number of conversations. Despite occurring on different days, they invariably started the same way.

Me: "Please, do the operation."

Dr. Wilson: "No."

Me: "Why not?"

Dr. Wilson: "As I have repeatedly explained to you, Carol, you do not have what we thought you had. I do not think my surgery can help you."

Me: "Please?"

And inevitably concluded the same way.

Dr. Wilson: (as he started to walk away) "No. I'm sorry."

Dr. Wright came into my room. It was the beginning of the third week of my stay in the hospital. "Dr. Wilson wants to see you in his office." *What now?* I thought. I suppose he just wants to reaffirm how much he does not want to do the surgery on me. I pulled my robe on over the chip on my shoulder and walked down the two flights of stairs to where he was waiting.

The office door was open. Books, papers, and journals were piled high everywhere. Dr. Wilson sat behind a desk that was barely visible with all the stacks. I could not tell from his expression why I had been summoned.

I removed some papers from the chair catty corner to the desk and sat. I looked at him expectantly.

"Carol, tell me again why you want me to do the surgery?"

Again? Why doesn't he just rub it in my face that he doesn't want to do it? Geez.

"Because I know what is in there, and I know your surgery is the appropriate one for it."

"What will you do if I refuse to operate?"

"I am fixated on your procedure. I know it is the right one. I'm not prepared to have any other surgery. I know that yours is the only one that might work."

I knew why he asked me that. Many times pain patients are willing to let anyone do anything. He wanted to be sure that it was not a matter of my wanting anyone to do any surgery. It was not. I *knew*, absolutely knew, within myself, that his operation was the right one. It had to be. After all, it was similar to what Dr. Osterholm had done the first time, and his had worked.

Dr. Wilson stayed quiet for a minute or two. With his hands holding up his chin, he appeared to be deciding.

"All right, Carol, I'll do the surgery." I started to smile. "Let me finish. I want to be very clear with you about the chances."

Well, I know he'll make 'em bad. I thought to myself. *Maybe he thinks I'll opt out then.*

"There is only a twenty-five-percent chance that this will help you. I do not believe that it will. It could make you worse."

"I know you don't want to operate, but I truly know that this is the right thing to do. I really appreciate that you're taking what I'm saying into consideration. Thank you. Thank you."

"I'm afraid there is another problem." *Uh-oh.* "Your insurance is not going to pay for you to stay in the hospital just to wait for a surgical date, and I cannot make room on the schedule for you until at least next week. If you stay, you will have to pay out of pocket."

"Oh, I can't do that. I don't have any money, not even if I left. I couldn't pay for a hotel room."

"I'm really sorry. The only thing I can suggest is that you talk with Social Services. Maybe they can help you find a rooming house or something."

I left his office overjoyed . . . and desolate.

Social Services tried, but they could find nothing, at least not in my price range. Dr. Raskin and the Inderal came to my rescue.

He had planned on starting me on it in pill form. Instead, he proposed that it be given to me as an injection. That would require continued hospitalization. I had only one problem with that. I am phobic about needles.

"I'll take the pill. I would rather take the risk of my insurance refusing to pay than have a shot."

When he realized I was serious, that my fear of an injection outweighed my fear of the bill, he started me on the pills. As I expected, it did nothing for my pain, but it did allow me to remain in the hospital. At the end of the week, a utilization review committee member came to my room. "You need to know that your insurance benefits will be cut off within the next few days if surgery is not scheduled." Finally, luck was with me. Dr. Wilson could do me the next week.

The wait for the surgery was very hard. Actually, just being in the hospital again was difficult. I would spend long hours with my nose pressed up against the window. Longingly, I stared out at the Golden Gate Bridge and the passersby. I hated watching people, hurrying back and forth, living their lives. My imagination worked overtime, thinking of how they spent their days and what their lives were like. I wanted to be with them. With only a slight shift of my eyes, I would catch a glimpse of the trees blowing, the trash moving along the sidewalk. It only took that minuscule glance to remind me that the pain would not let me enjoy the outside. It did not matter what I remembered. I had to give it a try.

I took a pass for the afternoon. I walked around Haight-Ashbury, Chinatown, and Ghirardelli Square by the wharf. I enjoyed being outside, but I had to drug myself heavily. The chance to see parts of San Francisco that I heard about pleased me. I found myself enjoying almost none of it.

The wind was as strong as it had appeared from the window. Even after realizing how bad it was, I refused to give up and go back to the hospital. I intended to see the sites, even if it killed me. It didn't, of course, but the pain was unrelenting. By the time I returned to the hospital, I had taken so much codeine I fell straight into bed. At least, I had accomplished two things. One, I had seen parts of California. Two, the pain of the day forced me to let go of the fantasy that the pain would not interfere. I had to have the operation.

As long as I was going to be under anaesthetics, I asked Dr. Wilson if he would do one other thing. I wanted my eye opened. He sent an ophthalmologist to my room. I explained what I wanted and why. "I can't stand the way it looks!" He agreed to do it, adding, "But I do not think it should be done. It is well protected with the tarsorrharphy. If I take it down, there is a twenty-five-percent chance that it will immediately go bad." Didn't matter. I wanted it done.

The more I thought about it, the more scared I became. Only

twenty-five-percent chance that the surgery would work. Twenty-five-percent chance the eye would go bad. I could only deal with one bad percentage at a time. A few hours before I was due to go to the OR, I called the eye surgeon. "I've changed my mind. Please don't open my eye." He was more than happy to oblige.

Before I could go to surgery, I had to sign a consent form. I knew in my mind that I was doing the right thing. I also remembered what my father told me about the way I had acted before Dr. Osterholm's procedure. I was afraid my unconscious might try to thwart me again. Just in case, I called Dr. Wright to my room. I told him about the incident. "No matter what I might say before the surgery, my signature supersedes anything. No matter what, you go ahead with it."

Even though I was sure within myself that the operation was necessary and appropriate, I needed some support in going through with it. I called Carolyn and Edna. They both wished me luck. They each told me they backed me in my decision. It was not enough. Maybe the nurse could help me out.

As the orderly rolled me down the hall, Sharon walked alongside. "I know you may not believe it, and I know it is not your position to say anything about my decision, but I really need to have someone tell me right now that I am doing the right thing."

She looked me straight in the eye. "I can't tell you that." I hoped that she would understand that I was asking for some psychological support. *Perhaps,* I thought, *she's thinking of my lawsuits against Dr. Martinez and Dr. Jannetta.* "I'm only asking you to say the words. They don't mean anything. I just need to hear someone say them before I go down." It was the first time I had outrightly asked a nurse to give me emotional help. I should have realized, based on past experiences, it would be refused.

A few hours later, I awakened in the recovery room. The first thought I had was of my eye. I was afraid they might have forgotten that I had canceled my request to have it opened.

"Is my eye open?" I asked the nurse.

"Yes, your eye is open." She did not know that "open" meant the taking down of the tarsorrharphy.

"Oh no!" I cried. "I told them not to do it. Why did they do that?" I was inconsolable.

She looked at me strangely for a minute, then walked away. She returned a few minutes later. "Your eye is not open." She must have called Dr. Wright or Dr. Wilson and asked what the heck I was talking about. "It is still closed," she assured me.

I was filled with relief. The other question, whether I had made the right choice in going ahead with the surgery, was answered by Dr. Wright before I even had a chance to ask. He came over to my litter. He looked down at me and smiled. "You were right."

Dr. Wilson had entered an area away from where Dr. Osterholm had operated. He, too, found vascular anomalies. Before he was forced to stop, because he was too close to the brain stem, he decompressed as many of the vessels as he could.

There was no discernible change in the pain. I remained in the hospital for eight additional days, to recuperate. Then I flew home.

A few weeks later, I called Dr. Wilson's office as he had requested. That was when I learned my father had not stopped his efforts to interfere with my treatment. After identifying myself, the secretary, Chris*, did not ask how I was feeling or if everything was okay. Instead, she said, "Is your father feeling any better?"

"What are you talking about?" I replied.

I could hear her audible gulp. "Well, your father was very upset about your surgery. He called here a number of times to tell Dr. Wilson that he could not do the operation. He told him, 'If you operate, there will be big trouble.' Finally, Dr. Wilson refused to accept his calls. He was very upset and worried about you. His last call here was fifteen minutes before Dr. Wilson was to start your operation."

I had not known about any of this. I apologized to her for the inconvenience. She said that it was all right. "He was very upset, and I hope he is feeling better now."

I tried to talk to him about his behavior. As in all my at-

tempted conversations with him about the pain and my disability, he refused to discuss it. His feelings about my situation were
very strong. There was nothing I could say or do that was going to
change them. I liked to think that when the pain lessened, he
felt better about it. Regardless of whether it was from an operation or merely a change in the weather.

CHAPTER NINETEEN

It was June. Summer normally brought a reduction in the pain. I was able to reduce my codeine to only two and three a day. I was not able to distinguish if it was the surgery or the lack of wind and cold that was helping. I like to think it was Dr. Wilson. If so, the coming fall would be just as easy.

As with the first surgery, my head had again been shaved. This time, the barber compromised—between all and nothing. On the right side of my head, all my hair was intact.. My left side was totally bald.

Even though things were better, I still could not tolerate touch to that side of my scalp. I could not wear a wig or turban as I had the first time. The reactions to my unusual coiffure were varied. There was the woman who turned to her husband and pointed at me as they were stopped at a red light. In a loud voice, I heard her say, "She must have had an operation." Some folks just stared. And then, there was the strange man in the ice cream store.

Within two weeks, I had grown what looked like duck's down. Before the surgery, my hair was down past my shoulders. After I got home, I cut the hair on the right side to just below my ear line. I thought it might look a little less odd.

"Who did your hair?" I heard as I turned from the ice cream counter.

"Excuse me?"

"Where did you get your hair done?"

"Nowhere." I was not in the mood to explain to some stranger about my surgery.

I was amazed by his persistence. "You can tell me. I won't tell anyone."

Given the new fad of punk hairdos, maybe I did not look as weird as I felt. I decided to ignore him. When he asked the third time, I finally answered.

"I did not have my hair cut. I had brain surgery, and my hair is just starting to grow back."

Astoundingly, he asked me a fourth time. "I won't tell anyone. Where did you get it cut?"

Evidently, the names of hairdressers were so important that I had made up a surgery, so I would not have to divulge the name of my stylist. I gave up and went home.

I stayed there and waited for my hair to grow back. I also waited for another way to address the pain.

Before I went to California, one good thing had happened. After watching another television show, I refound a friend I had not seen in years, since before I had moved to New York. Jay, a veterinarian, was a most unusual woman. Dark-haired, dark-eyed, and American, she looked Indian. She wrote Sanskrit and specialized in Indian dance when she was not working in India or Africa.

PBS had shown a play by Wendy Wasserstein entitled *Uncommon Women*. Jay was the most uncommon woman I knew.

I vacillated about calling her. She would ask me, "What have you been doing?" The idea of saying, of admitting out loud, that I was disabled was nauseating to me. I would also have to admit to the disfigurement. I did not want to do that. It was something I hated to say out loud. I also did not know if I was willing to be seen by her.

I screwed up my nerve and called. I was happy that I did. I found her to be the same person that I remembered. She still lived outside of Philadelphia, an-hour-and-forty-five-minute train ride from Manhattan. Since Edna lived so far away, Jay became my main source of support. With her, I did not have to worry if I looked too ugly or seemed too drugged.

I needed the support, even more than before. It was starting to become more real to me that the pain might never go away.

Many of my thoughts centered around two themes: When I wake up tomorrow, the pain will be gone; or, this is really a dream. When I wake up, it will be over. I found I was becoming less and less able to find sustenance in them.

I could continue to hope for a cure. Hope and reality were not synonymous, after all. The probability was getting stronger that this was the way it was going to be. I had always gone into a new surgery, thinking about the first one. That had worked. There was no reason for this one not to. But I had not looked at the literature before, other than the article that Dr. Jordan had given me in Pittsburgh.

I went to the medical library at the New York Academy of Medicine. I took a pocketful of codeine and a feeling of dread with me. Dread that I might find what I was looking for; the truth of what I had; a truth that might spell the death knell for my dreams of being okay again.

There were volumes and volumes, article upon article. Trigeminal neuralgia had been around for a very long time. An awful lot of people had tried an awful lot (literally and figuratively) of treatments.

I learned that my symptoms were typical of tic, with the exception of my young age at its onset. The spontaneity of the first pain. The horror and intensity of it. Remembering where you were, what you were doing, the time of day, the day itself—that is a major sign. My worry that I never was awakened by the pain— maybe that meant it was psychological—another known sign of tic. If a patient is awakened by the pain, it is most probably not trigeminal neuralgia. I did not find anything about the eye pain and little about the constant pain, but it could not be denied. The authors were describing me.

I also read that the benefits of surgery often lasted only two to three months. Dr. Schatz was not being kind when he had told me to call if I had a problem. He had known the operation would probably fail after a few months.

Hope is a funny thing. I was not deterred by the articles. I still, really and truly, except when the doubt crept in and it was harder and harder to stave it off, believed that there was that one operation out there that would provide me with my miracle cure.

In the meantime I had to get through the coming months.

As soon as the summer ended and the weather started acting up, so did my pain. I increased the codeine back up to eight to ten grains a day. Once winter set in, I averaged fourteen per day.

The weather was one problem. The other was my face.

I wanted my eye opened. I was afraid that once I forced them to open it, it would go bad, and I would lose it. Just as the eye doctor in California had warned. The fear was not as strong as my hatred of the way it looked. Each time I broached the subject with Dr. Arentsen or the residents at the clinic, they told me the chances were not good enough. My eye would most probably not be able to protect itself. "There's a good chance you will end up losing that eye."

I was legally blind in the left eye, from amblyopia or "lazy eye," since childhood. I did not know if a complete loss of vision would be any different. The day I treated myself to a Broadway show, *Peter Pan*, I realized there was somebody who would know the answer.

Sandy Duncan played Peter. I remembered having heard, years before, that she had vision in only one eye. My decreased sight in the left had given me problems with depth perception. I was always a good driver except when it came to parking. I could never tell exactly where the other car ended and mine began. Over time, I hit (never hard) eleven parked cars. If that happened with minimal vision, I asked myself, what would happen with none?

Ms. Duncan flew across the stage eight times a week. If she could do that without problems, maybe the loss of sight, in what was a bad eye to begin with, would not be such a big deal.

She kindly invited me into her dressing room after the show. To my surprise, I did not feel nervous about talking with her. We talked about the show for a few minutes. Then she asked me why I had left a note requesting to see her.

I had mentioned visual problems in my note. "I am considering having surgery on my left eye," I said, "that might result in the loss of the vision in that eye. I know you have sight in only one eye. Has it stopped you from doing anything?"

It did not, she said. She had absolutely no trouble flying or driving. Without depth perception, I assumed the walls would look as though they were coming straight at her. She assured me that was not the case.

It was her next question that turned me into a quivering wreck. It was the same reaction I had every time I heard the question. "What do you need the surgery for?" I told her about the pain. About what had happened to my face. I stammered. I blushed. I shook. I was wearing my sunglasses. In response to her questioning look, I took them off.

She was truly kind; she looked at me without wincing or glancing away. "I don't have any problem with my vision loss. I think you should consider having the surgery. It would help you cosmetically." We talked for another minute or two. Not only was she a good actress, she was a nice human being. And she was right. I would look a lot better.

It was important to me to know that if the worst happened and I lost the vision, it would not be so bad. I thought that was all I needed to quiet my fear. It was not. I could not go through with it. I left it closed.

The codeine, the pain, and the disfigurement were soon to become an even greater problem.

One morning, I opened my mail. Lying between the junk mail and brochures was an invitation to my tenth-year high school reunion.

Jay and I had met in high school. We decided that she, Tim, her husband, and I, would go together.

I read the questionnaire Gwen, one of the organizers, sent me. I did not want to answer truthfully. In truth, I could not answer truthfully. Not and keep any semblance of pride. I decided to turn it into a joke. To the first question, What is your vocation? I wrote, "Jack of all trades." To the second, What is your avocation? I wrote, "Master of none." Not very funny, but it was still better than the truth.

I worried about how people would react when they saw me. These were people who had known me when I looked fine. Strangers looked and stared. I had people offer me tissues, thinking that I was crying. One woman insisted on taking my arm and escorting me. She declared me blind. Some folks came right up to me. "What's wrong with your eye?"

If strangers asked, what would people who once knew me when I was considered "cute" say?

I always had an idea somewhere. I realized there was something I could do to make myself look somewhat better. I went over to Dr. Schatz's office. I asked Jeanette if she would ask Dr. Schatz if there was a way I could have my face washed. It had been a long time since the last operation. There was a large dirt build-up. I hoped he would know someone who would anaesthetize me in his/her office. It could only be done asleep.

Jeanette returned from talking with him in the backroom. "He says we'll arrange to have you come into the hospital for anaesthesia." Unbidden tears sprang to my eyes. "No. I just meant for somebody to do it in their office." "No, he said that's not safe. It has to be done in the hospital." What choice did I have? If I wanted to be clean, there was none. "Okay. Whenever you can set it up, I'll go."

I went to the Wills Eye Hospital Short Procedure Unit, where

they did day surgeries. It was necessary for them to put me completely "out." Once "under," the nurses washed my face, hair,
and scalp on the left. Once the nausea and hangover from the
drugs ended, I was very happy. I was squeaky clean.

I knew a clean face would probably not be enough to draw
eyes away from the disfigurement. I was always known as a "fuddy-
duddy." This night I would be something else. I resolved that all
looks would go to my body, not my face.

Normally, I wore clothes that were a little long, opaque and
high necked. I went to Macy's and returned, a few hours later,
with a sheer burgundy wraparound dress. The hem in the back
fell past my knees. It sloped a few inches above them in the
front. The sleeves were short. The neckline went down past my
cleavage and then some. There was no room for an undergar-
ment. For the first time in my life, I went without.

We arrived late. Dinner had been finished long before our
entrance. Much of the talking and remembering had been done
during the meal. We had not realized that a meal was going to be
served. We must have glossed over that part of the invitation. I
was happy that we had missed it. I did not need or want the
humiliation of trying to eat. The paralysis made it too difficult a
task to do in public. Especially with people I had known back
when . . .

A hostess showed us to the main room. We were asked to
sign in at a table where we would find our identification tags.
Each one bore a name and a yearbook picture. The sight of my
face, a face seventeen years old that moved well, worked well,
and did not have pain. It was more than I could bear. I excused
myself. Looking neither left nor right, I walked to the ladies' room.
As soon as the door closed, my eyes welled with tears. I ripped
the picture to shreds. With all the force I could muster, I threw it
into the trash can. I felt consumed with sadness and anger. It was
the first time since the Jannetta procedure that I had looked at a
picture of me. It brought home to me how great the difference
between what had been, what was, and what might always be. I
waited for the feelings to subside. When they did not, I forced

them down. Down my throat and into a thick hard ball that stayed in the pit of my stomach. Then I went back to the party.

My life might be terrible. My face looked awful. The pain was severe. I was darned if I was going to let anyone else know. Luckily, the music was very loud. I did not have to answer any questions about my lengthy absence. No one asked about my missing ID. I was able to get away with nodding a lot.

Everything was going along smoothly. And then, one of my former classmates came up behind me.

I did not hear him. Suddenly, out of the corner of my eye, I saw two hands heading towards my face. "Guess who?" he said, a smile in his voice. His hands came around to the front of my face. They started to close in. He was going to put his hands over my eyes. Over my left eye!

I whipped around. "Don't do that!" I shouted. He had triggered the pain.

My attacker was Vince. He and I had been good friends in school. He had wanted to become a doctor. He had. I don't know if he chose to ignore my outburst because he had made a quick medical decision upon seeing my face. Maybe I had given an unspoken signal. Whatever, we both tacitly agreed it had not happened.

We talked a bit about what he had been doing. We said how good it was to see each other. The conversation differed none from any of the others I had that evening. Every time someone asked me what I had been doing, I quickly turned the question back around to them.

I felt strange about the way people were responding to me. It could have been a result of my paranoia about the way I looked. Or, it could have been the same thing everyone said to every one else. "You look just the same. You haven't changed." I knew that was not the truth. I knew I was still recognizable as Carol, but there was no question that I no longer looked the same.

Emotionally, the pretense that I looked fine, and hearing about the successes most of my classmates seemed to have, made the evening wretched. Jay and Carolyn suggested that only the people who were successful decided to come. Both told me it was brave of me to go. I could have chosen to hide. Maybe. I did not think courage had anything to do with it. I was curious. I wanted to know what had happened to the people with whom I had spent so many years. I only hoped they would not express a similar curiosity towards me. Most didn't, or at least elected not to ask.

Jane and I had been very close. As I was getting ready to leave, she handed me her phone number. "Please call," she said. "We can get together for lunch." I wanted to. It would have been fun to catch up with an old buddy. But I knew I would not call. If I did, I would have to tell her about the pain. I could not do that.

The loneliness I felt, as I said, "Sure, I'd like that"—knowing that I never would—did not differ from the loneliness I felt all along. Since the paralysis, it was even more important, to me, that I pretend to be normal. Keeping up the pretense meant not going out to eat. It meant not using my face too much. It was doable only if I stayed alone. Or if I found people who seemed to understand.

That's what had led me, a few months before I left for California, to get involved with the people from the cult.

CHAPTER TWENTY

I was not a particularly religious, spiritual or superstitious person. Like a Christmas or Easter Christian, I chose each year on which High Holy Day I would go to synagogue. It was either Yom Kippur or Rosh Hashanah. Never both.

Jan, and Blanche, the friends I had made at *House Beautiful*, had tried to awaken a religious interest in me. What they told me about Judaism seemed to make some sense. My whole world was upside down. If the world I could see and touch could not help me, maybe a spiritual one could. For the first time in my life, when I was in New York Columbia Presbyterian Hospital, I asked to see a rabbi.

For some reason, in each hospital, the chaplain would come to visit. Each time, I told them I was Jewish, but they were not deterred. They still, very kindly, would return often, popping in to say, "Hello." Ironically, it was the rabbi, for whom I had asked, who never came. Maybe God or Kismet was trying to tell me something.

In the beginning of 1980, I thought fate had found me.

I was returning home from another appointment with Dr. Schatz. I left his office with the usual pat on the hand and a prescription for codeine. At that time, we were still waiting for word from Dr. Wilson.

Because of the touch-induced pain, plus my exquisite sensitivity to light, I always sat in the same general area. And always in the direction in which the train was headed.

The right side of the train and the inside seat allowed me to sit with my right eye against the window. That kept the sun from shining directly into my left eye. Sitting away from the aisle protected me from someone accidentally brushing against my face.

It was late fall, close to the holiday season. The train was jam-packed. Just my luck, the only available seat was an inside seat on the left side. The sunlight would pour directly into my eye.

I was very weary. I tried to stop myself from doing it, but each time I saw a doctor, no matter who, I was crushed to leave the office without leaving the pain behind as well. The sense of disappointment, anger, and frustration, the lack of control over the pain and my fate, was fatiguing. I did not have the energy to wrestle with the task of asking someone on the other side of the train, sitting in the seat they found comfortable, to trade with me.

It was standing room only. I needed to make a quick decision. Which was worse? The fear of someone setting off the pain? Or the pain of the glaring sun streaming into my left eye? The fear of my face being touched was the stronger one.

There was only one visible seat left. I excused myself so my soon-to-be seatmate could give me room to get to the seat. As I edged past her, I noticed an open book sitting on her lap. It was a musical score.

She appeared to be young, about my age. She turned toward me. "My name's Monica*." I introduced myself in return. Then we engaged in the normal chitchat of strangers forced to spend time together.

I pointed to her book. "Are you a musician?" "I'm a singer," she said.

I was excited to learn we had something in common, especially music. "I used to sing. It was only in local dinner theater. But that's why I moved to New York, to pursue it professionally."

She was easy to talk with. I found myself losing some of my protective shell. As I became more comfortable with her, she asked the question I hated to answer. "What do you do for a living?" I did not like saying the word out loud. Something about her accessibility gave me permission. "I'm disabled right now."

She expressed her sorrow over that. "Do you think you'll be able to sing again?" "No," I replied. "Even if I didn't have the pain, the disfigurement will never allow me to try and go back on a stage." My face and heart ached. It hurt so to say those words. To announce the truth.

Monica honed in on what I was feeling. Somehow, she recognized my desperation, my feeling of isolation, of apartness from the world.

"I belong to a group that meets once a week. All of us are in the performing arts. We have actors, singers, and dancers." This piqued my interest. "Why don't you come one time? I think you'd enjoy meeting them."

It sounded almost too good to be true. When she added, "The group's basis is religious." I could feel my bubble of excitement burst.

The words "group" and "religious" did not belong together in the same sentence. Not without raising some questions.

"I'm Jewish. I doubt I would fit in." *That should take care of this,* I thought.

"Oh, that doesn't matter. We're not of any specific denomination."

My sense of loneliness, aloneness and purposelessness was very strong. I missed singing. I missed being with people who sang. My mind, always looking for an out, went back to the rabbi who never showed. *Hmmmm,* I thought. *Maybe this time I've found an answer.*

My mind listed the reasons I should be wary. My emotions shouted, *Listen. This is what we have been searching for. Maybe this is a "sign."*

It was the only seat available. Her book had been open so that I could see she was involved in music. She sang. It was so easy to believe. It *is* a sign.

I needed to believe that the world, and my life, had some

structure and meaning. That necessity overrode my rational mind. It was telling me, *This is too good to be true. Be careful.*

Oh be quiet! I told it. Hope was the only voice I wanted to hear.

"I'd like to join you. At least, to come to one meeting," I said.

"Jessica* [her roommate and sometime singing partner] and I will be there at the next meeting. It's a week from this Saturday," she replied. "I hope you'll be there."

The meeting was to be held in one of the members' apartment. Monica was waiting for me in the lobby. Jessica met us at the elevator.

The owner of the apartment, Jill*, was an ex-Rockette. Janet* and Linda* were both Broadway "gypsies," dancing in the chorus of a successful musical. Nicky* also sang. Michael*, one of the four men present, worked for a national TV network, in the advertising department. The other three were also involved in the entertainment industry, either in front of or behind the cameras. My unemployment and disfigurement made no difference to any of them. They welcomed me into their group, arms wide open and accepting.

The meeting began and ended with a prayer. In between, the Bible was read and discussed. Then there was a general discussion.

Linda began by explaining their philosophy. "Carol, we believe that the Bible is the literal Truth. All of life and thought evolve directly from it."

Each person was given a chance to express their thoughts. They assured me that my opinion was valuable. "What do you think of what you have heard today?"

I was feeling very uncomfortable. "I have to tell you, I don't believe the same things that you do." "That's okay," Jessica said. Mark chimed in, "Give it some time before you make any decision. Okay?"

Everyone was so nice to me. Jessica and Monica invited me to their home for dinner. Sometimes I would go uptown and meet them at a diner for coffee. They knew I was hurting for money. I brought a cake I had made to one of the meetings. They enjoyed it. "This is really good. You could sell these." A week later, Monica called me. "Can you bake three cakes? We need one each for three different Broadway casts. I told them you charged thirty dollars per cake. I hope that's all right?" It certainly was.

They presented me with a gift of the Bible. Often they called, just to see how I was doing. This was something totally new to me. People caring enough to make sure I was okay. Someone calling just to let me know they were there for me. With no family that cared, and no friends nearby, it was a godsend. It was a nice feeling. It was a relief. It was making me nervous.

As kind and accepting as they were, I was beginning to have some suspicions about their purpose. My accepting the literalness of the Bible might not be as innocuous as it seemed.

People often seemed compelled to offer me their spiritual beliefs. On a different train ride, years before, my seatmate noticed that my left eye was tearing. Because of the numbness, I was never aware of it. After offering me a tissue, she told me she was a Buddhist. She was convinced, and tried to convince me, that if I chanted, I would find "the answer" and cure to my illness. Ever ready to find relief, I tried it. It didn't work.

That happened during the course of an-hour-and-a-half train ride. These people were sticking with me over a much longer period of time. It was hard for me to understand. Why would anyone continue to befriend me? Who would want to be my friend once they realized that I was not a very interesting person?

My life revolved around doctors, hospitals, and two in the afternoon. What did they want from me? I was not sure. If they were a cult, I assumed they would try to get money. But that could not be it. They knew I had no money.

Their focus seemed simple enough. I didn't have to be rich or be the life of the party. All I had to do was accept the reality of their fundamentalist beliefs.

Monica, Jessica, and the others, often mentioned that there were other similar prayer groups throughout the country. All the groups belonged to a larger umbrella organization called "The Way." "All of us are praying for you. We are all asking God to heal you, physically and spiritually." I had to do only one thing to have this cure bestowed upon me. I had to accept the Truth of their path. "God is ready for you, Carol, ready to take away your pain, your disfigurement. You only need to believe and accept."

That was a hard promise to ignore. The pain would be gone. I would come to know God. I would look normal again. I could not ask for more.

These were mostly performers. Maybe God *had* brought us together. What better way to show me His Grace than by putting me together with people who were doing with their lives what I had always hoped to do?

The night the three of us went to the "Take-A-Stand Caravan," my hesitations overcame my desperate hope.

On this night, many of the individual groups would come together as one. Monica assured me that it would be fun. "The most important thing, though, is that you'll get to share with us. You'll get to see the grace that comes from believing together."

Everyone was nice, but I had an odd sensation of déjà vu. Unti, it came to me. I *had* seen this before. It was a real-life scene from the movie *Elmer Gantry*. We were exhorted to sing and pray. People raised their hands in praise. They stood, individually and together. They shared their stories. They told tales of witnessing. One after another told of how they had been helped by their membership in the group. The ecstasy was contagious. The air buzzed with joy and the Glory of God. And the glory of the group.

Coffee and cake were set out on a table in another room. Once the meeting ended, Monica took me by the hand, steering me over to the refreshments. She led me over to a tall, attractive, dark-haired man. "This is Bob*. He is one of the national leaders." He smiled and took my hand, the one that Monica released over to him. He looked directly into my eyes. "I hope you're enjoying being with us. Are you a new member?" "No." He smiled again. "Do you share in our beliefs?" "No." He smiled a third time. He laid a hand on my back. He patted me softly. "Give it time."

I liked these people immensely. They were kind, giving, and seemed genuinely nice. There was only one problem. No matter what the conversation, sooner or later, they turned it back to their beliefs, or rather, my lack thereof. Their way was the right and true path. If I could only accept, they said sorrowfully. The subtext was sent to my unconscious: "If you had the right belief, you would be healed. Your suffering is your fault as long as you refuse to acknowledge the One True Way."

They were praying so hard for me. They wanted me to acknowledge all their work and effort. I was being unrepentant. "If only," they said. With my acquiescence and the help of God, the pain would stop. With my capitulation, and God's help, the paralysis would go away. Only an ingrate would turn away from such an offer.

A part of me fed right into it. I knew what the miracles of modern medicine had done to me. I wanted and needed to know there was another way out. If it did not involve doctors, so much the better. As an agnostic, I could see that I could be at fault. I did not know if God existed. If He did, maybe my refusal to acknowledge Him was the reason I was being punished. Suffering, like evil, needs a reason for being.

I was being pushed into making a decision. At least, that was the way I felt. A decision about something that defied logic. I wanted to be healed. I prayed, in my own way, to look normal. I needed friends who cared about me. I did not want to know that all of their kindnesses were a ruse. My need was too strong, too insistent. Still, something did not feel right.

None of the other people I knew in New York had ever heard of the group. Until I met Monica, I had never heard of it either. It had been heard of in California.

They did not desert me once I left for San Francisco. They continued to support me with phone calls and cards. I happened to mention to one of the residents that I had received a letter from Jessica. I casually mentioned that she was a member of a group called "The Way."

"The Way!" he spat out. "You mean the cult?"

It was not as though I was an innocent. The idea that they might be part of a cult had occurred to me. It was something that I tried not to think about too frequently. Sadly, many things come with a cost. Even possible friendship.

One of the first things I did after I came home was to call Jessica. I wanted to maintain the friendship. We had music and performing in common. I thought that Jessica, Monica and I had truly connected. Maybe the group and the friendship could be separated.

We had a very nice conversation. How was I doing? How was she doing? Anything special going on? Had they performed anywhere recently? It was the sort of phone conversation you have with a friend. Until I asked her, "Are you a cult?"

As I had with Dr. Jannetta, I anticipated a variety of responses. She might deny it, she might laugh. Heck, she could even admit it.

"We are not a cult!" she screamed into the receiver. "How could you say that! How could you even ask me that!"

It never occurred to me that the question might feel to her like a lit explosive. "I really need to know. I'm beginning to have questions about it." I worked to keep my voice steady and calm. I hoped to quiet her anger. "I really like you and Monica. I'd like to remain friends. It's just that I can't join in your belief system."

Well! She told me what I could do with that. Then she slammed down the phone.

I regretted losing these people. For the short periods, when they stopped proselytizing, when they talked about their lives, careers, and dreams, I felt a connection. As with all cults, though, the connection was only a lure. They did not want me. They only wanted my mind and allegiance. I was never even asked for money.

And once more, I was alone.

I still saw Dr. Schatz occasionally. I had the summer, or Dr. Wilson induced (I was not sure which) reduction of the pain. That was good. I walked a lot. I spent more time outside. I hated the heat of a New York summer. The pain loved the absence of breeze.

Once the fall and its wind returned, so, too, did the intense pain. And, again, the pain took away my choices. I decreased my time outside. I increased my codeine.

I developed a high tolerance for the drug. I was taking up to fourteen grains a day. A normal dose was one grain every four hours. It never helped the pain. I took them because they allowed me to maintain a false sense of control. I never left the house without putting two or three pills in my pants pocket. As long as I knew I had the pill, I could chance a slight breeze. If the pain got worse, I could pretend the way to make it better was sitting in my pocket.

Dr. Schatz and I agreed to try other medications. Percodan, another narcotic, worked no better than the codeine, which meant not at all. That was not completely true. The fog in which I felt enveloped was a function of the codeine. It sometimes caused me to forget whether you crossed on the red or the green. The haze, when I took enough, made me feel a degree or two away from the pain.

I tried Haldol, a major antipsychotic. Hopefully, it would affect the pain-signaling chemicals in my brain. It did not. Again Dilantin, again no effect. Again Tegretol—the fourth try, again no benefit. Again, awful side effects.

We talked again of surgery. One by one, each operation I suggested was dismissed. Too risky. Too esoteric.

"There is one other thing you could consider," he said. It was an operation. The one I did not want to hear about, any more now than when I had first been diagnosed by Jamshyd. One similar to the one I had seen and remembered so long ago from the TV show, *The Bold Ones*.

Dr. Adams had earlier dismissed the idea of electrode implantation. Not if stopping the constant pain was my first priority.

Dr. Schatz and Dr. Wilson were not sure they agreed. They suggested I contact Dr. Hosobuchi, Dr. Adam's associate. His specialty was deep brain electrode implantation.

CHAPTER TWENTY-ONE

Both Dr. Wilson and Dr. Schatz suggested I write to Dr. Hosobuchi. He wrote back to tell me he had two procedures he could offer. One was a major surgery. His letter read, "I do not recommend it. It has a high failure rate and high risk potential." The next paragraph contained the words I both expected and feared. "The other is brain stimulation. You have a choice of either. I strongly recommend the latter."

I did not want an implant. The idea of having a machine sewn inside my body was repulsive.

Before I wrote him, I had seen a weekly news show. When the announcer said the subject was brain stimulation, I thought I should watch it. When he said the surgeon was Dr. Hosobuchi, I had no choice. I had to watch it.

I kept the set on. I heard some of the words. I saw the patient being prepped. Then I turned away. It was too gruesome. I could not listen or see.

Now, it was imperative that I know what it was, exactly, and how it was done.

The production company was located in Mid-Manhattan. I called their office. I spoke with a secretary. "A few weeks ago, you showed a segment on Dr. Y. Hosobuchi and a brain implant procedure. He's offering to do that on me. Is there a way I can come to the office and view the tape?" "No."

I asked to speak with someone higher up. They, too, said it was not possible. It is simply not done.

When I want or need something important, I am like a dog with a bone. The more it is pulled away from me, the harder I hang on. Undaunted, and uninvited, I went to the office. I had the look of a person who suffered paralysis. I also brought Dr. Hosobuchi's letter with me.

A production assistant came down to the office. She greeted me, looked at the letter and told me to wait. "It'll take a few minutes to locate the tape," she said as she walked away. Ten minutes later, she escorted me to a small room. In it were a chair, a console, and the tape. My stomach clutched as she turned on the set.

Dr. Hosobuchi's face came on the screen. He was dressed in a surgical gown, mask, and gloves. The camera pointed down at the patient on the litter. She was wide awake. It was then aimed at her open skull. My stomach clutched and churned.

I wanted to turn away. *Why can't it just all go away? But the pain! I can't do nothing. I have to do something. There must be a way to stop it. I would be willing to agree to almost anything. If it could fix me.*

My hands gripped the arms of the chair. I forced myself to look at the screen. I watched the electrodes being put inside her head. I listened as he asked her, "Where do you feel it? Where is the pain now?" *My God, the same questions that Dr. Brisman and Dr. Martinez asked. The same torture! No!* The word reverberated in my head. I spoke it out loud. "There is no way. I can't allow somebody to do that to me!"

The tape ended. I stood up. I swallowed a number of times. I worked at getting my face into order. I did not want them to see the horror I felt.

I was able to get my things together. I walked out into the hall and passed the receptionist. "Did you find what you needed?" Sadly, I smiled. "Yes. I did. And I wish I hadn't."

I knew I did not want the electrodes. Seeing it in color reinforced my hatred for it. Despite how disgusting it was, I realized I had harbored some hope that it was something to which I could agree. No matter how ludicrous, hope always snuck in somehow.

Dr. Hosobuchi did not want to do the surgery. I was stuck between a rock and a hard place.

A few months prior to the letter and the tape, I realized there was something I could do. Something that might make me feel and look better. I wanted the tarsorrharphy opened. Dr. Arentsen was not ecstatic about doing it. After all, it was doing what it was supposed to do. My eye was in good shape, neither infected nor eroded.

I convinced him to go ahead. He agreed somewhat to go along. "The only way I'm willing to do it is if you agree to my opening only one side of it." Half is better than nothing, so they say. It was not. It helped neither the loathing of my appearance nor the pain.

I went back to him. "I want you to undo it the rest of the way."

"As soon as I open it, you run the risk of an infection. The eye can completely dry out. It could erode, even ulcerate. You could end up losing your eye. You have no feeling in that eye. You wouldn't know if something was wrong." I knew that. "I know. I understand the risk I may be taking." With the hatred of it straining my voice, I pled, "You have to open it. I can't stand the way it looks."

He looked at me with sympathy. "Is it really that bad?"

"It's horrible!" I cried out. I couldn't stand the way I looked. I hoped the pain would lessen. I was petrified by the idea that I could lose my eye. "Please, I want it opened."

My theory was proved wrong. The pain did not get better. I did, however. My stomach no longer cartwheeled when I accidentally caught sight of myself in a mirror.

Other visual effects of the paralysis remained.

I thought I was being overly sensitive. The day I asked a policeman for directions, I found out that was not so.

He gave me the information I needed. After thanking him, I started to walk away. I noticed he did not. "Do you mind if I ask you a question?" he said. He had been staring at my face. Strangers often stared. Some asked outright, "What is wrong with your face?" or "What is wrong with your eye?" The kinder ones offered a tissue or advice. One sweet lady decided that I was blind. She took hold of my arm and led me off the subway train.

His question I did not expect. "How old are you?" It was kind of impertinent. He was a policeman. I had been taught you always speak respectfully to the police. I decided to be coy. "How old do you think I am?"

"Well," he said. "Your left side looks like you're twenty-six, but your right side looks like you're thirty. Are you twenty-eight?" Yes. I was.

The right side continued to age as time and pain took its toll. The left side couldn't show age, or anything else, since it continued to refuse to move.

My age was becoming a big problem for me. I tried not to look in the mirror. When I did, I got the same confusing information that the officer had noted. The signs most people use were missing from the left side of my face. The events that mark the passage of time were absent from my life.

Most people start jobs, graduate school, get married, have children. They celebrate anniversaries and birthdays. They meet deadlines, get promotions. I had none of these.

I could not work. I had no husband, no children.

I did not celebrate my birthday. There was no point to it, no reason to rejoice. Just the start of another year of pain. Three hundred sixty-five more days of being alone. My life was an exercise in futility.

Each year, Edna sent me a birthday greeting. She usually called as well. Every couple of years, one or the other of my siblings would send a card. I never heard from any of my five nephews and one niece. My mother might send a gift certificate. One year, it was for $50.00 at Bloomingdale's. That was a nice gesture. Except that I was stealing toilet paper from ladies' rooms. I needed money for necessities, not niceties. If she called, it was usually a few days late. Even when it was acknowledged, it was done in a way to hurt me. To remind me I did not have a family.

My life was like a record with the needle caught in a groove. My problems were always the same. I had surgery, more or less, annually. The operations may have been different, but the results were always the same. I started the year with pain. Surgery was offered. Drugs were tried. I raised my hopes. I went into the hospital. My hopes were felled. The year ended with pain. A bagpipe wail, played over and over.

I felt better with my eye opened. It was still obvious that I had a facial deformity, but I felt as though I looked less disfigured. Sometimes, if I held my head a certain way, I could catch a glimpse of the way I used to look.

It had been a number of months since the last operation. I looked worse around the eye. My forehead was discolored. A thick solid crust of greasy dirt had settled. Because of the pain, there was nothing I could do about it. At least, at home.

The dirt was not merely a problem because it looked so awful. After three or four months of build-up, my eye would become infected or dry out. That made the pain worse. My belief was that the dirt was getting into the eye.

The reason, whatever it was, was not important. I cared only about the eye getting better. Then the pain could go back to the baseline level.

The infections and dryness stopped within a few hours of my face being washed. The washing had to be done at the day surgery department at Wills Eye Hospital. Every three to four months, I would take the train to Philadelphia. Sometimes I would stay at my parents' house. My father would leave me off at the hospital. A few hours later, after I awakened from the general anaesthesia, he would pick me up. I stayed overnight at the house. Two days later, I would get back on the train to New York. A face washing is so inconsequential. The doctors and nurses had more important things to do. Yet they never treated me as though I was there for a piddling procedure. I was treated like an old friend. In case

I forgot, which I sometimes did, Dr. Anya or the nurses kept shampoo in their lockers.

As with the pain and surgeries, this, too, became a cycle. The dirt built up. The eye went bad. The pain increased because the eye was bad. I had general anaesthesia. My face was washed. The cleaning helped the pain. I looked better. The eye behaved itself. Then, in about two weeks, the dirt started to visibly accumulate. The eye couldn't take it. It would go bad. Back I went to have my face washed. Round and round, I went.

In October 1981, I raised my hopes once more.

Dr. Hosobuchi and I decided I would try his surgery. We were not in agreement as to which one. I had now spent three weeks a year, every year, in a hospital. This time, I intended to make at least one change. I would not allow my father to sabotage either me or the surgery.

No one but Carolyn knew that I was going back to California. I was able to save up enough money to fly. After I arrived and was settled in my room, I walked down to the nurses' station. "No one knows that I'm here. If anyone calls, please do not let them know that I'm here." I told them what had happened with Dr. Wilson. "I don't want Dr. Hosobuchi to go through the same thing." The head nurse assured me Dr. Hosobuchi could handle it. "I'm not going to give him the chance to find out." Knowing that neither I nor Dr. Hosobuchi would be bothered by my father made my stay a little easier.

This stay did not fit the pattern. I was there for surgery. It was a definite. None of the tests were repeated. Dr. Hosobuchi knew what I had come for. He knew what he wanted to do. He did insist on conducting two tests. Every patient had to go through them before he would operate. We still debated. He continued to advocate the implant. I continued to insist on the operation.

I was given a shot of sodium amytal. This would not be the truth serum interview I had been forced to undergo when my shoulder was bad. The nurse asked no questions. I was told,

"Let me know when the pain stops." If the pain remained until the drug put me to sleep, it was a sign of organicity. It did. I had passed the first test.

For the second, I was given alternating doses of morphine and placebo. I would not know which was which. Janine*, the nurse, told me the test was not to see if I was a malingerer. Of course, if the placebo helped, the pain might well be psychosomatic. She told me the order in which she had given me the two after the test was over. I only responded to the morphine. It made me feel weird. It took me somewhat away from the pain. It did not stop or minimize it. Once again, it was determined that my pain was from the trigeminal neuralgia and damage from prior surgeries. The pain was not in my mind. It was in my brain.

A day later, Dr. Hosobuchi walked into my room. He stood next to the bed. "I think you should let me do the implant. It is much less dangerous than the surgery." I did not care. I did not want anyone sewing metal into my brain.

The "major" surgery was called a trigeminal tractotomy. He would have to cut deep into my neck. That was where the path (or tract) of the trigeminal nerve was accessible. Once there, he would cut the nerve. Finally, someone was offering to cut the nerve. That had always seemed the most sensible thing to do. If the nerve was cut, there was no way it could communicate with any part of my brain or skin. With the nerve cut and killed, there could be no pain or sensation. I knew this was the right answer.

He did not agree. "If you have the implant and it doesn't work, I will still be able to go back in and do the tractotomy." A very tall, handsome man of Japanese descent, he was dressed this day in a brown-beige suit. His manner was soft and quiet. In his nicely modulated, slightly accented voice, he continued, "If you have the tractotomy first, I have shot my wad." I laughed at the incongruity of his words with his style. It did not change my mind at all. I told him I would only agree to the tractotomy.

He put me on the surgical schedule. He still expected to do the implant. He told me, though, that the choice was still mine.

I called Dr. Schatz. "What do you think I should do? I really don't want the implant." He apologized. "I don't know what to tell you." I thought he might say that. It was nice to talk with him, but I wanted his opinion. His refusal was of no help. I needed to hear a medical person second my decision.

I was walking down the hall, headed nowhere in particular. Just trying to think out what I should do. As I rounded a corner, I looked up to see someone I knew. I liked this person. It was someone in whom I had faith. "I have a problem. I don't know who to talk to." This person asked me, "What's the matter? Maybe I can help?" It was nice to have someone ask me that. "I don't want the implant, but that's what Dr. Hosobuchi wants to do. I know the tractotomy is what I need. What do you think I should do?"

This individual smiled. "If you don't tell anyone who advised you, I think you're right. I think you should go for the tractotomy."

Oh boy. What a relief. It felt so good to have someone help me with the decision. "Doctor-patient confidentiality," I said with a laugh. "I won't tell anyone."

During the week before the surgery, I repeatedly asked about possible side effects. Even though he was set on the electrodes, Dr. Hosobuchi talked with me about the risks of the other. "There is a ninety-five-percent chance that you won't be able to walk after the surgery. You won't be paralyzed, and it should be transient. The instructions from your brain to your legs will be temporarily disturbed. If it happens," he added, "it should only take a few weeks of therapy to fix."

That warning and knowing that he was entering my brain through the top of my spine was very scary. *Could I be paralyzed?* Dr. Jannetta had trained me very well. Every time I saw Dr. Hosobuchi, whether in my room or in the hall, I stopped him. "Is there a chance I can be paralyzed from this?" He assured and reassured me, "That is not one of the risks."

By the seventh time I asked, he must have realized that I needed to hear a "yes." "Yes," he said. "There is a chance of paralysis. It is very, very small." I did not want to wake up and find I had been lied to again. His answer scared me, but now I knew the truth. I could prepare myself, just in case.

The day of surgery arrived. One of the floor nurses came to the room to help me get ready to go downstairs. "Dr. Hosobuchi is waiting for you. He has the OR all prepared for the implant." He was ready for me to agree with him up to the last second. "Wait a minute. I'm not having the implant. I told him I wanted him to do the tractotomy." "Okay," she said. "I'll call the OR and tell him." She had a bit of reluctance in her voice. She returned to the room a short time later. "He's getting set up to do the tractotomy." To his great credit, he accepted my refusal.

As always, an orderly rolled me down to the pre-anaesthesia room. The IV was put in the back of my right hand. I was taken to the operating suite. A couple of nurses moved me onto the surgical table. The anaesthesiologist, plunger in hand, said, "You're going to go to sleep now." The sounds of the room and the thoughts in my mind swirled farther and farther away. My last prayer before losing consciousness was very concrete.

Oh, God, please don't let me wake up paralyzed.

CHAPTER TWENTY-TWO

Every surgery required me to go to the neurosurgical ICU. This time was no different. I awakened to an array of blinking and beeping machines. None were attached to me. I only had an IV in my arm. If you needed peace and quiet, this was not the place to be. Most of the beds were filled. It was very noisy, very bright. The lights hurt my eye as they always did. I looked around, trying to see who else was in the unit. I turned my eyes left to right to see if the pain was still there.

That answered one concern. Did they fix the pain? I shook my head in frustration and disappointment. No, it was still there.

I fearfully moved my toes. They wiggled. The movement was still there. I was not paralyzed! A foam brace was fastened around my neck. I was not allowed to get out of bed. The nurses insisted I use a bedpan when the need arose. Nora, in particular, was very kind and attentive. A tall, short-haired blond, she personified what one hoped to have in a nurse: kindness, compassion, and care. After three days, I was allowed to try and get out of bed. Dr. Hosobuchi had not exaggerated. I could not walk. I was like a newborn colt. My legs splayed all over the place.

On the fourth postoperative day, Joan took care of my discharge from the NICU. She sat me in a wheelchair. She wheeled me to my room on the regular nursing floor.

A physical therapist came to my room every day. The exercise was simple. She took my arm. Together, we walked up and down the hall, over and over again. Dr. Hosobuchi's cut went through some of the fiber tract of the central nervous system.

These fibers carried the command to walk from my brain to my legs. The repetitious walking would reignite the connection. The rehabilitation was primarily to get my brain to remind my legs how it used to be done.

The rehabbing of my walking started me thinking about my face.

In the past, various doctors told me that a right-sided facelift could help. It needed to be done every ten to fifteen years. It would help the problem that the police officer noticed. It would give better age symmetry to my face.

I had never talked with a plastic surgeon. No one had suggested it. It had never occurred to me. I always thought of the damage as a muscular thing. It would get better on its own, or not at all. Neither Dr. Jannetta nor anyone else ever suggested therapy, exercise, or reconstructive surgery.

I asked Dr. Hosobuchi if he had any ideas. He nodded affirmatively. "The accessory nerve [#11], the one that shrugs your shoulder, can be connected to your facial nerve. When you shrug, the left side of your mouth will smile. It would look coquettish if you shrug when you smile."

It took me less than three seconds of thought. I did not want another operation. The idea of another doctor fiddling around with another major nerve? *No, no. Who knows how I would end up then? And shrugging if I wanted to smile? No, I don't think so.*

There was only one thing I needed immediately. That was to direct my energies toward recovering from the surgery.

I was so disappointed. I fell into the trap I unconsciously set for myself every time. My conscious mind worked hard at reminding me. *I'm not going to let myself get caught again. I want it to work but,* I hated having to remind myself, *I have to keep remembering that it might not.*

I forgot. *How could it not have worked?* I cried inside myself. The despondency was overwhelming.

I looked across the room at the patient in the bed opposite

mine. She had been very ill. Her surgery worked. I felt very happy for her. I hated her for her success.

I could not walk at all for the first few days. I was forced to stay in bed. Even trying to sit up was difficult. I was dependent on the staff, for everything.

John* and Mark* were two of the nurses. I could not get to a bathroom to shower or bathe. Marcy* told me there was a shortage of staff. "If you want to get a bath, only Mark or John can do it." For three days, I insisted I would only let a female nurse help me with the bath. "I'm sorry, but we don't have anyone to do it. It's either John or Mark or no one. I'm sorry."

It felt like they were trying to teach me a lesson. A nurse is a nurse is a nurse. After three days, I felt so grimy I could not fight it anymore. "It doesn't matter who. Can you send someone in to help me take a bath?" John came into my room. He looked at me. "Are you sure?"

He scooped me up from the bed, almost cradling me. He carried me into the bathroom. He stayed as I undressed. Then he lowered me into the tub. "I'm sorry. I know you're a nurse. I shouldn't have fought letting you do your job."

I stayed in the warm water for a long time. It felt so good to be clean again. I hit the red button at the side of the tub. "Yes?" a voice answered. "I'm finished with the bath. Can you send John back?"

He knocked on the door. He walked into the room, carrying a towel. He reached down to the tub. He gently lifted me up and out. He stood, letting me hold on to him as I dressed.

It was all too much to take in. The pain, the loss of independence, the lack of control, I grieved for what I had hoped, for what I had lost. When I have pain and I can't make a sound, it is because I am physically incapable of doing so. My vocal cords literally closed down. For the first time in my life, the emotional pain took my words from me.

Little by little, I became more independent with the use of a cane. As I gained back my physical control, my words returned. The depression remained but no longer enshrouded me.

I did not feel well. It was not from the surgery or the afteref-
fects. I had a slight fever. I felt "sick."

I never learn my lesson.

I hate being in the hospital. Logic and sense are irrelevant to
me when the chance is there for me to go home. My recovery
period was over. I was ready to be discharged. A resident, Dr.
Wiser*, asked me if I felt well enough to leave. "Sure," I said,
lying. "I'm fine."

I flew home. I slept for the entire flight. I assumed I would
feel better after I got home. It always takes a few days to get back
on your feet again (as it were).

Little by little, instead of feeling better, I felt worse and worse.
I could not put my finger on what was wrong. I had the general
fatigue feeling you get when you're ill. I waited for it to go away.
Three weeks later, my low-grade fever turned into a high-grade
fever, 103 degrees Fahrenheit. I had a terrible headache that
worsened with changes in my position, especially when I tried to
stand. I felt incredibly weak. I wished I had family to call, but I
did not. New York City was in the middle of a severe snowstorm.
Even if it had occurred to me to ask a neighbor for help, there
was no way we could have gotten to a hospital.

I was too sick to pretend everything was okay. Meningitis is a
possible complication from brain surgery. My symptoms were
those of meningitis. I knew I needed help.

Two ambulance attendants rang my doorbell an hour and a
half after my call to 911. I opened the door. "What's the trouble?"
one of them asked.

"I think I may have meningitis."

He looked at his partner. His eyes turned up to the ceiling.
"What makes you think that?"

"I have a very high fever and a postural headache." They
did not look impressed. "I had brain surgery three weeks ago."
The smiles vanished. They moved to stand aside me, one to the
right, one to the left. They walked me out to the waiting ambulance. I sat in the back as they drove me to St. Vincent's Hospital,
a few blocks away.

The ambulance attendants brought me inside. I was taken to an examining room. Someone came in with a gown in her hand. "You need to change into this." I sat on the litter, gowned and waiting for help to come.

A nurse came into the room. I breathed a sigh of relief. Now, I was on my way to getting better. She would prepare me for the doctor. Then I could go home with a diagnosis and prescription. That was not why she was there. "We need this room. We're going to have to put you out in the hallway."

I stayed in the hall for four and a half hours. A nurse came over to me. Now I would get help. "We're going to move you off here to the side. You'll be seen as soon as we can get to you."

I was so thirsty. I had not had anything liquid in hours. The fever made the thirst worse. Every time I saw someone who looked like they worked there, I called out to them. "Please, can you get me a glass of water?" No one could or would. I had to find a way to get it myself.

I leaned over and freed the railing lock. I looked over the side of the bed. The floor was a thousand miles away. I cautiously maneuvered myself over to the side of the bed. Gingerly, with the help of my cane, I lowered myself from the height of the litter to the depth of the floor. The fatigue and my coltish legs fought my effort not to fall. Success! I forced my legs to walk me over to the water fountain. It was so good, the water a coolant to my body turned into a furnace.

I returned to the litter and hoisted myself up. I lay back down. I tried to figure out why I was being ignored. I said, "I think I may have meningitis" to the nurses. All I could think was that they thought I was making a big deal out of a cold. No one had a lot of time to spare for a problem so mundane.

A resident stood at the side of the litter. "I hear you're not feeling well. What's wrong?" I told him about the fever, the headache, and the surgery. Within two minutes, I was in an examining room. Within five, Dr. Collins* had a spinal tap tray in his hand.

"You have to have a tap. We need to check for infection or leakage." I got into position, on my side with my knees drawn up to my chest.

"Have you ever had a spinal tap before?" he asked me. "Only two," I said. As though most people had more, rather than none.

"Please. Warn me before you put the needle in, okay? Please?" I hated having things done to me, especially when I could not see when and what was being done. "I'm injecting the local anaesthesia now." I knew that would hurt, and it did. We waited for it to take effect. "Okay, stay very, very still. I'm going to put the needle in now."

I was scared and nervous. Not because it hurt, which it did not. The fright came from not being able to control what he was doing to me. I fought to stay in control of myself. "Okay, I'm finished but don't move yet." I heaved a sigh of relief. It was not that bad. Best of all, it was over.

"I have to do it again. We didn't get enough fluid." *Oh no.* "No. Please don't it again. Please don't," I pleaded. Once was enough. I was so tired, physically and emotionally, from all the struggles over the past few weeks, maybe even the last few years. I was defenseless, my emotions rushing to be heard. As he helped me get back into position and pushed the needle back into my spine, I cried, "Oh please. Don't do it again."

The tap showed neither infection nor leakage. I had to stay in the hospital though. The admitting diagnosis was "rule out meningitis."

It was not that, a cold, or the flu. I had "posterior fossa syndrome." The symptoms mimic those of meningitis. It is not uncommon after a neurosurgery to that area of the brain. Unlike meningitis, it is benign.

I stayed in the hospital for a week. For the first few days, I was as sick as a dog. In addition to the other symptoms, I developed horrendous nausea. The mere site of food made me ill. My problem walking made it hard to get to the bathroom in time.

After two days, I called my father to tell him where I was. In case something unexpected happened, I figured someone should know where I was. There was no one else for me to call.

I had one friend in my apartment building. David lived on the same floor. He and I talked often at the mailbox. I would go to his apartment or he to mine every few months. We would sit, schmooze and have a cheese-and-tea tasting. I trusted him implicitly. It did not occur to me to call him. Our friendship was inside the building. It did not extend farther than that.

It is a lesson I learned from my family. I am on my own. Even when there was someone I could call, I did not think to do so. If I did, it would most probably be refused. Or impinge on their plans. The last thing I ever wanted to be was a bother. Not calling or asking assured me that I would not be hurt. It was so deeply entrenched in me that the idea of reaching out, except to those paid to care, was an almost-unknown thought.

There was no treatment other than an IV, the codeine for my face pain, and aspirin. I was discharged five days after my arrival.

I returned home feeling better. I left with a fever of 99.6 degrees Fahrenheit. Dr. Duggan, the internist to whom I had been assigned, did not think the temperature was a reason for me to stay. Neither did I.

With the exception of the fever, I felt fine physically. I still had the pain; the surgery did not touch it. It was time to return to dealing with it. It was also time to work on regaining my footing. Being in the hospital and feeling so ill had kept me from practicing my walking.

I used the cane, which helped a lot. Since the problem was not in my legs but in my brain, I talked to it each time I walked. "Right foot, left foot, right foot, left foot." After three months, they finally got together on the subject.

Occasionally, my legs would buckle or go the wrong way. I sometimes fell while practicing in my apartment. I wobbled when I walked down the street. I looked more like Charlie Chaplin than me. Once I collected myself, I reminded my feet, and via them, my brain, "Right, left, right, left," and they, sometimes reluctantly, obeyed.

I met with Dr. Schatz. I hoped he had something else I could try. I also had a very important question I needed to ask him. In the article given to me by Dr. Jordan, the author detailed the signs and symptoms of the syndrome he believed I had. These included some patients going blind and/or becoming paralyzed. The idea was more than I could bear. During every appointment, there came a time when my voice trembled, my eyes clouded. "Am I going to go blind? Will I become paralyzed?" "No," he answered each and every time. "That's not what you have." The article detailed the kind of vascular malformations I had. The other signs and symptoms, such as retardation, organic psychiatric difficulties, seizures, and other associated brain abnormalities, had nothing to do with me.

Dr. Schatz had never misled me before. After maybe the tenth time he said, "No." I finally believed him.

There was nothing I could do to change the pain. I continued to take the codeine. The pain was made worse when my eye dried out. Because it was happening frequently, I started to go to the Manhattan Eye, Ear, and Throat Hospital. Dr. Schatz knew Dr. Odel, a neuroophthalmologist who practiced there.

Dr. Odel called me into an exam room. A number of residents and fellows lined the walls. I told him my history as he asked. I always said it as fast as possible. If I got it over with quickly, then it did not sound quite so bad. He took the sheaf of papers I handed him. He looked them over. He read copies of letters sent to me from Dr. Schatz. As he read, his face made the same expression of "wow" that I had seen on so many others.

He was nice, the kind of doctor I expected Dr. Schatz to know. His dark hair and dark eyes nicely complimented his dark suit jacket. He asked me many of the same questions I had been asked before. I listed my surgeries for him. I enumerated all the different kinds of therapies and drugs that had been tried.

He agreed to continue giving me prescriptions for the codeine. "I think it would not be a bad idea to try the Tegretol again." This would be my fourth try for this drug. I hated the way it made me feel. Each time, the side effects were somewhat less, but it still made me feel cloudy and tired. "Well, it's the fourth time, but . . . okay."

It surprised me how fast the feeling of the drug wore off this time. After about a week, I was not sleeping all the time. My mind was not cloudy. The pain remained the same.

Three weeks later, I knew there was a change. Not one spontaneous pain. Not yet. It was too soon to celebrate. The pain could never be trusted to keep its apparent promises.

Five more weeks went by. Still no spontaneous pains. After four months without the lightning, I was convinced. They were gone! No more savage unbidden slicing! No more sudden attacks from out of the blue! For the first time since Dr. Osterholm's surgery had stopped working, I could relax.

I needed to continue my vigil against floating leaves, errant hands illustrating a point, coats and sweaters thrown about recklessly. Touch still triggered the pain. But I no longer had to fear the secretive attacker hiding inside my head. My trigeminal nerve, my enemy, had been rousted by Tegretol. Yeah, Tegretol!

The constant and eye movement pains did not change. They were what kept me from working, going to school, leaving the house when the weather was bad. My ecstasy over the absence of the lightning was profound. It let me breathe freely, without fear.

My delight ebbed as I realized my life had not changed. Anger, despair, and life weariness returned.

I called Dr. Schatz. "Isn't there anything I can do?" I could almost see the shrug I heard in his voice. "I'm sorry, Carol. I'm running out of ideas" The line stayed quiet as he tried to think of something. "Maybe you can try hypnosis again?"

He knew that both times it had been tried, it failed. Nevertheless, something is always better than nothing. I asked him for a referral.

Dr. Schatz gave me the phone number of Dr. Clorinda
Margolis. She was the department head of the Jefferson Hypnosis Center. Three weeks later, I had my appointment. Dr. Margolis
and I went into a consultation room. A pretty woman, her face
appearing younger than her gray hair implied, she said, "Tell me
about your situation with the pain." She sat with me for one session. The appointment would let her decide if hypnosis was
appropriate. After listening to my story, she agreed that it would
not hurt to give it one more try.

I returned the following week to meet Jenny Myers.* She
greeted me out in the waiting room. She was young, maybe a few
years older than I. She walked me back to a room that contained
two chairs.

It was nice, for a change, to know I would not have to un-
dress or let someone touch my face. Already I was better because
my level of fear remained low. We agreed to meet once a week.
Jenny explained how she worked. Before we started, she wanted
to give me a test. It would show if I was hypnotizable. And how
deep into a trance I could go.

This test was unlike Dr. Speigel's. I did not have to roll my
eyes. She asked nothing of me that could worsen the pain. She
had me sit back comfortably in the nicely padded armchair. She
spoke in a soft, somewhat rhythmic voice. Slowly, I was lulled
into a trance state.

"Your right arm has helium balloons tied to it," she told me.
"Let the balloons raise your arm. You don't have to do anything.
The balloons will do it all." I smiled inwardly. How silly. My arm
did not think it was silly. It rose, slow and steady, until it was
loosely hanging in the air. It made no attempt to fall back down.
"Your arm is floating on the air. Slowly, it can lower itself until it
is lying back on the chair." It complied.

"I have a list of words that I am going to tell you. I want you
to remember them." After she read the list, she added, "You will
not remember the words."

After fifteen minutes or so, she gave me directions that brought me up out of the trance. When she asked me to repeat the words she had spoken, I remembered only three. "Do you recall the word 'refrigerator'?" No, I did not. She asked about other words. To some, I would reply, "Oh, yes. I do remember you saying that one." I laughed at the fact that the instruction had taken. It surprised and amused me that I did not know all the words. "That's a good sign. It tells us that you're able to go into a deep trance state." It seemed this was a good portent.

Every Saturday morning, for the next three months, I took the train to Philadelphia. Jenny lulled me into a trance at each session. The third time was not the charm. The pain remained the same.

I found it to be enjoyable, something I had not experienced with Dr. Sacerdote. Using Jenny's words, I would sometimes put myself back into trance during the ride home. Hypnosis is a state of concentrated attention. I did not worry about missing my stop. I was always aware of all that happened around me.

I liked Jenny. I did not want to quit. The problem was the expense. The Amtrak fare was $50.00. Jenny's fee was $25.00. It was being raised. The next visit, it would be $50.00. There was no way I could continue. I. was deeply disappointed, but there was nothing I could do about it.

I went back to see Dr. Schatz. He gave me more prescriptions for more drugs. None helped.

Some articles refer to TN as the "suicide disease."* The literature cites a statistic of fifty percent to eighty-five percent of sufferers attempting/completing suicide. I was ready to join that number.

At least once a day, I put myself in a trance. My instructions were simple. "There is only one way left to try and stop the pain. It is okay to do whatever you have to. It is okay to die."

I started doing it while I was still seeing Jenny. I decided I should tell her. It was not a "cry for help." I wanted her to know that I did find benefit from what she was teaching me.

Sometimes she misread my cues. Often, the worse I felt, the brighter the colors of my earrings and clothes would be. She tended to comment. "You must be feeling better. You're wearing such joyful colors."

I felt I needed to be explicit with her about how she had helped me. I wanted there to be no misunderstanding but that I appreciated what she had given me.

She was not happy about it. "I don't like that you're using this as a weapon, but I can't stop you from using it any way you want." That was how our last appointment ended.

I had no family with whom I could talk. I was not going to tell Edna my plans. My relationship with David, my friend from the apartment building, did not extend to discussing something like this.

I continued to see Carolyn. We were four years into the therapy. The only way I could talk about what I planned to do was to say it to a person who was paid to hear it.

"I'm seriously considering suicide as a way, hopefully, to stop the pain." A therapist's job is to be objective and available. Carolyn was both. She was also supportive of my plans. She said she knew of a therapist who did LSD therapy with people who are dying. She also suggested I might want to talk with a thanantologist.

My past efforts at suicide, although emotional in cause, helped make the conditioning process easier. Then, I wanted out of life because I could not take the emotional, verbal, and physical abuse anymore. This time, suicide was a therapy. I prepared to induce my own cure. I remained open to other possibilities as well. After all, the side effect, death, was not the point. The point was to get rid of the pain.

Dr. Schatz had no idea that I worked each day at self-help. Unaware of my plans, he suggested that I consider entering a pain clinic.

The main thing I knew about pain clinics was that they helped people by using treatments such as biofeedback, exercise, physical therapy, and massage. The pain conditions that were helped were usually from the neck down. I did not see how they could be applied to facial pain. But, then, you never know.

Dr. Nelson Hendler owns and runs the Mensana Pain Clinic, in Stevenson, Maryland. It is a private clinic. As a result, it is very expensive.

The financial terms almost closed off any chance of my going there. "We're a private clinic. As a result, some insurance companies will pay for the medical treatments. None pay the room and board." I explained about my finances, or lack thereof. He was very kind. "I can waive the non-medical fees. We might be able to help you. As long as your insurance agrees to pay the medical costs. I'd like to try."

I called both of my insurance carriers: Blue Cross/Blue Shield of Pennsylvania and Medicare. I was afraid it would be like pulling teeth to get them to agree to pay. Instead, it was easy. I explained what therapies were offered. "That's no problem. We cover that kind of thing."

The day after my thirtieth birthday, August 16, 1982, I arrived in Maryland. I was ready to embark on what I believed to be my last chance. And my next to last choice.

CHAPTER TWENTY-THREE

I took a taxi from the Baltimore Amtrak station. We rode for twenty minutes. The driver took me past magnificent trees, lush grounds, and large homes. Finally, we pulled up to what appeared to be a mansion. It sat high upon a hill. I saw no sign announcing Mensana Clinic. Nothing indicated that we were entering a medical facility. Up we went into a long driveway. As we turned left, I saw a small parking lot. I still saw no sign. I could not believe this was the clinic.

I knocked at the outside door and found it open. I entered a small vestibule. Past it, I saw a large room with a secretary sitting at a small desk. I was in the right place. As I identified myself, a short, dark-haired, overweight man entered the room. I was surprised when he identified himself as Dr. Hendler. From what I had heard and read about him, and the clinic, I expected to meet quite a powerhouse. Instead, I found a smiling, soft-spoken, young man. In fact, he was only a few years older than I.

"Why don't you take your things up to the room? When you come back down, we can talk." I walked up a flight of stairs. I turned right. A door was partially opened. I pushed it. My mouth hung open in delight. As magnificent as the building was, nothing prepared me for the elegance of my room.

It was enormous, almost twice the size of my studio apartment. Next to the door were two beds spaced a few feet apart. A few feet past the ends of the beds was a sitting area, containing two chairs and a small couch. A fireplace at the opposite end of the room completed what could rightfully be called a salon.

This was not a clinic. It was not merely a converted manse. It was heaven.

I was disabused of that notion a half an hour later when Dr. Hendler and I had our first interview.

He asked the perfunctory questions: Describe the pain. What does it feel like? Where is it? What treatments have been tried? Did any of them work? I answered some in shorthand since he knew a little about me from our telephone conversation.

"How do you feel about the pain and what has happened to your life?"

I did not intend to start our relationship with a lie. "I'm going to try anything you offer me. I want to get rid of the pain. But I have to tell you that I will commit suicide if I can't get relief."

I was surprised at how easy it was for me to talk about it. Whenever I had to talk about my two adolescent attempts, I always stammered and hesitated. They embarrassed me. I had to gird myself to even say the word. Now that I knew it as a legitimate option in a legitimate situation, the words tumbled easily off my tongue.

"Are you saying that if I cannot help you, you'll kill yourself?"

I needed to make it very clear to him that it was not an issue of his, personally, being able to help me. "I'm not saying that if you cannot help me, I will kill myself. I am saying that I will try to stop or help the pain by doing whatever you suggest. If the pain doesn't respond, and there are no medical options left, then I'll have to initiate the only other thing I can think of to try and stop the pain." I could not have anticipated his reaction.

"If you're telling me that you're going to kill yourself, then I will have to have you committed to the hospital."

This was definitely not going well.

The interview concluded with nothing resolved. When we

met in the hall a short time later, I stopped him. "How serious are you about your threat to have me committed?"

"It is not meant to be a threat. I don't mean to be facetious, but I am as serious about it as you are."

This was very upsetting.

I returned to my room and called the ACLU and the Legal Aid Society. I asked the person who answered what my constitutional rights in a situation like this would be. "Could I be legally committed given the fact that I have a legitimate medical reason for committing suicide?"

The possibility of my self-induced death was a function of my pain. It was not a result of psychiatric impairment.

The people I spoke with were unable to sympathize with my situation. The man from Legal Aid told me, "If you're thinking of suicide, then you are crazy. You should be in a hospital." The ACLU could offer me nothing.

The next day, Dr. Hendler told me he had received a call from the man at the Legal Aid Society. He was upset, he told Dr. Hendler, and thought he should know about my call.

I kept my anger under control as I replied, "I'm not going to let you commit me. I don't think this is an issue of instability. That is why I wanted to find out what my legal recourse is if you attempt it." I continued, "I'm not making threats because I think that will force you to stop the pain. I am saying that I will do everything within my power to relieve it. If I can't find a way medically, then I will have to take matters into my own hands." Dr. Hendler made no attempt to interrupt me. "I'm not going to kill myself because I want to die. I don't know if death will stop the pain; no one knows what happens at or after death. I can only hope there's no pain. My death would be the side effect of attempting to stop the pain. It's like any operation. I can only hope that it will be successful. It is not a side effect that I want. It's something that can't be helped."

He said he agreed that my problem was not primarily psychiatric. What I said made sense but, "I don't like it." He added,

"I talked with the psychiatrist for the Court of Maryland about the possibility of having you committed. He told me that there'd be no point. They could only hold you for ten days but then you would have to be released if you could not be certified mentally ill. Given that your threat of suicide appears to be a response to a specific situation, the court couldn't hold you, and the situation after discharge would still be the same."

I told him I was greatly relieved to hear that.

Now that the threat of psychiatric incarceration was over, we were able to move on to therapy.

The treatment at a pain clinic is very different from that of a hospital. Dr. Hendler was both a psychiatrist and a pain specialist. As such, he prescribed both medications and psychotherapy. All patients were scheduled to meet with him once a day for injections and/or talk. We were also required to attend group therapy three times a week with Mary Davidson, the social worker.

The most important therapy for me was being with other chronic pain patients. This was the first time that I had ever talked with other people who had constant pain. It astounded me to be with others who had been through equally harrowing medical experiences.

There were eight other patients in the clinic during my stay. Each one had his own share of stories about misdiagnoses and mismanagement. More than one person told me about their pain being made worse by one or more medical interventions. Everyone had been through the emotional pain of being told their pain was psychological. All had been given treatment advice from one or more family members or friends: If you would just change (something) you would be fine. Every one of them had met up with at least one Miriam (my sister's mother-in-law who told me I just needed a job).

It amazed me that even though none of us shared the same body area or type of pain or diagnosis, other than the diagnosis of chronic pain, we all had the same basic story. Doctor to doctor, pill to pill, surgery to surgery, each of us could empathize with the other.

For the first time, I did not have to censor myself. I did not have to be afraid I would not be believed.

Sherry*, an intelligent and creative middle-aged woman who sometimes sold real estate, suffered from severe back, neck, and shoulder pain. Mark*, a gentle man in his thirties, was no longer able to work as an ambulance technician. He had sustained a severe back injury in a work-related accident. Linda* and Stephanie*, both housewives, also had bad backs as did college student Melissa. Both Jenny* and Belinda* had abdominal pain, and Mike* had a bad wrist. None of our faces indicated that we had constant pain. Yet, each of us had various things we were physically incapable of doing. Without knowing the things we could not do, anyone looking at any of us would be surprised to hear how severe our pain was. This was demonstrated most clearly by Mark, one afternoon at lunch.

We were talking about an episode of *The Odd Couple*, a television show we both enjoyed watching in rerun. He was saying something about the plot line. He did not sound like he was in pain. He did not look like he was in pain. I had absolutely no inkling until I saw the sweat breaking out on his forehead. His back had gone into severe spasm. He felt no need to make mention of it.

There were some times when we did have trouble accepting one another's pain complaints. One afternoon, Sherry and I had what might be called a pain competition.

She was upset because she had not been able to garden the day before. She had been unable to get down on her knees. "Could you do it another day instead?" I asked her.

"Yes," she said. "But I couldn't do it yesterday, and there will be other days that I also will not be able to do it."

"I don't understand why you're so upset. The things I can't do today, I could not do yesterday, and I won't be able to do them tomorrow. At least you know that there are times when you are able to do the things you want."

We were both in pain. We both grieved over what we had lost. It seemed hard on occasion to sympathize. I envied her for the things she could do. She found it dismaying that I could seem so heartless.

Sadly and unwittingly, I seemed to be responsible for a large amount of psychological stress in everyone. Not because they thought I was heartless. It was because I was considering suicide. I decided that, unless asked, I would not mention my plans for death. It did not seem appropriate. I knew it would be upsetting. I also assumed that there was a large probability that it was not an unknown thought to the others.

At the first group therapy meeting, Mary introduced me. She asked me to tell a little about myself. Introductions in group were different than in the hall. Telling some of what I already told others in a formal group meeting took on a different aura. When I finished, Mary asked me, "What will you do if the pain cannot be relieved?"

It was an honest question. One that deserved a truthful answer. I thought hard about what I intended to say. I did not want to start out by lying. "I will kill myself."

The faces around me looked stricken. Those comfortable talking in group turned to me.

Jenny and Belinda told stories of the times they had contemplated suicide. They talked themselves out of it by reminding themselves of the days with better hours, weeks with better days. "If you could get through the bad times by thinking about the better ones, it might help."

It was a good idea for the others. "For me, there are no better and worse times. I always have the pain. It never gets better, it only gets worse." The truth of my life: Yesterday, today, tomorrow, I never have a respite. The others looked at me sadly. The discussion wound down. Mary dismissed us all. As I rose to leave, she stopped me.

"I have to tell you—I never ask patients what they'll do if

nothing can be done. I asked you because I had a feeling about what you would say."

I seemed to have unsettled everyone. I felt unsettled, too, but there was nothing I could do about it.

Sherry and I realized we were not coming from different places. She, Mark, and I developed a close relationship. Often, the issue of my suicide would come up. "You know, you should write a book about chronic pain, about what you have been through." Dr. Hendler and Mary seconded the idea. I think they hoped the time it would take to write a book would forestall my plans for death.

It would have been a relief to everyone if I would just say I changed my mind. I knew I could not lie. It was something I could not say. Not unless we found a treatment that worked on the pain.

One afternoon, Jenny stopped me as I was leaving the group therapy room. "Can I talk to you?" She turned away from me. She circled the room. She picked up a magazine from the coffee table. She made no effort to look at it. She put it back down on another table. She did not say a word.

Only one subject could make her this uncomfortable. Only one subject might seem unbroachable.

I decided the best way to handle it was to wait her out. Finally, she found her voice. "Are you really planning on killing yourself?" I did not think she wanted a mere "yes" or "no."

She was obviously agitated. I waited to see if she would say more. "I've thought about doing it a lot of times."

She had a life vastly different from mine. Her pain allowed her to work on and off. Most importantly, she had a family.

"I don't think my answer is an answer for you. I definitely don't want you to think I advocate suicide as a way out of the pain."

I tried to explain my thinking. "You know, there's no way of knowing if death will end the pain. There's always a chance you can end up in a worse position.

"Also, our lives are different. I have no one to whom I am

responsible and no one for whom I have responsibility. That would make a big difference in my choices."

She nodded her head. She stood as we talked. She could not keep her hands or feet still.

"Are you thinking about it?" "Yes," she said, her eyes looking at the floor.

"Are you planning on doing something soon?" She looked me in the eye for the first time. "No. I'm not ready to do anything right now." I felt a little less guilty. I stirred up a hornet's nest. I feared what someone might do. Jenny, at least, had no plans for attacking herself.

"You know, you can talk to me about this, or anything else, anytime. Okay?" She thanked me. With nothing left to say, she left the room. I went in search of Mary.

I found her in her office. "I just talked with Jenny. She told me she's thinking about suicide." Mary said she was aware of that. She then added something people often said to me. "You are so perceptive," referring to my understanding of what Jenny had wanted to say. "It was pretty obvious. Otherwise, I don't think she would have been so uncomfortable."

My perceived intelligence and sensitivity was often used as a weapon against my inability to work. It was often cited as a reason for me not to commit suicide. "You are so intelligent. Why can't you find a way to work? Why can't you find a way to live?" They liked to ask the question. They never proposed an answer.

In case the idea of writing a book or my innate intelligence did not result in a change in my plans, Dr. Hendler decided to start me on some medications in an effort to affect the pain.

He wanted me to take a test before deciding which drug/ drugs to try. I was handed a pink pill, Dexamethasone. This drug affects the blood cortisol levels. Six hours later, he drew a blood sample from my arm.

The level of cortisol helps determine if a person has a biologically induced depression. It would clarify if I was depressed—which I was—because of the pain and my life situation, or if the depression was endogenous (of biological origin).

The results were borderline. The number was high but not elevated enough to support a psychiatric diagnosis.

We met for therapy sessions five days a week. We discussed the same issues over and over. How do you feel about your pain? What can be done about your life? Is there a connection between your feelings of sadness and the pain? I never evaded the truth. "I've had problems with depression most of my life, definitely a long time before the onset of the pain."

One day, I had an insight. Much of the time, I tried to hide my despair behind a fake upturn of my lips that I tried to pass off as a smile. This time, I entered his office with a real smile on my face. "Dr. Hendler, I've had an epiphany! You know how so many of the doctors have tried to convince me that the pain is 'all in my head'? You know what? I finally realized they're right! It IS all in my head. That's exactly where the pain is. It's in my head."

I felt good about my insight. I could finally put the psychosomatic accusations behind me. The problem is that depression is characterized by feelings of hopelessness and helplessness. "Dr. Hendler, I think that could also be the definition for chronic pain."

He sighed. He shrugged his shoulders. He readied himself to fight those two emotions within me.

CHAPTER TWENTY-FOUR

Dr. Hendler and I spent a lot of time talking about my possible suicide. I wanted to look at it from every angle. I needed to make sure within me that, if I had to act on it, it would only be a response to the pain. If it was from emotion, then it would not be appropriate. He agreed with that.

"What do you think happens after you die?" he asked me.

"They put you in the ground and the worms get you." I had not changed my belief that death was the end of life, despite the teachings of Jan and Blanche and the intended indoctrination of the cult.

Both of us were Jewish. He, much more than I. "What do 'we' believe happens if you kill yourself?" His answer was not comforting. "Your soul floats through eternity. It is never able to settle."

I did not like the idea of that. I sought pain relief, not peace per se. It would be nice if my death could result in a surcease of both pains—physical and emotional. Nice, but not decision-changing.

He started me on drugs again, hoping to change my mind by changing the pain. It seems I had run the gamut. The names of the drugs were different, but the actions were the same. The one that lowered blood pressure lowered my pulse, as before. It did nothing to reduce the level of pain. The anticonvulsant had no effect. The psychotropic moved neither my mind nor the pain. A new one, hormonally based, did nothing.

One of the patients underwent sodium amytal interviewing. This seemed to be a way to be sure that the idea of suicide came only from the pain. I was clear within my own mind that if I committed suicide, it would not be a response to an emotional problem. I was certain of this consciously. Could I be reacting psychologically on an unconscious level?

"Could we try an interview? Just so I can make sure?"

I felt nervous when I entered the office. I knew about "truth serum" from movies. I recalled seeing *Captain Newman, M.D.* This was a movie about a psychiatrist at a military psychiatric hospital. Bobby Darin was injected with the drug. Gregory Peck, playing the title role, asked him to go back, in his mind, to the trauma that was causing him to be psychiatrically ill. Bobby Darin started to tell what happened, reliving it all, the emotions and the physical sensations. It was heart wrenching to watch. Would I react the same way?

No, I did not. He asked me about the pain. How bad was it? Why are you thinking of killing yourself? Do you have plans? What are those plans?

Everything I said during the interview indicated the pain was the sole reason for my willingness to kill myself. My conscious mind agreed with my unconscious. If not for the pain, I would not be ready to die.

The patients with pain below their necks were taught to use the biofeedback machine. I agreed to give it a try.

The biofeedback room was upstairs in an area away from the hubbub of the clinic. The light was somewhat low. A chair was placed in front of a square machine. I sat. Sheldon, the staff psychologist, turned on the machine. It lit up with a dim light. He picked up a pad that was attached to the machine with wires. As per his instructions, I wrapped it around my fingertip.

The movement of the lines on the screen indicated its temperature. My job was to make it warmer. If I could succeed in doing that, hopefully, I could learn to manipulate my blood vessels. Most patients use it to teach their bodies to relax. That was not my goal. Relaxation was not the culprit. Blood vessels were.

I tried it for five days. I succeeded at raising the heat of my fingertip. The rise was so miniscule that the three of us, Dr. Hendler, Sheldon and I, agreed there was no point in continuing.

Dr. Hendler made an appointment for me with a neuroophthalmologist. Dr. Neil Miller, a tall man with dark hair and a clean-shaven face, was on staff at the Wilmer Eye Institute in Baltimore. In case he did not have any ideas, I came armed with a theory of my own.

If you have pain and nothing helps, what do you do? Removing my eye might be a solution. The idea disgusted me, but what if it was the answer?

"Dr. Miller, what if you took out my eye?" "No way. Even if I were willing to consider it, you would need a prosthesis. It would have to be hooked up to your eye muscles to allow it to move." "Oh no, then. That wouldn't work. That's why I thought getting rid of it would help. No eye, no movement. A false eye would still cause the pain then." One more theory, one more hope. Gone in the blink of an eye.

"Also, you have vision in that eye. I would never remove a seeing eye." I had very minimal sight in my left eye. It is amblyopic ("lazy eye"). I could read the big "E" on the eye chart. Some days, even the second line. That was vision and, therefore, an ethical "no-no."

"I have to tell you. You have the worst case of this I have ever seen." That was not nice to hear. Still, it was better than the common: "I have never seen this before."

His words as to my future were not much better. They were more acceptable to me than the doctors who dismissed me saying, "It can't be that bad." His parting words were similar to those of Dr. Rothman.

"What do your other patients with this, do?"

He looked at me for a few seconds. "They decide they can't

stand it anymore." I said nothing. I looked back at him. "They decide they cannot take it." Another vote for suicide as an alternative. Another hoped-for, yet unwanted, solution abandoned.

Part of an occupational therapist's job is to help clients "reach functional independence within his/her environment." The problem was not within my environment. It was without. Julia* had not been taught anything about someone like me.

If only I were a different kind of person who was content to sit at home. If only looking out the window was all I needed to feel a part of the world. If, if, if.

Since I was not . . . since I needed to be in the world . . . Julia, creative Julia, found a way to keep the world away from me.

I sat at a table. Julia walked around me. She unwound a tape measure. Placing it across the top of my back, she measured the width of my shoulders. Standing away from my face, she "air" measured it—length, width, and depth. The last she needed was the length from the bottom of my neck to the top of my head.

I looked through some therapy magazines she brought with her. As she pointed to photos, she asked me, "Do you think this might work?" I did not see any that could serve our purpose. We picked a part of this one and a part of that. Julia added suggestions of her own. I helped her to refine them to meet our very specific criteria.

I returned to the clinic. I waited to hear from her. She said it might take her at least a week, maybe a little more.

"Carol, I think I've got it. Can they drive you here today?" Could they? If no one could I was willing to walk the several miles to see what she had done.

It was a work of art. Nothing more than a visor, in the strict sense of the word. This visor had a shoulder harness. I put it on. Around my chest, over my shoulders. The fit was fine. On each shoulder, a holder extended upward from the strap. Inserted into each holder was a stick of wood. Attached to the wood was a large, curved piece of transparent plastic. It covered temple to temple, from the middle of my cheek to two inches above my scalp. It was magnificent.

I wanted to cry for all the work she had put into this. She had nothing to gain except her satisfaction and the complete turn-about of my life, if it worked.

I went upstairs. I walked to the doorway that opened onto an outside walk area on the roof. I wore the harness. I placed the visor wood attachments into the holes. I held my breath in antici-pation of joy and freedom. I walked out the door. It was a gorgeous day. There was a breeze.

The breeze caressed the areas of my head that were not cov-ered—my hairline, by my ear. It snuck in under the plastic. It worked its way over and around the left side of my face. It smirked and flitted, setting off the nerve endings, one by one, hundreds by hundreds. It swirled and danced, joyous in its victory. Mali-ciously, it caressed my face. It wiggled and giggled as it made its way across. It whistled a sound of freedom as it liberated itself back into the day. My mind keened with the sound of defeat.

I could not bring myself to tell Julia it did not work. She smiled when she saw me reenter the room. Her eyebrows lifted as her face widened in expectation. I heard the unspoken, "And?"

"Um, it did help a little, I think. It was hard to really tell, though. I could feel the air over my scalp and that did give me, um, ah, uh, some of the pain. I was thinking I could take it home with me. Then I would have time to really give it a good try." "I'm sorry it doesn't seem to be helping. Let me know if it works." I took it off, and we folded it. As she handed me the bag it was in, she wished me well.

Mary Viernstein was another therapist. Something I had not known existed, a psychologist who specialized in pain patients. A tall, willowy, short dark-haired woman, she was a godsend.

The people who tried to "therapize" me, excluding the clinic people, all came from the perspective that their patients were physically healthy. Many of their diagnoses and recommendations arose from that prejudice.

Pain and disfigurement do not live in harmony with the normal psyche. If I had acted "normal," then I would have been crazy. Mary understood. Constant pain pounds away at you. Day after day, year after year. We talked about it. She heard what I was saying. Even when I could not say the words. She translated the feelings showing in my face and body. "The pain is a horrible, scary, and overwhelming thing, isn't it?" Yes, it was. And, now, someone else really understood what was happening to me.

Sheldon had me take a number of psychological tests. One, developed by Dr. Hendler and very specific for back pain patients, was the Hendler Back Pain Scale. I answered questions such as, "Did the pain develop suddenly or slowly?" and "Was there a precipitating event?"

Back pain rarely occurs without an accident or movement, etc., preceding it. On those occasions, it may have a sudden onset. Many times, the cause is an accumulation of bad body habits (such as poor posture). Tic is the exact opposite. The first pain is spontaneous and unprovoked.

The results were that I was an "exaggerating pain patient." If I had back pain, probably so. For tic pain, there can be no exaggeration. Both men agreed with me.

The Beck Depression Inventory found me to be depressed. They could have used the results to force me into the hospital.

It was self-administered. Statements came in increasing levels of depth. You picked the statement which best indicated your feelings. They were rated zero to three.

"I do not feel sad," "I do feel sad," "I am sad all the time," and "I am so sad or unhappy that I can't stand it" were the choices for the first question. I picked number two. Number three was wrong. It was not the feelings of sadness I could not stand. It was the pain I could not tolerate. Nowhere was there room for an asterisk to explain the reason for the one you picked.

Item 14 read, "I don't feel that I look any worse than I used to," "I am worried that I am looking old or unattractive," "I feel that there are permanent changes in my appearance that make me look unattractive," and "I believe that I am ugly." I was permanently disfigured. Of course there were changes in my appearance, and of course I believe I am ugly.

The other items to be rated were mostly off point as well. Number nine addressed suicide. "I would like to kill myself." "I feel that the future is hopeless and that things cannot improve." Those statements were appropriate to me. Dr. Hendler, Dr. Rothman,, Dr. Schatz and others, . they said, "Yes, I do not think there is anything else to do for you." Hopeless and helpless. Definition of depression. Reality of my pain.

I continued to work with Mary Viernstein. She did not want me to kill myself. She worked diligently on trying to dissuade me. She had an office in Manhattan as well as at the clinic. Ironically, it was two blocks away from Carolyn's.

She offered to continue seeing me at her New York office. Knowing she would be there for me might help me change my mind. "I appreciate it. I would like to do that. But I won't make any commitments as to what I'll be doing until I get back home. If nothing has changed then, neither will my decision."

Dr. Hendler allowed me to stay for thirty days. All of the treatments and therapies he could offer had been offered. None helped. There was nothing more to be done. I shrugged my shoulders. "I don't see any other option. I will kill myself when I get home."

Maybe this was not as strong a drive or as thorough a plan as I thought. We were in the therapy room. "I want you to do a psychodrama about your suicide. I want you to show me exactly how and where you will do it." Gulp.

I felt very silly and uncomfortable. It was strange enough, his wanting me to do some acting. A scene of my self-imposed death . . . that seemed unthinkable.

"I know you feel uncomfortable. I'd like you to try anyway."

I giggled. This is so silly.

I had spent a lot of time thinking about how and where I would do it. I wanted to die at home, surrounded by the things I knew. The reality was that there was no one who would miss me, not for a while at least. My body would lie in the apartment until someone noticed a death had occurred by the smell. The sensible thing was to go to a hotel.

Dr. Hendler wanted all the details. "What hotel?" I knew which I intended to use. I did not want him to know that, so I named another.

"What floor are you on?"

I said the first number that popped in my mind. "The fifteenth." I was still smiling and feeling very foolish.

"What is the room number?" I stopped smiling. I was in the room. It was no longer a game.

"Describe the room for me."

"There is a large bed and a bureau attached to a desk. A round table with chairs is off to the side."

"Where are you in the room? Tell me what you are doing."

"I am sitting at the desk."

"Do you have any luggage?"

"No. There's no reason for me to bring anything."

"Are you writing any suicide notes?"

"I'm not sure. I'm still debating about that."

"What and to whom would you write?"

"I've been thinking about that. Maybe Dr. Schatz, to thank him for sticking with me for so long. I haven't decided whether or not to write a note to Jude and Charlie [my parents]."

"What are you doing next?"

I saw myself opening my purse. "I'm taking the pills out of my pocketbook." I was no longer acting out a scene for a doctor. The drama had become the here and now. "I go over to the bathroom to get a glass of water so that I can take them."

"I have to ask you this. Are you wearing lingerie or have you put on makeup?"

"No. Of course not."

"I didn't think you would, but I had to ask." Sometimes people attempting suicide get dressed up or put on makeup, hoping to be found in time. That was not something I wanted to happen.

He became quiet. No more questions. Not until after I said, "The pills are starting to work."

I remained sitting in the chair. In my mind, I lay down on the bed, my eyes closing, going away from the world.

"What happens now?"

I was blind to the next events. "The maid finds me. An ambulance or the police are called. They come and take me away."

"See yourself on the litter as they carry you out. Are you breathing?"

In my mind, I had succeeded. There was no more "I." "One hopes not."

I saw a look of sorrow on his face. I felt sad, too. Clearly, this was something my mind had accepted. Something I was very willing and ready to do. Unless something else could be found and tried to stop the pain.

CHAPTER TWENTY-FIVE

Dr. William Sweet was a neurosurgeon. He worked at the Massachusetts General Hospital, in Boston. He is known as "The Father of Trigeminal Neuralgia Surgery." I was aware of him. In fact, I had my own nickname for him. I called him "Mr. Tic."

His name had come up in the past. He was the "Court of Last Resort." If he could not help me, no one could. I would never have seen any doctor after him. Now, of course, I had seen the rest. He was all that was left.

There was no point in seeing him now. Everyone agreed that all that could be done had been done. He was also seventy-two years old. I had severe reservations about someone that age holding a knife to my brain.

Dr. Hendler called me to his office. "I'm going to call Dr. Sweet. Maybe he can offer you something." I told him why I would prefer not seeing him. "There's another reason, too."

I contacted a lawyer in 1980 about suing both Dr. Martinez and Dr. Jannetta. My father sent me to an attorney he knew, Jonathan DeYoung. Mr. DeYoung and I talked. He referred me to another attorney in his firm, Catherine Lecky.

Ms. Lecky said she would send the records out for a medical review. A number of surgeons refused. They did not want to become involved in any case against Peter Jannetta. The lore of physicians refusing to testify against each other was based on fact. Our doctor of last resort was Dr. Sweet.

He agreed to review the records, primarily the ones regarding Dr. Martinez's rhizolysis. That was one of the surgeries Dr. Sweet had developed. A few days after cashing the check from my lawyer, for $500.00, he spoke with her by phone. "I can't make a comment one way or the other. The record lacks sufficient information for me to make a determination."

It seemed to us that the inadequacy of the record was an indication that something was awry. Neither of us believed Dr. Sweet was telling us the real reason he would not testify. I believed he did not want to get involved. I was sure he would not want me as a patient, knowing I was suing two of his colleagues.

I told Dr. Hendler all of it. "When I talk with him, I'll ask him if that's going to be a problem." We waited three days. He did not call back. Feeling there was no point in waiting any longer, Dr. Hendler went ahead with my discharge. I would be leaving the clinic the following morning. As I walked back towards my room, I saw Sheldon standing on the stair landing. "I hear you're leaving. I wanted to tell you that I'll understand if you commit suicide. But I hope you don't." Mary agreed with that sentiment. Dr. Hendler had nothing more to say on the subject.

The next morning came. I thought about what I would do. It seemed stupid to go home and wait for a few days to go by before I took action. I finished packing and said my good-byes to Sherry and Jenny. We talked and hugged. Then they left the room. "We'll see you downstairs before you go."

I lay down on the floor. I put myself into a trance. I was beginning to start the instructions to myself. *It's time to die when I get home. It's time to stop the pain. There's nothing left to be done. When I get home, I will be ready to take the pills. I will be ready to die.* In the midst of repeating the mantra, my phone rang.

"Carol, it's Dr. Hendler. I just talked with Dr. Sweet. He says he has a surgery for you." I did not think Dr. Hendler would resort to this; making up something in a last-ditch effort to save me from myself. He must have sensed my thought.

"I'm not making this up. He wants to talk to you. After you get home, he wants you to give him a call."

I did not return to my trance. I had said any and all options. If there was truly a possibility of a surgery that could work, how could I refuse?

I talked with Dr. Sweet, by phone. I reminded him of the lawsuit. "Will that be a problem for you?" "No. I want you to come into the hospital. I have a surgery that could help you. It's what we call a mesencephalic tractotomy."

I knew what a tractotomy was. It was the procedure Dr. Hosobuchi had performed. The mesencephalon is in the center of the brain. He was offering to cut the nerve at a deeper inward level. That might work. "I'll come. Thank you."

I called my parents from the airport a few minutes before boarding the plane to Boston. My mother answered. I needed to have someone know where I was. I needed to not have either of them pull the same behavior they had before.

"Listen, I'm going to the hospital for surgery for the pain. I won't tell you where. Not unless you promise me that you will support me, not try and hurt me like the other times."

"What hospital?" she asked me. "I won't tell you. Not unless you promise. I am totally serious. I'm not willing to go through the things that you two have done before, especially what Charlie did when I was in California.

"I need to have an answer because they are calling my plane now."

"Okay. I promise we'll help you. We won't interfere or cause trouble. Okay?"

I hoped I could believe her. "Okay. I'm taking you at your word. I have to board now. I'll be in MGH (as it is known) this afternoon, around four o'clock."

On October 8, 1982, I arrived at Massachusetts General Hospital in Boston. The building looked very old. I realized from the exterior that I should not expect the shining modern facilities that I had found in other hospitals. Still, I was not prepared for what I saw once I arrived on the neurosurgical floor.

MGH is very well known. It is an institution with worldwide recognition and respect. Many medical breakthroughs occur there. It is renowned for its up-to-the-minute research. I expected a modern hospital setting, at least, once I got to the neurosurgical floor.

What I found was a throwback to the 1950s or beyond. The walls were painted dark green. The rooms were tiny. Mine was so small that the two beds were set in the shape of an "L." The head of my bed sat only a foot or two away from my roommate's feet. The room had no bathroom facility, just a sink. The nurse pointed, "To shower or use the toilets you have to go around the corner and down the hall." Once I got there, I found a room that reminded me of the lavatory in the girls' gym in high school. There were three toilet stalls and three showers.

I was disturbed by the lack of privacy. It made me realize that I had developed certain routines to get through each hospital day. One of them involved the shower. I could not comfortably employ the method in a ladies' room open to everyone.

At home, I always sing in my shower. In the hospital, I continued to do it when the bathroom was in my room. When it was not, the single facility in the hall had a lock to keep everyone else away. If upset or in a bad mood, I would find some happy song. If things were going relatively well, I sang whatever found my fancy.

I walked out of the room. I stopped the first nurse I could find. "Don't you have any rooms that have a bathroom in them?" "No, we don't. What's the problem with the one we have?" "Aside from the obvious, that's the one place where a person can have total privacy. That's really important to me." I told her about my need to sing. She said that she saw no reason why I should feel restrained from doing so, even in their public facility.

I had a very good reason. I would not, and could not, do it where I thought someone might hear. Since my face had been paralyzed, I dreaded anyone hearing me sing. I did not think I could take hearing someone comment on my voice. If they heard me, based on past experience, they might compliment me. As far as I was concerned, once Dr. Jannetta took my face, as I had come to think of it, he took away any chance of my singing again in public. The last thing I wanted to hear was someone reminding me of what I had lost. I went back to my room and shouted into a pillow. I hoped it would help to relieve my frustration about how horrible this place was. It worked. I felt calmer. The calm left me shortly after I met Dr. Sweet.

It was rare for the attending physician to see me on my first day of admission.

Dr. Sweet arrived in my room an hour or so after I had unpacked. Except for his white hair, he was the opposite of all my expectations. Given his name and his willingness to let bygones be bygones, as it were, I expected a large, compassionate man, kind of Santa Clausish. Slightly built and bespectacled, he asked me how I was. His next question gave the lie to his concern for my well-being.

"Why are you suing Dr. Martinez?"

"My litigation has nothing to do with this hospitalization," I said, taken aback. "I'm curious," he replied. He was curious? He knew exactly what it was about. He told my lawyer and me that he had read the entire hospital record.

I did not know what to do. I came to him for help. He held out hope. Now, he held out, what? I was not sure what he wanted from me.

I decided to answer. Maybe, he would be satisfied. It would be brought out into the open. We would not have to talk about it anymore. It should not interfere with any of the medical decisions. After all, he told me it would not, when we talked on the phone. I repeated what my lawyer wrote in the letter asking him to review the records. He looked me in the eye. His mouth was set in a straight line. "I will do everything I can to defeat you."

Oh no. Not again. *This cannot be happening. He said he would help me. He knows how. Now he's holding the litigation against me. What am I supposed to do?*

The lawsuit seemed to be his main concern. Every day, for the first three days, he came to my room. Each time, he performed a cursory neurological examination. His main concern was the lawsuit. Over and over, he asked, "Why are you suing Dr. Martinez?" He knew why. Maybe he hoped I would slip up. If asked enough, I might change my "story." On the third day, he did not ask, he commanded. "If you pursue your lawsuit against Dr. Martinez, I will have to testify totally in favor of him." This was totally at odds with what he had said to my attorney. And totally antithetical to his reassurance to me that the lawsuit would have no effect on his taking me on as a patient.

His interest in the suit against Dr. Martinez did not seem to extend to the one against Dr. Jannetta. His apparent anger about the former seemed to bring out two aspects of his personality. One was a sense of loyalty to his fellow physician, regardless of the circumstances. The other was the paranoia in himself.

On the second day of my stay, he told me he had not decided what surgical intervention, if any, he might offer. Just in case, though, he had drawn up a special surgical consent permit. It was written strictly for me. He said he had no special plans for me. The heading and contents of the permit told me something completely different.

The heading read LEUKOTOMY. Leukotomy? He said a mesencephalic tractotomy when we talked.

The text defined the purpose. It read:

"The goal of this operation is to stop or reduce both pain and the PSYCHOLOGICAL STRESS (full capitalization mine) of illness and incapacity." The next two paragraphs explained how a metal electrode, to conduct electrical current used to destroy fibers in the frontal lobe of the brain, would be inserted in my brain. The paper ended with the potential risks. "The value of this operation I cannot predict IN YOUR EXTRAORDINARY CASE (full capitalization mine) and indeed am unable to be sure that there is any chance whatsoever of success. There is a small risk of death, paralysis, or other severe complication. There is a greater risk of some lesser complication whose precise nature I cannot predict. SOME REDUCTION OF EMOTIONAL CONTROL OR RESPONSIVENESS OR IN MEMORY OR OTHER COMPONENT OF MENTAL PROWESS IS THE MAIN TYPE OF COMPLICATION THAT MAY OCCUR (full capitalization mine). THIS IS LIKELY TO IMPROVE IF IT APPEARS. There is also, unfortunately, a possibility that good pain relief may not last."

Dr. Sweet may have said that he had no specific plan in mind, but he evidently leaned towards the leukotomy. The word itself sounded no more, or less, scary than any other operation. Until I learned the layman's word for it.

Leukotomy is another name for a mini-frontal lobotomy. I began to wonder if he did not want the surgery to affect my "mental prowess." If it affected my memory, the last thing I would do was make a good witness. It seemed clear to me, from the last paragraph, that his main objective might not be pain relief but release from a possible lawsuit. Obviously, if I sued Dr. Martinez and Dr. Jannetta, who was to say he might not be next?

I worried about the way doctors would accept me. Dr. Wilson and Dr. Hosobuchi made me feel my concern was groundless. To my knowledge, they were both aware of the litigation. Neither mentioned the suit and both their surgeries had carried high risks. I could not believe I was now with the best of the trigeminal neuralgia surgeons. I always feared him because I was afraid he would tell me he had nothing to offer. I gave no thought to a possible problem with his mental status.

I did not take my intuition seriously that pain relief was not his only goal. My first clue should have been his preoccupation with the lawsuit. My second should have been his reaction to my request for my usual pain medication.

I had been taking codeine continuously, with the exception of the three months after Dr. Osterholm's successful surgery. Each doctor I spoke with told me they were not concerned with addiction. The first order of business was to try and stop, or at least reduce, my level of pain. If addiction did occur, like Scarlet O'Hara, we would worry about it tomorrow.

I told Dr. Sweet that I had brought codeine with me. "In the other hospitals, they've always let me take my own," I explained. "It's easier than constantly calling a nurse." I took approximately eight grains a day. It was unfair, I thought, and other doctors agreed, to both the nurses and me, to have to ask them every hour or so for medication.

"I'm not going to let you take your own pills," he replied. "You'll get addicted." I was dumbstruck. I had been on the drug for six years. If I read or went out in bad weather, I would often take one grain an hour, four times the normal dosage. I had no reason to believe I was not addicted. I also had no reason to stop the pills. "I'm only going to write for half a pill every four hours. You won't get it automatically. Only if you ask for it." That was not acceptable. I continued to take my own, the same way I did on the outside. I would not lie about it directly. As long as no one asked if I had taken any—I would not tell.

One afternoon, he told me I would be going outside the hospital to a testing center. I would be given an intelligence test. There would be other studies as well. It was important, he said, to have the results before the operation. "I haven't agreed to it yet," I reminded him. "Well, it's important to get the results for when you do."

I knew an IQ test required reading and eye usage. I did not know what the others were. He said psychological and neurological testing. Some would need me to use my eyes. I expected he would give me trouble about the codeine. "If I'm going to have to do these tests, they're going to make the eye pain much worse. I'm going to need more codeine, to take with me." He shook his head. "No. I'm not going to give you any more codeine." Why would a doctor put me in a situation that he knew would be painful? Why would he then refuse to give me enough pain medication to get through it?

I had a feeling Dr. Sweet's interest and mine were not one and the same.

CHAPTER TWENTY-SIX

Dr. Ray Maciewicz seemed more in tune with my needs. A light-brown-haired, clean-shaven, young man, in his middle thirties, he was of average height and appearance. It was his demeanor that made him attractive. I was immediately captivated by him because he had nothing to say about my litigation. The second thing in his favor: He did not argue with me about the validity of my pain.

Because of the numbness in my face, Dr. Sweet insisted I could not have pain when my face was touched. I explained to him, again and again, that I could not identify where or when that part of my face was touched. All I knew was that when it was, the pain would be triggered. He refused to believe me. Dr. Maciewicz, even if he had trouble understanding, accepted it.

Our first interview lasted quite a while. He wanted my complete story. He had no trouble until I got to Dr. Hosobuchi. I explained that the surgery had worked. "The spontaneous pains stopped." I told him the operation was a failure. "I still have the constant background pain and can't tolerate touch to my face. I still can't work. That's not my definition of success." He countered that as long as the spontaneous pains were gone, I had had a successful operation. "It makes no sense. If the pains stopped, then you should be better." He wrote in my chart, "[I] had not 'improved behaviorally' as a result of the loss of the spontaneous pains." He listened but did not hear. How else could I explain his utter lack of comprehension?

"How are you feeling emotionally?" I felt no reason to withhold information. I assumed Dr. Hendler made a point of discussing the possibility of my death when he first spoke with Dr. Sweet. It had to be written somewhere in my record. "If I can't find relief, then suicide will be the answer. I don't want to die; I want to stop the pain. I will do whatever is necessary to accomplish that." He was no more ready to accept death as an answer than anyone else had been. "It's my opinion, then that you should strongly consider having the operation Dr. Sweet wants to do."

I was seen by an ophthalmology resident. He had nothing to offer.

Dr. Fisher, the neurologist, looked the way I had expected Dr. Sweet to look. A heavy-set, white-maned man, he had the compassion and sensitivity that Dr. Sweet seemed to lack.

We spoke for about forty-five minutes. I told him the same things I said to everyone else. "The pain is horrible. Suicide is an option if all else fails. I came here because I want to avail myself of all possible options. It's not that I want to die or kill myself. I just need to get rid of the pain." He gave me all the time to say all I needed to say. Then he told me what I did not want to hear. "I think you should consider Dr. Sweet's surgery." I really took a liking to him. I hoped we would talk again. I wanted to try and make him understand why the leukotomy was not appropriate. He never came to talk with me again. He did stop by my room once more. "I just wanted to say 'Hello.'" He had seen me merely as a favor to Dr. Sweet. He was not a part of the "team."

The psychiatrist was next. The first interview lasted forty minutes. The first fifteen minutes or so, he asked about my medical and family history. The remainder of the session centered on the pain and my reactions to it.

I did not mind talking with Dr. Bouchoms. A tall, dark-haired man, he retained a little of his New Zealand accent. He wore an expression of interest. I did not get the impression from the first few minutes that he had a hidden agenda. He quickly straightened me out.

"Do you consider the pain to be 'an old friend'?" he asked.

Friend? "No." That was definitely not one of the words I applied to my pain. It was a concept totally foreign to me.

"How has your family responded?"

"They don't care."

"What makes you feel that way?"

"They do not call, send cards or flowers, or show any interest in the outcomes of the surgeries. They have no interest at all. My father has tried to sabotage other medical situations. He consistently tells me and my doctors that, 'All she needs is a good psychologist.'"

This professional listener closed his ears to my words. "I think your history with the pain and all of the operations you have had, this is how you are trying to get your family to pay attention." *Huh?* If I was someone looking only to get attention, Dr. Schatz, Dr. Wilson, Dr. Jannetta, Dr. Hosobuchi, et al., would have seen that. They do not do repeated brain surgeries on psychogenic complaints. They would not have seen a strange landscape inside my brain. The surgical records were available. All one had to do was read them to know the truth. Unless they had an agenda that required them not to believe me.

His preformed conclusions became obvious when Dr. Maciewicz walked into the room.

I was glad to see him. I had to ask a very important question.

I was upset from Dr. Bouchoms's pronouncement. I was uncomfortable and hesitant. I was afraid Dr. Maciewicz would be mad. I figured Dr. Bouchoms would use it against me.

"Dr. Maciewicz, Dr. Sweet is refusing to give me any extra codeine to take with me to the testing center. I have to have extra. I can't do all that eye work without having enough pain meds. I just can't."

Dr. Maciewicz was not the doctor in charge of my case, only a consultant. I did not know if he even had the authority to take care of it. All the more reason I was amazed, pleased, and relieved, by his answer. "Okay."

The three of us talked for a few more minutes. Then Dr. Maciewicz left. Dr. Bouchoms did not ask me why I had expected

Dr. Maciewicz to give me trouble. He had his own explanation. "You're behaving deceptively to your 'caretakers.'" This was his term for the doctors who had taken care of me previously.

It was a term he enjoyed. "You have a history of 'splitting' your caretakers. It is obvious from the notes I read from your first hospital stay at Jefferson Hospital."

The notes read that I had refused to see a psychiatrist when the suggestion was first made. Two days later, a new note was written saying that I had requested to see one. "That's contradictory behavior."

"No, it isn't. I asked to see Dr. Lanes after Dr. Osterholm said, 'I don't think we can help you' and then handed me the OR permit. I thought hesitating to sign until I had a chance to discuss the contradiction with Dr. Lanes made a lot of sense."

"Well, that does sound reasonable." When I had a chance to read the hospital record a day later, I found his written word did not match his spoken one. His note read, "Past history of splitting of caretakers."

He ended the interview by telling me his feelings on the advisability of the leukotomy. He confirmed my worries about the possible effects on my psyche. Surprisingly, given all of his prior statements to me, he said, "I don't believe that your pain is primarily psychosomatic. I think the benefit of surgery to you is questionable. I don't think you're depressed enough, or anxious enough, for me to make that recommendation." His chart note confirmed his remarks. "I doubt further Rx will be helpful."

The neuropsychiatric testing was done at the MIT Research Center. It was a twenty-minute ride away. The ward clerk arranged for a cab to pick me up in the lobby of the hospital. Both days, the nurses handed me my chart before I left the floor. As I waited for the cab, I read it.

The first testing, a neurological examination, was the only time I did not have to make the pain worse.

After the neurologist finished her exam, I was escorted to a testing room. Nancy, the tester, introduced herself. She explained that the first test would evaluate my level of mental health. It consisted of questions to determine how well I functioned emotionally. Along with this questionnaire, she gave me the Beck Depression Inventory, one of the tests I had already taken at the pain clinic in Maryland. Both required reading.

Dr. Maciewicz let me bring along five grains of codeine. By the end of the five-hour session, I had taken all five.

The next test was worse. The WAIS, or Wechsler Adult Intelligence Scale, assesses intelligence. It requires both reading and writing. For the first part, Nancy asked the questions. I only needed to look at her. The second section was more difficult. She handed me a picture. I had to identify either what was missing or what did not fit. To find the answer, my eyes needed to search the picture, right to left, up and down. The pain was too much.

I wanted to complete as much as I could. I was on the verge of tears. From the pain. From the awful feeling from the codeine. From the frustration and anger of not being able to finish. As much as I wanted to get it over with, I had no choice. "I can't do any more. I'm sorry," I said sniffling. Nancy was nice about it. "It's not a problem. You can only do as much as you can do. Do you think you can do more tomorrow?" It was hard for me to say, "Yes," but I did. She handed me my chart. I went outside and waited for the taxi.

I would have been a complete fool not to read the chart. I was awed. I saw Dr. Bouchoms's note about my "contradictory" behavior. He called my behavior deceptive. This was the deception: telling me one thing and writing the exact opposite in the chart—the permanent record. A handwritten note followed on the next page. It followed the three-page typewritten summary of his findings.

"She says she considers herself to be an actress," it read. The note was damning, without the added information that I was a trained singer/actress. In that context, my pain behavior could certainly be construed as conscious, or even unconscious, acting.

I arrived back in my room. I went directly to the nurses'

station. "I need to talk to Dr. Bouchoms." He was in my room a few minutes later.

I wasted no time on the niceties. "Are you a doctor or do you consider yourself to be a doctor? I was paid as an actress. I don't consider myself to be an actress. I *was* an actress. You don't consider yourself to be a doctor. You are a doctor. I expect the same." The next time I read my chart, the page was gone.

Before he left, he told me he wanted me to take an MMPI. This was the same psychological test Dr. Marquette had given me in Jefferson Hospital in 1979. He handed me the booklet. I handed it right back to him. "If you want me to take this test again, it'll have to be read to me." He refused. "You have to do it yourself."

That was not acceptable. I put it down on the desk. I went and lay down on my bed.

Joan*, a nurse, came into the room. She pointed to the booklet. "Dr. Bouchoms wants you to have this finished tonight." "Well, like I told him, someone will have to read it to me if he wants me to take it." "No. Dr. Bouchoms wants you to do it yourself."

"If he wants me to take it, then he's going to have to get someone to read it to me. I'm not going to set off the pain when it's not necessary." She shrugged and walked away. A short time later, she came back. She said nothing about the test. "You have to go over to the Ophthalmology Department. They want to look at your eye." "Fine. But I'll only go if you get me more codeine. They have to touch my face; I have to use my eyes to do some of the exams. That increases the pain. I need to have the pills for it." "I'm sorry. You have taken your codeine for the day [the five pills I had taken during the testing at MIT]. The doctor has not written for more." "Okay. Then I can't go." She realized I was serious. I suggested she call Dr. Maciewicz. As before, he did not argue. He wrote for more pills. I took one. Then I walked over to the eye doctor's office. As before, he had no suggestions.

The next round of tests at MIT was not for five days. While I waited, I saw another consultant and tried more drugs. Dr. Sweet,

Dr. Maciewicz and I had repeated, repetitive discussions about pain medication. Dr. Sweet had not changed his position. Dr. Maciewicz, although accommodating about the pills for MIT, was less agreeable once I was back in the hospital. Neither wanted me to have the amount I needed. I had not had this conflict in any of the other hospitals or with any other doctor. In fact, when the question of the amount of narcotic did come up, I was usually told, "Whatever it takes to help your pain is what we want to do." Even at the pain clinic, where reduction or stoppage of narcotics is a major goal, Dr. Hendler agreed there was no point in lowering or stopping the codeine. It was only with Dr. Sweet and his cohorts that I was met with argument and a brick wall.

I told Dr. Sweet, Dr. Maciewicz and Dr. Bouchoms, "I'm more than willing to try other pain meds. I don't care if they're narcotics or not. I have always hated the way the codeine makes me feel. If you can give me something that's not a narcotic and works, that would be great." They had none. Nonetheless, they would not give me enough codeine to moderate the pain during the pain-increasing activities they insisted I complete.

I succeeded in changing Dr. Bouchoms's mind when it came to finishing the MMPI. We went in circles for three days. Each evening, I would find it lying on my bed. Each night, I returned it to the nurse. Each morning, it reappeared on my bed. Each time, I told the nurse I would not do it unless someone read it to me. The third night, Dr. Bouchoms capitulated. An aide from his department came to my room. We sat on the bed, she reading, me answering. An hour or so later, it was completed.

My emotional state was not helped by dealing with Dr. Sweet's anger and irrationality about my lawsuits. Not a day went by when he did not bring it up. His behavior took away all the reserves of calm and hope I had when I arrived in Boston. I was becoming an emotional wreck.

As I went from test to test, from Dr. Bouchoms to Maciewicz to Sweet, it became clearer and clearer to me that I was becoming incapable of making a major decision on my own. Particularly as to whether I wanted to undergo surgery or not. We were not just discussing the possibility of pain relief. We were talking about potentially diminishing my emotional, mental, and intellectual functioning. I needed help.

I called Dr. Hendler. "I don't know what to do. Dr. Sweet is acting so strange. All he wants to talk about is the litigation. I felt so centered when I left Mensana. Now I feel like I'm going crazy, he is making me so confused. The surgery isn't what he said it would be when we talked on the phone. Dr. Hendler, I need your help. What he wants to do is like a lobotomy. What should I do?"

"I can't help you. I can't tell you what I think you should do." I felt devastated. I thought of Dr. Hendler as an ally.

I called Mary Viernstein. She was not a medical doctor but counseling implies guidance. I asked her to guide me. "What do you think I should do?" I was on the verge of tears. "I don't know which way to turn." She offered me no more direction than Dr. Hendler.

Much later, I realized that neither could have advised me. If they suggested I go ahead, I might lose some of my mind and intellect. If they told me they thought I should not, there was the possibility of my suicide. At that time, I could not appreciate the subtleties inherent in counseling me. I understood the conundrum into which I had placed them. Nevertheless, I hoped they could at least reassure me. Again, I was reminded of how utterly alone I was.

I had to go back to MIT and finish the testing. I knew I would have trouble with the pain. Dr. Sweet, not Dr. Maciewicz, wrote the codeine order. The nurse walked out with me to the lobby. As she handed me four pills, she said, "Dr. Sweet says this is all we can give you. It has to last you for the whole day." *Not again.* I did not even try to argue. "I have to go back to my room for a minute."

I was rationing my own pills, in case something like this might happen. I rushed back, not wanting to keep the cab waiting. I opened the top bureau drawer. I lifted up the top of the box in which I had hidden them. I broke five of them in half and put them in my pocket. Now, I was ready for Nancy and her tests.

She put five squares on the table. Each had a picture on it. "Rearrange them so they make a story." I might have liked doing that, before the pain. Looking at each one, picking it up to be certain of the little things that might make a difference in where it went (the clock in the corner, for instance), the eye howled. It continued as Nancy collected the story I made. We repeated this three more times, a different story board each time.

"Are you ready to do the next test?" No, I was not. But I had to.

I had noticed a map on the floor when I entered the room. It had not been there the last time. She pointed to it. "I'm going to give you directions I want you to walk on the map, following them." That was something I could barely do before the pain started. I loved getting lost when I drove. It was a good thing, too, because it happened a lot. Reading the map, finding the markers, looking up to hear Nancy, looking down to walk, my eye bellowed, *Stop it. Stop already!* Soundlessly, I spoke to it. *Please. It'll be over soon. Then I won't have to do any more. Please, please stop hurting.*

My jaw clenched, my mouth grimaced. Sometimes I had the feeling that, if I could just shut the left eye tight enough, the pain would stop. I closed and reclosed it, never hard enough. Never enough to stop the pain.

It was obvious that I was in severe pain and very drugged. "Would it be easier for you to come back and finish this another day?" *Yes. No.* "It will be just as bad either way. As long as the tests require me to use my eyes, it doesn't matter." I was fighting the urge to cry. The scream stuck in the back of my throat longed to be released. *Help me. Please.* It echoed over and over in my mind.

Thoughts ping-ponged across my mind. *Which is worse? If I*

stay, the pain will be so bad. If I leave, I know I'll have to do this again. I can't. I can't come back and start it over again. I just can't. Tears flowed inside me. "Let's just get this done."

She handed me a page filled with rows of numbers. *Oh no! I can't be hearing what I'm hearing.* "I need you to copy the numbers exactly. The grid on the bottom of the page is where I want you to write them. You have to put them in the same order."

This was a test made to torture me. My eyes flicked up to the top of the page and down to the bottom. Five blocks into it, I had to rove through the grid, finding where I stopped before. I kept sneaking one hand into my pocket, capturing half a codeine pill and slipping it into my mouth. As always, it did not help. I only felt very cloudy and far away, the way I always did.

Finally, the last test! "This will be it. You'll have to use your eyes though." She handed me pictures of body parts. "I want you to find these places on your own body." The looking was not that bad. I knew where parts of my body were located. I only had to look at the pictures Nancy held. My hand went where it needed without visual clues from me.

Then, the nicest words I could hear. "That's it. All the tests are done. We'll send the results over to Dr. Sweet."

I was very interested in how I had scored. I waited for the results, but no one talked with me about them. Or about anything else. So, I was totally unprepared for what happened the following night.

CHAPTER TWENTY-SEVEN

I spent most of the next day in my room, watching TV and thinking. I had to figure this thing out. Was Dr. Sweet really trying to help Dr. Martinez? Was I a pawn? I could not understand why he agreed to take me on as a patient when he was so adamant about his feelings towards me. Towards the lawsuit. Could someone really be willing to operate on someone, so a fellow doctor might get out of a lawsuit? MGH was turning into the twilight zone.

I thought things could not become more bizarre.

At about 5:00 P.M., a lab technician knocked on my door. "Hi. I'm here to draw blood."

She placed her basket containing the needles, tubes, and tourniquets onto the bedside table. No one told me I was having more blood work done. "What's it for?" I asked her.

"This is for your pre-op testing. For the surgery tomorrow."

My jaw dropped. My eyes bulged. "Surgery! I'm not scheduled to have surgery."

"You'll have to talk to a nurse about that. I only know what I was told to do." She held out the request form for me to read.

The words were right. The request was totally wrong! "I'm not having surgery. I never agreed to let them do anything."

She reached for my arm. "I have to take your blood. I'll get in trouble if I don't bring back a full tube." I pulled it back from her grasp.

"No. I'm not going to let you take any blood. I'm not having surgery!"

She repeated her plea, "My boss'll be mad if I come back without the sample." I knew she wanted me to feel guilty. "Well, all right." I said resignedly. I held out my arm. "You can take my blood. There is no way there is going to be any surgery! I can tell you that right now!"

Marsha*, one of the nurses, came to my room a little bit later. "How are you feeling tonight?" How was I feeling? "I am very, very upset. I cannot believe someone scheduled me for surgery. No one bothered to tell me. For that matter, no one bothered to ask me even!"

Dr. Sweet never talked with me about proceeding with surgery. I never talked to him about agreeing to let him operate. No resident came to the room. No consent form was offered. None other than the original one Dr. Sweet brought to me at the beginning of my stay. I never agreed to surgery, the contents of the form, or letting him do anything, at all, to me.

Even if I had or someone misunderstood somehow, there was still no way I could go for surgery. No anaesthesiologist had come to see me. That is a prerequisite before every operation. They need to know your history. They have to ask you personally how you react to the drugs. To which ones do you have a bad reaction? It cannot be done without his/her knowledge of me.

None of the above mattered. Because the most important piece of information was missing. What surgery did they think I would allow? What did Dr. Sweet think he was going to do to me?

I wasted no words or thought. "Marsha, this is my last chance for pain relief." I never cursed. Not in public or private. My sense of control and self-esteem were so compromised. I felt close to the edge. I was developing the mouth of a truck driver. "This is being treated like a s——tty game, and everyone else is calling the shots.

"I never agreed to any surgery. I never even talked to Dr.

Sweet about what he wanted to do, and what I didn't want him to do. Not, at least, in reference to letting him go ahead and operate on me. I don't know what is going on here."

"I don't know what to tell you," she said and left the room.

Never one to learn my lesson, I thought another talk with Dr. Bouchoms might help.

He came to my room that evening. "There is one more drug we can try." This was Clonidine, another blood pressure drug. "If it doesn't help, then I would suggest you proceed with the surgery. With the leukotomy." He added a caveat. "If you drop your lawsuit, we will do the surgery."

What? Could I be hearing him right? It's craziness!

Dr. Sweet had an ax to grind. I never expected a psychiatrist, someone whose entire professional life depends on his ability to be objective, to try and blackmail me.

This was consistent with his earlier behavior. Again, his last statement contradicted what he had said only a few minutes earlier.

Before he introduced the subject of my lawsuit, I asked him, "If I were your wife, would you let me have the surgery?" No equivocations, no hesitations. "No."

How could he reconcile the two?

I was told the surgery could alter my mind. A psychiatrist said he would not let someone he loved have the operation. Dr. Maciewicz said somewhat the same a few hours later.

We were in my room. "If I were your wife," I queried, "would you let me have the surgery?" Not quite as forthcoming as Dr. Bouchoms, his response was equally unequivocal. "We just got divorced."

It was a way of getting out of answering the question. I felt he was indirectly telling me he would not want her to have it. Two of the major players were saying, "Yes, I advise the surgery," and, "No, I would never let someone important to me go ahead with it." Was it any wonder I was confused?

My confusion only worsened when an orderly, pushing a litter ahead of him, came into my room. "I'm here to take you down for surgery. You ready?" It was not his fault. I told him, in nicer words, that I would not be going with him.

The next day, Dr. Sweet came to my room. For the first time, he talked about the specifics of the operation.

It is a two-stage procedure, normally done with the patient awake. In the first part, two holes are made in the skull. In my instance, it would be in the area where I had the pain. "I usually inject local anaesthesia in the area." I tried to explain why that would not be possible. "I couldn't tolerate that. I have never been awake for surgery. I can't take the chance of my face being touched and the pain being triggered. Besides, I could move from the pain being set off. That could be very dangerous." He brushed aside my objections. The reason became clear the next day. He did not believe I had touch-induced pain.

He came to my room while a medical intern was visiting me. The young man knocked on the door, an unusual occurrence in itself. "I'm Dr. Marcus*. I've been told you're an interesting patient. Would you mind if I talked to you for a while?" Not at all. Anything to relieve the boredom.

We spoke about many things. His interest and attention seemed sincere. He was still there two hours later when Dr. Sweet walked into the room. "I find it interesting that you say you cannot stand to have the left side of your face and scalp touched. I think I need to reexamine you.

"Close your eyes." I did as he asked. And he touched my left scalp. I flinched and quickly pulled away. He had triggered the pain.

"I did not touch you," he said. "You just imagine that you have the pain there." With that, he turned on his heel and left.

Dr. Marcus kept quiet while Dr. Sweet was in the room. As soon as Dr. Sweet left, he said, "I saw what he did. He did touch you."

"Please, can you tell someone? This is ridiculous. He sets off the pain then says it's all my imagination."

He took a deep breath, "I know he touched you, but I can't say anything. I'm leaving for Belgium to continue my studies. I just can't get involved in this, especially against someone like Dr. Sweet."

My parents had arrived at the hospital shortly after the "pre-op" blood had been taken.

The day after Dr. Sweet denied the pain he had caused by touching my face, he took the three of us into a small conference room. He said he wanted to explain the surgery. Instead, we got a forty-five-minute diatribe on why my suit against Dr. Martinez should be dropped. For the first time, he also mentioned my suit against Dr. Jannetta.

"Why are you suing him?"

"That has nothing to do with why I'm here."

He repeated the question.

As with my first discussion with him, I realized it would be easier to answer than argue. "Two doctors have told me that facial palsy is a complication of the microvascular procedure."

Before I could say anything else, he pounded his fists on the table. With a raised voice, he shouted, "Who told you this?! They are totally wrong and I will show you!" At that, without any explanation, he rose and marched out of the room. My parents and I looked at each other. His behavior was making no sense. It only got worse when he returned a few minutes later. He smacked down on the table the papers he was holding. "This proves those two doctors are wrong!" The article contained nothing about the microvascular procedure or facial paralysis. It was a discussion and explanation on leukotomy. Four more times, without preamble, he would leave the room. Each time, he returned to continue his argument about the lawsuits. As hard as my parents and I tried to get him to discuss his surgery, we could not. There was no point in going on with the meeting. A few minutes after he left the room for the final time, he called me over to the nurses' station.

"I want you to read this note I'm putting in your chart. I want you to sign it." It was a rather unusual request but totally in keeping with the strange behavior he had displayed in the conference room.

The note read, "I have made it clear that I do not consider the continuation or discontinuation of a lawsuit against previous neurosurgeons as germane to my decision as to whether or not to recommend as myself [sic] to do any operation on this lady. I have emphasized: (1) that I have no knowledge directly of any of the conversations [sic] her and Dr. Jannetta [sic] and hence have no opinion as to whether or not his statements to her constituted adequate information to give informed consent, (2) that Miss Levy has told me that she was informed by Dr. Martinez that as a consequence of his procedure her eyeball might be numb & even have to be removed and that she might not only [sic] an anesthetic numbed area of her face, V1, V2 but this might actually be actually [sic] painful, an anesthesia doloroso. I regard this as an exceptionally clear statement of the risks of this procedure and one which is more detailed that I actually give even in the multipage document I give to patients describing this procedure. Consequently if she persues [sic] her lawsuit against Dr. Martinez I shall do my best to defeat her legal action against him.

Read to the patient as I have written it."

He signed it in front of me. "Now, I want you to sign it." I refused to do so. Not until I added a post script. "I do not agree with the validity of Dr. Sweet's statements. My signature only attests to the fact that he is the author of the note." He looked at my signature. I write like a doctor, very illegibly. He looked at me, snarling. "What is that? Sign it again!"

Amazingly—or more to the point, stupidly—I still harbored the hope that Dr. Sweet could help me. When suicide is the only other option, you grab on to any hope, false or real, that passes by.

My parents, unable to offer any help, left for home the next morning.

I was standing in the solarium. I was doing nothing, just looking out the window. Dr. Maciewicz walked in. "What are you thinking about?" "Nothing in particular. Just looking at what's out there." Looking, and saddened by the knowledge of all that I had lost. All that might never be.

I turned and faced him. "I don't want to die, you know. I just want the pain to stop. I have to do what I can to obtain that, even if it has to be death." My ridiculous hope in Dr. Sweet was mired in that thought, that something still existed that would let me live.

Later that evening, Dr. Sweet came to my room. "I've been thinking. We could do a radiofrequency rhizolysis with an anaesthetic agent. I can do it Monday." (Monday was two days later.) He did not wait for my answer. He left the room. And never referred to it again.

In another conversation, he talked about the possible side effects of a leukotomy. Initially, he said, "The procedure could make you more placid." Quickly, he returned to talking about the litigation. "I consider your attitude towards Dr. Martinez as totally unreasonable." As a non sequitur, he added, "The surgery will make you illogical." Shortly after he left the room, my father telephoned me. To my surprise, he said, "Dr. Sweet called. He told me the surgery might make you violent."

That night, on the nightstand, I found a note written by my mother. "I will support you in almost anything you decide," it read, "but I cannot support you if you decide to go ahead with this surgery."

None of us were sure what I should do. I was not prepared to consent to any procedure, especially if Dr. Sweet was the surgeon. Dr. Sweet was no more willing to operate on me. He told me I should go home for two weeks. Then I could come back if I decided to go ahead with the surgery. "I cannot do any operation on you at this time."

I did not know which way to turn. I knew there was a good chance that I would kill myself if I went home in the same condition I had arrived.

Marsha came into my room. "I hear you may be going home." I struggled to keep my voice steady. "If I go home, I'll kill myself." She looked stricken. I attempted to reassure her. "This is an option, not a threat." "You wait here. I'm going to call Dr. Bouchoms." He came to the room. We talked for only a few minutes. He was not bothered by my statement that I would have to kill myself. Not that I wanted him to be. I did not want to have to deal with a threat like Dr. Hendler's again. Dr. Bouchoms was aware of my plans. He did not direct himself to them. Instead, he suggested that when I get home, I contact a doctor in New York by the name of Foley.

Dr. Kathleen Foley is a pain specialist at the Sloan-Kettering Hospital in Manhattan. More than a year before I arrived in Boston, Dr. Schatz had suggested I see her.

It was not as easy as it sounded.

I called the office and asked the receptionist to have Dr. Foley call me. "I've seen a lot of other pain doctors and been on tons of drugs. Before I waste either her time or mine, I'd like to know what sort of therapies she offers."

"Dr. Foley does not make calls to people she has not seen." I was taken aback by her answer. I repeated that I would like to talk to her so that I would not waste her time. "It would not be worth it for her to see me if she can only offer things I've already tried." "Dr. Foley does not call patients she has not seen, and she is not going to call you." I was surprised at the level of annoyance and vehemence in her voice.

"Could you at least give Dr. Foley my message and let her decide?" With a loud sigh, she said, "All right," and hung up. I called back. "I think she needs my phone number if she is going to call me." I waited a week or so and heard nothing. I called the office again. I again requested that Dr. Foley call me. "If she can't or does not want to, would you ask her to call Dr. Schatz? He's the referring doctor." Neither Dr. Schatz nor I received a response. I attempted to give her one more chance. I went to the office and left a note. There was no reply to that either. I persisted because Dr. Schatz had suggested her. I trusted his judgment, but it was very clear, by this time, that she was not someone with whom I wanted to consult.

Dr. Bouchoms's suggestion that I see her did not overjoy me. The next day, Dr. Maciewicz and I talked. My discharge had not yet been arranged. "Maybe you could stay for a few more days?" "Why would I do that? Dr. Sweet is acting crazy. No one has anything here to offer me. In fact, if my release isn't taken care of very soon, I'll sign out AMA [against medical advice]." "Don't do that. I'm sure your discharge can be put through for tomorrow. I do think that it would be a good idea if you saw Dr. Foley though."

Two days later, Dr. Sweet and I had our final blowup. "Here are the names of three specialists. You should make an appointment with one of them." The first was Dr. Foley. The second, Dr. Wolfe, a New York psychiatrist who specialized in pain patients. "Dr. Wolfe probably couldn't help you." I knew that. I had seen his associate a year or two before. The third was a retired psychiatrist in London. He then talked about why he would not be operating on me.

"I have discussed the surgery over and over with both your parents and you. You rarely talk about pain."

"You never give me the chance. Anytime either my parents or I mentioned it, you left. All you ever want to talk about is the lawsuit. You're asking for a lawsuit yourself when you behave this way."

I meant that he was behaving in an irrational manner. I was not threatening him. He raised his voice. "You are a damn liar!" I wasn't sure I could control my anger. I put my hand out in front of me, trying to remind myself to stay in control. "I can't listen to you anymore," I said and turned away.

He came to my room later that day. "You should call Dr. Foley when you get home." "I have to think about that," I said. "You are wrong about your lawsuits, and you're trying to make trouble. These things are your fault." He continued in this vein for a few minutes. Finally, I could take it no more. "You are a real

S—T." I had never, ever called someone that before. "And you are a damned liar!" he loudly repeated. Shortly after, a nurse came to my room and told me my discharge papers had been signed.

And coincidence and television were never far away.

That morning, I had seen a pain specialist on one of the national morning news shows. He was being interviewed about the use of heroin in treating chronic and terminal pain. I did not recall which side of the issue he was on. All that was important to me was that he had no relationship with Dr. Sweet or MGH.

Although the sense of calm and centeredness that had accompanied me to Boston was nowhere to be found, I seemed to have an endless supply of false hope. I could not control myself. As I waited for my plane to depart, I went to the phone and made appointments with both Dr. Foley and Dr. Taub, the doctor from the show.

CHAPTER TWENTY-EIGHT

The first appointment was with Dr. Foley. I felt very uncomfortable about seeing her. Not only because I had had so much trouble with her receptionist. Dr. Sweet told me, "I spoke with Dr. Foley about an appointment for you. She told me that she hadn't accepted you as a patient when you called her [the year before] because she found you to be too disagreeable a person, based on what her secretary had said." Nevertheless, when I called to make the appointment, she agreed, I suppose for Dr. Sweet's sake, to see me.

She came out to the waiting area to greet me. She called my name. When I rose and walked toward her, she smiled and introduced herself. She was taller than I, thin with below-chin-length, very light brown hair. Over her pale blue dress, she wore a long white doctor's coat. She escorted me upstairs to her office.

As we rode in the elevator, I told her about the problems I had experienced with her staff. She did not say, "Well, I heard you were a very nasty person" or "Your experience was unique."

"I have gone through a few secretaries since you first called my office." She made no apologies for them. That was all right, though, because, so far, she gave me no indication that the behavior of her former staff was indicative of the behavior I could expect from her.

We spent most of the appointment in conversation. She wanted to know everything about the pain, its history, and my personal story. I did not get the impression that she had any preconceived notions. Fool me once, shame on you. Fool me twice, shame on me.

"Do you have a psychiatric history?" It was an expected question. I was honest in my reply. I had taken pills and cut my wrists in my second suicide attempt, at age eighteen. Although the damage was minimal, I did require stitches. Even twelve years later, the faint scars remained. I was taken aback when she directed, "Let me see your wrists."

I did not want to show her. One, because I was embarrassed by them. Two, and more important, it had nothing to do with my face pain. She stood in front of me. I was seated at the end of her examining table. I shook my head no. She said nothing, waiting for me to comply. I sat still, silent, looking at the floor. She repeated her request, this time somewhat more forcefully. "Show me your wrists." I did not want to, but the same feeling washed over me, as it always did when confronted by a command. What choice is there? I pulled back both blouse cuffs. She looked. She said nothing. She nodded her head. I re-covered my wrists. She turned the discussion back to the reason I was there.

I was impressed with the thoroughness of her physical exam. I expected to be rushed through. If she could not be bothered to return a phone call, my thinking went, I was sure she could not spend more than a few minutes in an exam. Mixed in among her many questions was a complete neurological exam.

Two hours after we began, she had all the information she needed. "I have two ideas. There are two possible therapies for you. I need to look into them first." The first depended on what, if any, research was currently being conducted at the National Institute of Dental Research (NIDH) involving facial or dental pain. The second was a behavioral therapy prescription.

She thought that it might be possible to teach me to do things, such as wash my face, in spite of the pain. It would require my entering another pain program. The therapy would consist of having someone touch and rub the painful area until I could tolerate the sensation. There would be no effort to change the pain itself. I would simply be taught to "grin and bear it." It was close to the philosophy that was behind the leukotomy. As Dr. Sweet put it earlier, "You will still have the pain. You just won't care that you do." She recommended the approach mostly for cosmetic reasons. If successful, it would allow me to wash my face.

To my surprise, I found myself liking her. I began to think that it really was her secretary who had been responsible for her not responding to my calls the year before. When I telephoned her, as she had instructed, to find out about the NIDH or the pain program, I realized it may well have been her. She did not call back. I tried again a week later. Again, no response. As I did the year before, I went to her office with a letter. No reply to that either. When I wrote and asked her to submit a statement to Social Security, it finally did not surprise me when I received no reply.

Dr. Schatz had a practice I appreciated. When he wrote to a consultant, or they to him, he always sent me a copy of the letter. A short time after my appointment with Dr. Foley, he sent me her report.

She had not told me that she thought the pain, or the periods of relief after Dr. Osterholm's surgery, and maybe Dr. Wilson's, were primarily a benefit of an improved psychological state. Indeed, she had given me no reason to believe that she thought the pain had a psychological basis. That is what she wrote to Dr. Schatz.

Sloan-Kettering is renowned as a cancer treatment center. Dr. Foley worked primarily with cancer pain. I did not expect her to be overly familiar with trigeminal neuralgia. I did assume, though, that she had some knowledge of tic and its treatments.

The literature states that it is not unusual for a patient's surgical relief to be limited to two to three months. She wrote that it was her belief that the short time of relief was not a result of the surgeries. It was, instead, due to "an improvement in her psychological state." The sentence most telling to me read, "She is somewhat appealing and likable in one's direct contact with her."

Based on what Dr. Sweet quoted her as saying, it was apparent that she had decided beforehand I would not be personable. The fact that she found me to be pleasant contradicted her preconceived notion. It gave me reason to believe that she had made up her mind, medically and psychologically, a long time before we ever met.

Neither Dr. Schatz nor I had any other contact with her. She followed through on none of her recommendations.

My appointment with Dr. Taub would turn out to be almost equally unenlightening.

I called for an appointment. The receptionist was very nice. She asked why I wanted to see Dr. Taub. She told me she could make an appointment. "The fee is two hundred fifty dollars. It needs to be paid in full at the time of your appointment. Otherwise, Dr. Taub will not be able to see you." No other doctor I had seen had this policy. I could get the cash, so I thought nothing of it at the time.

I took a train up to his office in Connecticut. Shortly after I arrived, Dr. Taub summoned me into his office.

His white hair matched nicely with his short white medical jacket. He wore gold-rimmed glasses. His somewhat shortish stature was obscured by the wooden desk behind which he sat. We spoke for about an hour.

Prior to the appointment, his secretary had mailed me a questionnaire. I was asked to describe what treatments I had undergone, what the pain was like, and other similar information. As I took my seat, I noticed the answered questionnaire lying on top of the desk. He was not going to merely accept my written replies. He asked me to explain and elaborate on each one.

After completing a thorough interview, we walked across the hall to an examining room. It was the first time in the six years, since the pain started, that I was given a complete physical exam. Except for the presence of a nodule in my thyroid gland, he pronounced me healthy.

We spent about an hour in the examining room. "Get dressed, and then I'll talk to you in my office," he said as he walked out of the room. I hurriedly put my clothes back on. I was eager to get to the ideas part of the appointment. I hoped he had some new ones. I was quickly disappointed. "I think you should try these medications again." He was talking about antidepressants and anticonvulsants. *Oh boy*, I whined to myself. To him, I said, "I don't want to keep repeating what's already been tried."

He attempted to reassure me. "I don't think you've ever been tried on these kinds of drugs, not long enough to achieve a response. I'd like you to try them again. This drug, Taractan, is an antipsychotic. It has the same type of action as some of the others, but it isn't one you've had before."

He held out the prescriptions. Reluctantly, I took them. "Give me a call in a month to let me know if they're helping." Then he told me to see his secretary before I left.

I sat down at her desk. I took out my checkbook. I started to write in $250.00. She looked up. "The fee is three hundred dollars." "But you told me when I called it was two hundred fifty dollars." "I know, but it's gone up since then." I was annoyed and angered that she had not called to let me know. Getting $250.00 together had been hard enough. Another $50.00 was a lot of money to me. It would be difficult to get. I would have to ask my father for it. Something I hated doing. I was tempted to argue. I was so disappointed in Dr. Taub's recommendation that I didn't have enough energy or desire for it. I gave her the check and left.

I was not sure what I wanted to do. His treatment differed not at all from the other doctors. I was not sure that there was even any point to trying it.

When I left MGH, I was feeling very agitated. Nothing had happened since to change my mood. I knew I had to do something. Suicide, the only option left, was not appropriate. I was too upset from what had happened in Boston. I knew any major decision I might make could well be a result of the psychological manipulation by Dr. Sweet and Dr. Bouchoms. I told Dr. Hendler, as well as Mary and Carolyn, and the people at Boston, that I would choose death only as a way to stop the pain. If I chose to do it now, I did not think I could know what my reasoning would be.

I decided it would not hurt to try the drugs Dr. Taub prescribed. The Tegretol worked on the fourth try. Maybe, this would work. There would certainly be no benefit in doing nothing.

While I waited for the time to pass, and to see if the drugs might work, I received a letter from Social Security. They no longer considered me disabled. Because I knew that I was, as did most of the medical people with whom I worked, I was very upset. If they cut me off, I had no idea where my money would be coming from.

I had not been singled out. President Reagan had decided the time had come to reduce the number of people on disability. The news reported story after story of legitimately disabled people removed from the disability rolls with no warning. People died, killed themselves, or became homeless because of their abrupt dismissal. I knew that, ultimately, I would be reinstated. I did not know how long the process might take.

The first step was to file for a reconsideration of their decision. If that was not successful, I would have to go to court. In the meantime, my last check would be in December 1982.

I filed for my recertification of disability on January 24, 1983. Shortly before that, I asked a number of medical people to submit statements about my level of physical impairment. Mary Viernstein wrote, "In my opinion, Ms. Levy is totally permanently disabled." Dr. Schatz's letter stated, "It would appear that termination of her benefits is not based on the medical information." Dr. Hendler's said that I had a "temporary total disability." Social Security had letters from three highly respected medical people, all of whom found me to be disabled. I thought they would make their determination on the medical evidence supplied.

I had been asked, on the form for reconsideration, to list all of my hospitalizations for the tic. I assumed they would look at all of them. Instead, they picked three.

Three months later, in April, I received another letter from Social Security. According to them, I was now able and therefore no longer in need of disability payments. On a separate sheet, they informed me of the medical sources on which they had relied.

The first was a report from Dr. Schatz. It was one I had not seen. Based on the letter he had shown me in January, I was sure he had written it in defense of my position that I could not yet work. The other two sources: The discharge report from the Massachusetts General Hospital and a statement from the Clinical Research Center left no question as to why I had been terminated. The latter did not address my physical ability to work, one way or the other. Dr. Sweet declared my pain to be psychological.

Without the monthly check, I did not know how I would survive financially. I filed for a second reconsideration. I had no idea how long it might take. I did not want to ask my father for money again, but I had no choice. To my surprise, he put no conditions on his answer. "Don't worry. I'll give you whatever you need until something can be worked out." I hated having to ask him. The last thing I wanted was to go back on the dole.

Disability was an allowance, but it came from the government. It allowed me to feel a measure of independence. All along, my father had been helping with the rent and medical bills. I paid all my day-to-day expenses. I told him I appreciated his offer, "but I hope it won't come to that."

In the meantime, I was following Dr. Taub's regimen. There was no benefit from the drugs. After a month of taking them, I called him. He increased the amount of one. "I want you to continue taking both of them. Call me again in a month, and we'll see where we are."

I called him two weeks later. Increasing the drug made me

feel very lethargic. He reversed himself. "I want you to cut the dosage in half. I'll see you in the office in two weeks." I was no better. Neither drug made a difference. I called him before the scheduled appointment. "You need to come in and see me. I can't keep changing your dosages by phone." A good doctor wants you to come in. As a result of my removal from Social Security, I could not afford to do that.

"I cannot continue to make adjustments in your medications without an exam." I was very uncomfortable. "I've been taken off disability. I'm waiting for a redetermination. I don't have any income now. I can't afford to see you until they put me back on."

"If you can't pay the fee, then I'm afraid I cannot see you." I had not expected him to say that. It was not a great loss. His suggestions had not helped.

As I waited to learn my economic fate, I continued to see Carolyn Perla and Mary Viernstein. Their fees were not an overriding concern.

Carolyn continued to see me for a greatly reduced rate. Mary had arranged a method of payment with my father. He assured her he would pay but, instead, he let them accumulate. No matter how high they got before Mary or I could convince him to pay she did not stop my therapy. "We can work this out." She did not want it to be something else about which I had to worry.

I maintained contact with Sherry, my friend from Mensana. She invited me to come to her home in Maryland for a few days. Mary saw patients in New York one or two days a week. The other days she saw them in Maryland. When she heard I would be in town she scheduled me for an appointment. She also arranged for a neurosurgeon she knew to speak with me. It was not for an exam. She thought he and I might have something of interest to share with each other.

Dr. Nagerry* was very nice and very direct. In a lilting Indian accent, he said, "I would have refused to operate on you two or three operations ago. Carol, there comes a point when a

patient should no longer be cut. Your point," he said, "was probably reached a few years ago."

We then turned to the subject of Dr. Sweet. He had very
distinct feelings about leukotomy. "It's an unethical procedure.
He is one of only eight in the States who still do this operation."

I felt the solid weight of all my conflicting emotions melt away.
I knew what Dr. Sweet wanted to do to me was wrong. I knew he
had other reasons to want to do it. But he was Dr. Sweet! How
could I have been so wrong about someone?

We talked a while longer. As he walked me to the door, he
repeated, "I don't think you should have any more surgery. You
have a real bad problem, but you can only be made worse at this
point."

He was right, of course. I knew no answer existed for the
pain. For all these years, I had hung on to one main thought. "If
Dr. Osterholm's surgery worked, someone else must be able to do
the same thing." I came to the realization, before I entered the
pain clinic, that I could not expect another surgery to work. When
Dr. Sweet agreed to see me, I was only too ready to raise my
hopes again.

It became obvious, once more, that all avenues for relief were
closed. Dr. Schatz continued to give me codeine prescriptions.
Each came with six refills. I still took eight to fourteen grains a
day. It did not help the pain. It continued to let me fool myself
into thinking I was doing something for it. I hated the way it
made me feel. It occurred to me the only benefit was in the act of
taking them. *Maybe,* I thought, *there is something I can do to
make me feel better.* I started taking half a pill instead of a whole.
The reduction would make no difference in modifying the pain
since it was not doing that anyway. I would feel less drugged.
That, in itself, was a gain.

Mary Viernstein and I met once a week. As a specialist in
pain patients, options were her forte. Unfortunately, as soon as
one was thought of, it had to be cast out. The reasoning never
changed. As long as I had eye and face pain, the usual pain

relief mechanics, devised for the body and motion, were of no help. Carolyn and I continued to maintain our twice-a-week schedule as we had been doing for years.

Seeing Carolyn was one way of getting through each week. She and I both agreed that we were not making any progress in the psychological problems that had originally brought me to her. The major reasons for that were the pain and the yearly surgeries. As soon as one ended, we dealt with the devastation that failure brought. Then we worked on dealing with whatever side effect occurred. By the time we made some headway, another operation would be proposed. We would work on preparing for that, or after, getting over it. I continued with her mainly because she was my primary source of support. With three siblings that did not care, and parents actively obstructing my attempts to become able, Carolyn was the only person I had.

Edna and I talked on the phone every once in a while. I felt she had long tired of this. Jay and I also talked often. We visited occasionally but mainly used the phone. Calling Wyoming and Philadelphia was not the same as having someone I knew whom I could touch and see. The other advantage to seeing Carolyn was the same one that had helped me throughout the pain. I had someplace I was required to be, twice a week. It forced me to get out of the apartment.

I spent most of my time waiting to hear from Social Security. I also tried very hard to get back my sense of self. Soon, enough time passed and Boston became merely a bad memory. Finally, the sense of calm that had deserted me in Massachusetts returned.

Once I reclaimed my feeling of composure and acceptance, I went back to the same position I held at the pain clinic. I would try and stop the pain myself.

The means would be relatively easy. My bathroom shelf had turned into a small pharmacy. I had a lot of drugs: antidepressants, anticonvulsants, antihypertensives, antipsychotics, and antipain. Usually, once I had no relief within a week or two, the doctor would tell me to stop whatever new drug he had prescribed. Rarely did I finish the contents of any bottle. I felt fairly certain I had enough to kill at least three people. There might even be enough left over to keep a fourth person feeling nothing for at least a month. There would be no problem with the physical means.

I wanted to be sure about the emotional means as well. I needed to be absolutely clear within myself that any effort at self-death was not an act of destruction. In fact, without making it seem glamorous, any suicidal act would have to be a form of self-love. It could only be to help myself, not to hurt.

Mary and I often talked about suicide. She was against it. She did everything she could to dissuade me. Although Dr. Hendler and the patients at the pain clinic had all talked to me about writing a book on the pain experience, she suggested it most often and strongly. I told her I would consider it. It would be a big commitment. If I agreed, it would force me to keep on living. If I started to write it, it would be something that I would have to see through to the end. She also had me speak with her husband, Larry, a neurobiologist, about what the future might hold for people such as myself. The bottom line for both was a well-meant—but appreciated for the feelings that prompted it— cliché that I often heard: There is always the possibility of a better tomorrow.

Sadly, tomorrow for Mary came much too soon. I saw her for the last time on February 24, 1983.

One afternoon in March, I received a call. The woman identified herself as Margie*. She was a therapist. "I'm a colleague of Mary Viernstein. I'm calling to let you know that Mary is ill. She's in the hospital. Her appointments will be canceled for a while." My stomach fell at the news. I was very sorry that she was sick. I hoped she was not too ill or in pain. I trusted her. I needed her to be there for me. My attention returned to the woman on the phone. "You can call me if you need to talk. You should hear from her soon about when she'll be back to work."

That day never came. Mary died during her postoperative period. Of all the people with whom I had worked, I felt the most comfortable with her. She was special. She seemed to understand pain, my pain, more than most. She cared immensely. She was there for her patients. She was there for me. It took me quite a while to recover from the loss.

Carolyn and I also often discussed my suicide. I felt I needed to wait until I had completed my mourning of Mary before I made any decision. Once I felt I was back on secure ground, I was ready to prepare myself, one more time, to die. Carolyn felt uncomfortable dealing with it on her own. To help her, and me, she suggested I call a man she knew. He was a thanatologist, a specialist in death.

CHAPTER TWENTY-NINE

His name was Dr. Mel Roman. A large-framed man with a lived-in face and compassionate eyes, he met with me for about an hour. He began the session by explaining that he was not a thanatologist. "I'm a sociologist. I have a special interest in working with people who are thinking of committing suicide." Carolyn wanted me to speak with someone who was more intimate than she on the concept of "rational suicide." In this, Dr. Roman was a specialist.

Of all the doctors, therapists, and nurses with whom I had discussed my situation, Mel was the first to accept my position immediately. He heard me out as to what I had been through. He listened to my reasons for pursuing death. He agreed with my assessment of my situation.

He told me about some other people with whom he had worked. He had helped them in attaining their deaths. I did not ask him if he meant directly or only through emotional support. It was not my business. I was also not sure I wanted to know.

One of his clients had suffered from severe depression. This man had made numerous suicide attempts before finally succeeding. Dr. Roman felt he had made the right choice. "He had struggled with his depression for such a very long time." It was an emotional pain that would not let go of him.

That was at the base of my own concern. I wanted to be absolutely sure it was the physical factor, not the emotional, that was leading me to suicide.

Again, television informed me.

I began by telling him about a PBS documentary. "I saw a program on 'rational suicide.' This woman had terminal cancer. She killed herself to end the battle and her pain. The show closed with a debate as to whether or not her suicide was from her physical pain or a response to her fear of possible future pain from the cancer.

"She talked with her family. They had long conversations and debates about it. It was her decision to kill herself. She felt it was preferable to enduring the cancer and a possibly long, very painful death process.

"The experts on the show questioned whether her cancer was as bad as she believed. If it wasn't, as some of them said, then she didn't die strictly as a response to her cancer. Some of them believed that her actions did not meet the criteria of 'rational suicide.' I kind of thought the same thing. It seemed to me that maybe she did kill herself before she had exhausted all her other treatment options.

Mel nodded. "Her name was Joanne Roman." The similarity in the name escaped me. "She was my wife."

I was so embarrassed. Here I was questioning the rationale for this woman's action. I thought through some of the things I had been saying. In the context of it being his wife, I felt awful. Particularly because, earlier in the meeting, I had said, "There is one other possible way out of my situation."

Dr. Taub wanted me to see someone about the thyroid nodule he had noticed. "You need to have that checked as soon as possible. It could be cancerous." I did not know at the time that thyroid cancer grows very slowly.

I mentioned it to Dr. Roman. "I'm not going to do anything about it. Maybe, it's my body's way of ending the pain." To learn that his wife's death was a secondary consequence of cancer! I visually kicked myself. Here I was, throwing his wife's story back into his face. And saying she had been wrong.

"Those doctors on the show didn't know my wife's entire story.

She did do the right thing. She died before her pain and suffering became unbearable."

We talked a while longer. We discussed rational suicide in general. We talked about mine in particular. I stood to leave. As he opened the door for me, he said, "If you need any help, give me a call." I did not know how literally he meant that. I appreciated the offer.

It was a beautiful day, and I decided to walk home. The kind of day that gives pause to any and all thoughts of death. My head was in a spin. I have always believed that suicide is the right of everyone. I also believe that psychiatric distress precludes rationality in deciding to kill one's self. I talked with someone who felt as I did about suicide being a legitimate choice. The problem was I felt Dr. Roman went overboard. I disagreed with him about the man with the disabling depression. *Suicide*, I thought, *cannot be rational under that circumstance.*

As I watched the show on PBS, I questioned the reasons for Mrs. Roman's suicide. I obviously did not have the information Mel had. Based on her own words, I felt she had acted too soon. Who really knew the truth? Only those most intimately involved.

I had a lot of thinking to do.

The next day, I acted on one of his suggestions. I called the Hemlock Society. This is a group whose sole purpose is the acceptance of "self-deliverance," their euphemism for suicide. They believe that people in end-stage illness should not have to suffer. Nor should they have to die alone because their death is by their own hand.

Although not terminally ill, my pain was permanent. I wrote them about my situation. I received back a newsletter. They also sent along a book. Authored by Derek Humphrey (one of the proponents of assisted suicide for the dying), it contained stories of other people's situations. It also gave a few recipes for death. None of them used the drugs I had at hand. I put the information in a safe place. It might come in handy.

As I waited for a determination from Social Security, I had a lot of time to make decisions. The reality of my life had not changed. Except to get harder and worse.

I took large doses of codeine. Breaking them in half only resulted in my taking them twice as often. I constantly felt drugged. The pain remained the same. I was as much a prisoner of it now as I had been for the preceding eight years.

I continued to debate with myself about my suicide. I knew it was the only answer, yet, somehow, there was still a part of me that wanted, maybe needed, to hang on. Nothing seemed able to extinguish that little spark of hope that always flickered, no matter how low, in the back of my mind.

I remained linked to my doctors. They could do nothing for me. Or rather, nothing new.

If I wanted the codeine, I had to see Dr. Schatz. If I did not want to lose my eye, I had to see an ophthalmologist.

Dr. Arentsen knew what he had been talking about. The tarsorrharphy, as disgusting as it had been, probably should not have been "taken down." My eye went bad two and three times a month. Each incident meant a trip to the clinic. Each visit meant allowing someone to touch my face. No matter which resident I saw, he/she had the same words for me. "You really need to seriously consider letting them put back the tarsorrharphy." *Uh-oh.* Every time I looked in a mirror, I was disgusted by what I saw. The times when I accidentally caught a reflection of myself, in a store window or an unexpected mirrored wall, I was horrified. My stomach retched at the site of my face. I could not tolerate the idea of disfiguring myself further.

Each time the dirt built up, the eye would get very bad. When I first had the general anaesthesia for a face washing, it was out of conceit for my high school reunion. When I had it done the second, third, and fourth time, the reason was medical. Each time I had it done, my eye would be well for an entire week. Sometimes, luck would hold. It would last for two. It soon became routine. Approximately every three months, the Wills Eye anaesthesiologist put me out. The nurses, always obligingly, gave me a shampoo and a face wash.

I received an answer from Social Security in May. They decided that the original decision was correct. I had been able to work since October 1982. As far as I could tell, the determination continued to be based primarily on Dr. Sweet's notes. His were the only ones that said my pain was psychological.

The letter informed me that I could mount another appeal. I did. As part of the process, I had to be seen by two government physicians. They also allowed me to submit more information from my personal doctors. It was the opinions of the two state-appointed doctors that counted the most.

The first doctor was a neurologist. Dark haired and in his early forties, he was very familiar with all the medical people I had seen. As I sat in the waiting area, I filled out a personal information sheet. One question asked who my present physician was. Dr. Chernin looked at the form as I entered his office. He noticed Dr. Schatz's name. The first thing he said was, "You know, my exam will not be as good as Dr. Schatz's." Soon, I felt like a who's who of neurosurgery. He repeated the name of the surgery I had. He said the surgeon's name. After each, he added, "Oh, I know [Norman or Neil or Bob]."

It had been years since Dr. Schatz had done a full neurological exam on me. Dr. Chernin gave me a very thorough, and good, exam. He gave me no indication as to what his recommendation would be.

The second doctor was an ophthalmologist. Dr. Forchheimer was a rather elderly man. Gray haired and bespectacled, he quickly disabused me of any fear I might have. It concerned me that, doctors or no, these people were on the government payroll. If they found me "able," they would be saving the government money. Dr. Chernin gave me no feeling one way or the other. With Dr. Forchheimer I felt a genuine concern about my personal situation.

He performed an extensive eye exam. There were parts of tests that I could not do. Some required too much eye movement. For others, he had to touch my face. He gave no argument. If I said I could not do something, he did not insist that I do it.

We talked about all my operations. I told him I still harbored some hope that another surgery would come along. "Someone," I said, "sooner or later, will know how to fix this."

"I agree with all the other doctors. I am very sorry. I do not think you should let anyone operate on you." We talked a while, about both my medical history and the history of my syndrome. When we parted, he did not tell me what his finding to the disability office would be.

While I waited for the decision, I felt I really needed to see a friend. I called Edna. I had been trying to save a little cash. It was (just) enough. Within a few days, I was on a plane on my way to her new home in Montana. The discount ticket fare required that I stay for at least two weeks. I was excited to be going. She was happy that I was coming. It would be great.

After one week, I had to go home. Talking, playing games, and sightseeing with Edna, Stan, and their daughter, Justine, was too much for my eye. The pain was unbearable. Between the pain and all the codeine I was taking to combat it, I was miserable.

It was all I could do to hold my temper in check. Any little thing that made the pain worse or forced me to concentrate set off my anger. It was not them. It was not me. It was the pain. I was with friends. I was away from home. I loved the beauty of Montana. How could it do this to me?

I called the airline. "I have a medical problem. I have the discounted fare, but I need to go home now, a week early. What do I need to do?" "The only way you can go is if you buy a full one-way fare ticket. You can only go back at the price you paid if you honor the time limits of your ticket." I could not do that. I had not saved up that much.

Truly a friend, Edna came up with an alternative. Since I could not leave, they would.

There was something a little disconcerting about my friends having to take a vacation from my vacation with them. There was nothing else I could do. The pain, the pain, the pain! It ruined everything. I hated it! They got to see Mount Rushmore. I did not have to see anything. By the time they returned, I felt ready to let the pain mount again.

I stayed through the second week. The three days off were just what I needed. Who knows? It may have been what they needed, too.

When I arrived home, my food stamp vouchers and some other expected dated letters were missing from my mail. I thought someone might have broken into my box. Prior to my trip to Montana, I had canceled a court date for my disability appeal. My major concern was that the court might have sent me a new date and the notice was in one of the missing letters.

I called the judge's office. I spoke with his secretary. I asked her if a new date had been set. "Just a minute," she said. She put me on hold. Soon, a male voice came on the line, "This is Judge Friedman." Oops. I did not know why she called him to the phone. "Um, I was just calling to see if a new date had been set for my hearing." Instead of a direct answer, he asked me to tell him about my case.

"I was removed from disability, and I do not think it was a fair ruling. The new date was for the reconsideration hearing." I explained about my condition, history, treatments, and current situation. He listened. "I'm going to put you on hold for a minute." A few minutes later, he came back on the line. "I have your file. I want to look at it. I'll call you back in half an hour." I did not know why he would call me back. I did not ask. I was not going to question a judge, particularly one who held my financial future in his hands.

A while later, my phone rang. It was Judge Friedman. "I've looked at your records, including the letters from both the state and your own doctors. You should never have been taken off. You're now reinstated. You should get a copy of my decision within a few weeks." I shook my head in wonderment as I hung up the phone. I could not believe it. After all my angst, all it took was one judge who was willing to look at the record in its entirety. A month later, I received the verification notice. I could breathe freely again. Finally, something was actively settled. I had something for which I no longer had to fight. Something on which I could rely.

I was still in limbo about how I would deal with the pain. Unsure of which way I should turn, I decided I would try to write a book. Since Mary's death, I felt that I owed it to her. Working on it meant that I could make no steps towards my suicide until it was done. I was still only able to use my eyes for fifteen to twenty minutes without severe pain. I neglected to consider how much time it might take.

One day, my neighbor, Steve, a professional writer, and I were talking. I asked him if he knew of a service I had read about. "Have you ever heard of this service, 'editor-for-hire'?" He was not familiar with them. "Why do you want to know?" I felt embarrassed saying it out loud. Especially to someone who wrote for a living. "I'm working on a book, but I don't really know how to go about it." "I know a book packager," he replied. "I think she might be interested in working with you. Let me give you her name."

He went back to his apartment. A few seconds later, he came back with her number written on a slip of paper. I took it and thanked him.

I went back to my apartment and lay the note on my desk. I felt torn. I made a commitment to Mary. I wanted the pain to end. If I called this person, I was making an active movement towards continuing the pain.

Occasionally, Steve and I met in the hall. Two or three times, he asked if I had spoken with the woman he suggested. The third time, it embarrassed me to say, "No." I had no choice. The same reason I agreed to so many things that were wrong for me. I went home and dialed the number.

MaryLee was very nice on the phone. We set up a date to meet. She was very nice in person, too. She was tall, dark haired, very pretty, and very intelligent. I sat at her desk while she read what I brought with me. It was one thing to be writing at home. Now, a professional was looking at it. My hands fought my effort to stop them from tapping at my knees. My lungs tried to force me to breathe. "I think you have something workable here." *Oh boy*. I smiled at her. Inside, I screamed, *Yeah!* We talked about the various forms a book, such as the one I wanted to write, could take.

We met a number of times as I progressed in the writing. It started out as an educational book: What therapies are there? What kinds of emotions does one go through? I interviewed and sent out surveys to other pain sufferers. I would collate the information. I would relate some of their anecdotes and stories. *This could work,* I thought. And it is much better than having to write about my life.

One day, we got together at a coffee house in Soho. She and I sat at a table. The sounds of the other customers filled the air. That person went to an audition. This one hates her dance teacher. "Did you hear what Cindy told me?" someone else asked her tablemate.

The smell of coffee and pastry tickled the senses. This was a perfect New York City tableau.

I had to fake it a little. I hate coffee.

The waitress brought us our drinks. MaryLee tasted her latte. I sipped at the chocolate, ice cream, and coffee concoction I ordered. It was in a coffee cup. I could pretend it was the real thing.

We talked, drank, wrote, and edited. I felt like an artiste. Sitting in the midst of a café, talking about writing, editing the first part of a manuscript. It was a New York fantasy come true.

As all good things do, this, too, came to an end. Unlike the sad way Mary left, MaryLee had a happy reason. She decided to work full-time on her own dream: writing a novel. To do so, she had to drop her book-packaging work. Which meant she had to drop me.

I worked on the manuscript halfheartedly. After a few months, I decided I could not do it. It was the sole obligation I had. It had been made to someone no longer able to know if I honored it. There was now only me to whom I had to answer.

CHAPTER THIRTY

I stopped seeing Carolyn.

She and I often discussed discontinuing therapy. It was always at my prompting. We both agreed we were not making progress. Nevertheless, she always suggested I give the process more time. I felt she wanted me to continue because she knew how alone I was and how difficult my life was. This time, I resisted. Interestingly, once I stopped seeing her, I made a friend. It was as though I did not need anyone else as long as I had her.

Laura and I were neighbors. We had often seen each other as we passed the hall. We started talking one day in the laundry room. It turned out that she had a medical problem that had not allowed her to work in some time. We each had plenty of free time.

I enjoyed having a friend nearby. I knew a number of people in my building. With the exception of David, diagonally across the hall, most of our contacts consisted of friendly chats as we collected our mail or threw out the trash. Many people knew, generally, of my medical problem. They knew I stayed home much of the time. When they looked at my face, it immediately told them something was physically wrong. I was frequently asked, "How are you?" No matter how sincere the question was, I always kept my answers on a superficial level. David and Laura were the only new people with whom I became informationally intimate.

Those who tried to befriend me did not have success. I spent years building up a facade. If the issue of my medical problems came up, I deflected it. I spent so much energy on erecting a wall. I was unable to break it down. With the exception of David and Laura, I permitted no one more than glimpses into my life.

My connection with her had me hoping that there was an emotional cause to my pain. The closeness was a tonic for me. For the first time in a long time, my pangs of loneliness were eased. If the pain was psychological, this would make it stop. It did not.

With the exception of having someone to talk and share with, my life stayed the same.

Every morning, when I awakened, before looking at the window or the clock, or around, the pain was not there. In the background, maybe, but I was used to that. Like a backache, you get used to the constant ache. It is the normal sensation. As long as you do not move, it is okay. And then you move. *Oh boy.*

It was the same for me. The minute I awakened. Before I opened my eyes. *Oh, I'm okay.* And then I open my eyes. And look around. Or the sun comes into my eye. And reality comes zooming back. *No, I'm not.*

Sometimes, after I washed, dressed, and ate breakfast, time long enough after I had been reminded, I could convince myself. *I bet it won't be so bad today. I bet I could go outside, even if it's windy. I bet ya I could do that.*

It was hard to keep the truth in the forefront of my mind. The first step outside brought it back. I fought to read past the time the pain got really bad. Maybe it can only get so bad. Then it will have to go away. It did not. It grew and grew. I swallowed half a codeine pill after half a codeine pill.

The pain brought on nausea. Tears sprang to my eyes. The pain caused them. The impossibility of denying the truth sent them down my cheeks.

Every time my eye went bad, because something had gotten in it or, more often, because it dried out because of its inability to close well, the pain got worse. By the beginning of 1984, the eye was rarely well. In February, I was advised by every member of the clinic who had examined me to have the tarsorrharphy put back.

I hated to do it. The idea of having the eye closed again sickened me. I told them, "No. I can't do that. Not again."

I went back and forth to the clinic. Sometimes, once and twice a week. It went bad faster. It took longer to heal. The pain increased with every incident. A familiar stanza ran through my mind. *I have no choice.*

I called Dr. Arentsen. He admitted me into the hospital a few days later.

The drugs dripped into my vein. The last picture I saw in my mind's eye was the horrible sight that accosted me the first time I saw "it." My eyes involuntarily closed.

I awakened a short time later. As soon as I could get up from the litter, I went to find a mirror. *Oh, Dr. Arentsen. Thank you.* He had taken the middle ground. I had not wanted it closed at all. He wanted it closed completely.

Only the inside corner of the eye was sewn shut. Instead of that disgusting opening in the middle, almost two-thirds of my eye was still open.

He took out the stitches a week later. "I'm really grateful that you left it more open. It's still awful, but it's less nauseating to me this way." "I'm glad you're happier this time," he said. I smiled and started to say something. He stopped me. "But, I will never open this again for you." *Well,* I thought, *we can cross that bridge when we get to it.*

I thought I would be safer with it closed, even if only partially. It took almost no time before I hated it, almost as much as before. I expected the benefit to my eye would make up for my loathing.

Even with it closed, it refused to behave itself. It continued to go bad. With less eye exposed and incredible health and strength despite what it had been through, it invariably cleared within a day or two.

I did not do as well as my eye. It took longer and longer to bounce back from each attack of increased pain. Finally, I could not do it anymore.

I made an appointment with Dr. Schatz. My eyes begged. My voice stumbled. "Please, give me something else. The codeine isn't doing anything."

My power game with the codeine no longer helped. "I can think of one other thing we can try that you haven't yet. I'll write you a prescription for opium." Opium? Addicts used to use that. I did not think it was available anymore. I did not want to take opium.

I returned to New York with a bottle of liquid opium in my purse. I had seen the movies. I knew what an opium den looked like. I knew what happened there. *Ugh.*

I stood in the bathroom. The opened bottle in one hand, a teaspoon in the other. "I don't want to do this." I said out loud. I was afraid of what it might do to me.

I poured the liquid into the spoon. The pain was stronger than my fear. I closed my eyes. I brought the dose up to my mouth. I swallowed the drug and my fear. I waited for hallucinations or euphoria. Instead, I itched and vomited. I was allergic to it.

I called Dr. Schatz. "You can take a Benadryl with it if you want to try it again. Take it a few minutes before taking the opium."

I figured I tried it once. It had not made me crazy or an addict. I waited a day. I awakened and waited for the pain to get bad. I never thought of taking it before the pain, when it might have staved off the worsening. Except for one incident where I thought I saw a mouse that no one could find any evidence of, the only effect I had was a very heavy sleep. In a sense, it worked. As long as I was asleep, I did not feel the pain.

Day after day passed. Almost nothing changed. My inabilities, disabilities, financial circumstances, aloneness—all the same. I arrived, once more, where I felt I had to do something about it. And, again, suicide seemed the answer.

There was nothing in my life that was of such a magnitude that it would inhibit me. I wavered as to whether or not I had an obligation to Mary (to try and write a book). The one thing that did change, a few months earlier was: They could be a problem.

I returned to visit Edna and her family earlier that summer, in Wyoming, where they now lived. Edna was teaching summer school. Stan was driving a truck. Justine was at daycare. My stay was shorter. I was alone for long periods of time. There was much less for me to do. That allowed me to tolerate the pain a little more.

I spent most of my time with Edna's pets. Samwise was a kitten. Each night, I tried to get him to sleep with me. A little tiny thing, he had a lot of fight in him. He did not want to stay with me. He hit and hissed, "Lady, let me go!" I always gave up and out of the room he ran. Oh well.

The first thing I felt and saw every morning was Samwise lying on my neck, snuggled up tight against me. I love kittens. I love dogs. I hate cats. I fell in love.

A few days after I returned home, I went to the animal shelter. Two orange kittens were sitting in a cage in a back room. One was all orange. The other had white paws and a white spot on his nose and chest. They looked at me with their big kitten eyes.

A few hours later, the two adorable four-month-old kittens were making themselves at home in my apartment.

Puss and Boots helped me through many hard times. Some times, it was only the knowledge that I had to feed and comfort these two little creatures that got me through the day.

They were my only responsibility. I thought long and hard about them. *What if I killed myself? What would happen to them?* I adored them. I would be able to find them another home if need be.

As I came closer to deciding the time had come to die, my father became ill.

He had not been feeling well for some months. During the summer, my mother told me that he had been behaving strangely. He was also feeling weaker and weaker. She thought he might have Alzheimer's. I would not have been surprised. I had seen him acting in ways that were irrational.

The three of us, Jude, Charlie and I, had gone to the mall. My mother walked away to another store. Charlie became frantic when he could not find her. I tried to calm him down. I explained that she was coming right back. He refused to believe me. Only when she returned into his line of vision did he become still. This was an Alzheimer's symptom.

It was not Alzheimer's. Normally that would be a reason to celebrate. But what he had was just as bad, if not worse. The diagnosis was ALS (Lou Gehrig's Disease).

ALS is a terminal disease. We did not know when he would die, but we all knew it would be coming. Before death came, his body would betray him. He would slowly lose the use of it. The mind is not affected. An ALS patient is aware of what is happening to him/her at all times. That is considered to be one of the horrifying curses of the disease. No matter how I felt about him, I knew my death would only serve to hurt him more. It might hasten his decline and demise. Until he died, I could not take steps to end my own pain.

By December 1985, a little over a year, he was in a wheelchair. Soon, he was able to move only his left hand. Then, only one finger. His death was imminent.

Because he had been sick for over a year and a half, I felt I had prepared myself emotionally for when the time came. I knew from past experience that my family would not be there for me, or let me be there for them. Once I quit Carolyn, I decided I would never go back into therapy. I had seen too many psychotherapists for too many years. Some contracts that you make with yourself are meant to be broken. Counseling would be a healthier choice than just assuming I would be all right.

I went back to St. Vincent's Hospital, this time to the psychiatry clinic. I had to wait until one of the therapists had an opening. At the end of December, I received a call. Dr. Muncey, a resident, could see me the last week in January. He and I met once. I had to cancel our second appointment. Charlie went into coma. Two days later, on February 3, 1986, he died.

As I had expected, I was prepared for his death. I did not need to do much grief work. I knew the real work I had to do centered on the pain and my plans for it.

I told Dr. Muncey that I intended to commit suicide. "There's no other medical option. I can't take the pain anymore." Once enough time had passed to let my mother get over my father's death, I intended to instigate my own.

I thought the course would be smooth and unbroken.

Dr. Muncey was a resident. His term at the hospital would be over in a year and a half. I expected that I would spend as much of that time as necessary to prepare myself, once more—and finally—to end the pain. Once again, my plans were interrupted.

Hope, my arch nemesis, got in the way.

CHAPTER THIRTY-ONE

Hope came in the form of Peggy, a petite anaesthesiologist at Will's Eye Hospital. She was often the one to put me to sleep for my face washings.

As always, I worked at keeping my feelings to myself. Especially because all of the people at the SPU (Short Procedure Unit) were so kind to me. I felt stupid and foolish, having to come to the OR just to get a cleaning. They acted as though I was there for just as important a reason as the patient getting a cataract removed.

I always smiled when I entered the unit. I was friendly. I acted upbeat.

The staff accepted my presentation. They may have known it was a mask. They let me keep up the pretense.

Peggy was not fooled. Or chose to not let me think she was. "I'm very worried about you. I've been praying for you. I've asked my children to pray for you, too."

I heard that often. From those I knew. From total strangers. Peggy went further. "I know a doctor at Jefferson who specializes in chronic pain," she said. "Would you think about seeing him?" I liked her. I truly valued her concern for me. Dr. Ericson, the acupuncturist, had been an anaesthesiologist. I was not interested in seeing another one. She was so concerned. I did not have the heart to say no.

I liked Dr. Woo from the moment we met. A young, gentle and attractive, dark-haired man, he told me he had a treatment that might be of some help. In 1978, Dr. Brisman had done his rhizolysis with Marcaine, a local anaesthetic. Dr. Woo proposed using Lidocaine, another local anaesthetic. Instead of injecting it into my face, he would inject it into my body.

I went to the recovery room, at Jefferson, once or twice a week. The therapy itself was not dangerous. In case of a bad reaction, though, it could only be done where oxygen and drugs would be immediately available.

Once I was settled, Dr. Woo, or one of his colleagues, would hook me up to an intravenous drip solution of Lidocaine. It took an hour to an hour and a half for the bottle to empty. There was no benefit after the first try. I agreed to do it seven more times in the hope that there might be a cumulative effect. It was not totally surprising to either of us that there was not. Repeating the advice of the others who had gone before him, he said, "I definitely think you shouldn't let anyone operate on you again." He added, "I'd like you to see Dr. Schwartzman. He's a neurologist here at Jefferson. He might be able to do something."

I did not want to change from Dr. Schatz. But it never hurts to get another opinion. My thinking was never changed by my experience. It hurt, a lot, with Dr. Sweet, Dr. Martinez and the others. I used logic to convince myself to see this doctor. *After all, I told Peggy I would see Dr. Woo. Dr. Schwartzman is his recommendation.* I called for an appointment.

An older man, he had white hair and a grizzled face. He sat behind a neatly arranged desk, his white doctor's coat unbuttoned over a blue lightly striped shirt.

He performed all the usual neurological tests. Close your eyes, put out your arms. Now touch your each index finger to your nose, in turn. Move your fingers, in order, the index first to the little one, very quickly, against your thumb, and so on.

As always, I passed. Doing any of the actions involved in testing the brain was never a problem for me. (Except for smiling and other movement requests that showed if the seventh cranial nerve was intact.)

"I was sure you wouldn't have any suggestions." It was a question as much, if not more, as it was a statement. As always, despite all the talks I had with myself (*Now, don't get your hopes up this time. You know you're always disappointed*), I had gotten my hopes up. They plummeted when he said, "This is really a tough problem." And rose again when he added, "I may have some ideas. I want to talk with Dr. Osterholm first. Then I want to bring you into the hospital for some tests. Give me a call in a few days." *Oh. Maybe. Maybe this time it will work!* I took the train back to New York full of plans for when the pain was gone.

I called Dr. Schwartzman a week later. He did not return my call. I called again the next week. He did not return my call. I tried a third time. He still did not return my call.

I met with Dr. Schatz. I told him about my visit with Dr. Schwartzman. I repeated his words to me about maybe being able to help me. Dr. Schatz moved his phone over in front of him. He picked up the receiver and began dialing a number. "I'll call him right now, so we can get this figured out."

I watched his face as he spoke and listened. I knew what he was going to tell me merely by his expression.

"Dr. Schwartzman says he doesn't have anything to offer you. There's nothing he can do." *Oh God.* "Once again, a doctor tells me one thing to my face. Then he gets me all excited because I think there is a chance I can be fixed. I don't understand why he said that to me, why he said he did have some ideas." "I'm really sorry, Carol. I don't know why he told you what he did." Neither did I.

It was, again, the end of the medical line. I tried everything that had been suggested. Dr. Woo and Dr. Schwartzman had been very long shots. There were no more shots to be had. I decided that my only medical contact from now on would be the psychiatric resident, Dr. Muncey.

Dr. Schatz had moved his medical practice to Florida for half the year. To make it easier for both of us during the time he was away, the residents from the Manhattan Eye and Ear Hospital wrote the prescriptions for my codeine. As far as I was concerned, I would continue only with the codeine and the shrink. I would not, I commanded myself, get my hopes up anymore. In fact, they had descended further. The benefit from Dr. Hosobuchi's surgery—the end of the spontaneous pains—had stopped.

In October 1985, I had two lightning attacks. I decided I would deal with them in the same way I had when the first pain came. I pretended they had not happened.

As they had in 1976, when they first occurred, they terrified me. Then my fear was not specific. I had no idea what the pain meant. This time, nine years and six neurosurgeries later, I knew only too well what could happen. Overtly, I succeeded in the pretense. Covertly, it may have been a different matter.

I met with Dr. Muncey once, and sometimes twice, a week. I often mentioned my intention to commit suicide, "if I can't find relief from the pain." As far as I was concerned, and had been told on numerous occasions, there were no new avenues of relief. My main purpose in seeing him was to clarify issues from my past. I believed that once I died, I would be aware of nothing. In that sense, it did not matter what I resolved. Nonetheless, I felt that I needed to be on an even and understanding keel before leaving life.

I had been going to him for four months when I developed a terrible problem with my eye. There was no respite from the increased pain each time it went bad. I went from dry eye to dry eye. I started feeling actively suicidal. I could not get a break from the pain.

The time for my death had not arrived. I was not where I wanted to be emotionally, but the pain was pushing me into a corner. Dr. Muncey recommended that I consider coming into the hospital. He would admit me to the psychiatric unit. I refused. I was darned if I was going to be locked up.

He was scheduled to go on vacation. Before he left, he asked me to think seriously about admitting myself. I felt so bad, emotionally and physically, that it was tempting. His absence gave me a chance to really think about, to evaluate, what was happening to me.

The problem was my eye. The residents at Manhattan Eye and Ear strongly advised me to have the part that Dr. Arentsen had not closed, closed. I did not want that—no matter how bad my eye got.

Or so I thought.

Finally, the pain overwhelmed me. I literally had no choice. I called Dr. Arentsen. "I want you to close the eye." He would not, until he saw it for himself. "Come in tomorrow, and I'll take a look."

One of the residents saw me first. I asked him what he thought. "Dr. Arentsen will have to see you before any decision can be made."

"Can it be closed this afternoon? Please?" I was virtually begging. The irony was not lost on me. I was pleading to have something I abhorred, done. It was not me. It was the pain. It spoke for me and through me.

"If it's done," she replied, "he can't do it for a day or two. There's no opening in his schedule."

"Your eye looks perfectly fine," Dr. Arentsen said when he examined me an hour later. I thought he would jump at the chance to close the eye. He had been so resolute about not wanting to open it in the first place.

"Please close it. It's the only thing I can think to do to try and lessen the pain."

"You do not need to have your eye closed," he said to my surprise and disappointment. "I do have time to do it this afternoon, but I won't. It's not necessary."

Dr. Schatz was the only one left. His office was on the floor below. I walked downstairs. I left Dr. Arentsen's office fighting back tears. By the time I got to Jeannette's, his secretary, desk I could not help myself. "I can't deal with the pain anymore." I was weeping. "Wait here," she said and walked to the back office. "Dr. Schatz says if you can wait a little, he'll be able to talk with you. It won't be too long."

I sat in the waiting room. I tried to look nonchalant. I did not want all the people waiting to see how upset I was. It was hard work. An hour or so later, he called me back into his office.

I could not wait until we made it to his office. "I can't take it anymore. I swore after Boston I would never go back into the hospital. Please. Admit me to the hospital."

No longer affiliated with Jefferson, he arranged for me to be admitted to the University of Pennsylvania Hospital, also in Philadelphia. I repeated my actions of nine years before. I took a train back to New York, packed a bag and returned, this time, the next day, May 23, 1986, to enter the hospital.

There was no proposal of surgery. I think he brought me in mainly to give me a break from dealing with the pain on my own. But, as long as I was there, he decided to try more drugs. Many of the names were new, but the actions were the same. We tried blood pressure drugs, psychotropic drugs, and more anticonvulsants. None were any more effective than the ones we had tried in the past.

I was standing next to my bed. A female resident was leaning back against the window, interviewing me. The night before had been a scary one for me. "I had one of the spontaneous pains last night."

"Was that the first time since your last surgery?" she asked.

Until that moment, I had successfully repressed the memory of the two times in October. Maybe the return of the pains and my forgetting them, or so I theorized to myself, was one of the reasons I was having so much more trouble dealing with the pain. The recollection of them made no difference. The level of pain remained the same. Valid or not, the insight seemed useless.

One of the consultants suggested I enter the pain clinic within the hospital. I decided to walk over and take a look. I walked through the door and picked up a pamphlet that explained the workings of the center.

As I read, a woman came over to me. "Hi. I'm Susan.* I'm one of the physical therapists in the clinic." I introduced myself in turn. "Are you considering coming into the pain center?"

I explained about my situation and the suggestion that I consider it.

I was not surprised by her response. "We're not equipped to handle your kind of pain. We do physical rehabilitation and behavior modification here. What we offer wouldn't be helpful for the kind of problem you have." "I kind of figured this would not be something for me but, thanks, anyway." I knew that there was nothing she could offer me. And yet. And yet . . . My mind kept whispering, *Maybe. Maybe. Maybe.* It was like the little engine that could. "I think I can. I think I can. I think I can." Only, it was able to say, "I knew I could" when he made it to the top of the hill. The last line for me was always, *I thought it could. Why can't it?*

I walked back to my room to wait for someone, anyone, to suggest something new. Instead, I was met with something old.

I had been admitted with the specific diagnosis of trigeminal neuralgia. Dr. Schatz had verified the definitive neurological basis for my pain. And still, the resident in charge of my care found it hard to believe.

I was lying in bed with a hot water bottle on my stomach. I had just taken it off when the resident entered my room.

"What are using that for?" he asked as he pointed to the bottle.

"I have really bad cramps."

"Oh. I thought you were putting it on your forehead for your face pain."

He was the first resident with whom I had spoken after my admission. "I can't touch this part of my forehead and face. If I or anyone or anything does, it causes really severe horrific pain. If I want it cleaned, 'cause it gets really dirty from the air and soap that falls on it when I wash the rest of my hair, I have to have general anaesthesia so the nurses can wash the area for me."

He looked as though he was paying attention. Nevertheless, he assumed that I was using the bottle directly on a place where I said I could not tolerate touch. Ten years and six surgeries later, I was still being disbelieved.

In addition to Dr. Schatz, my care was directed by Dr. Friedman, an anaesthesiologist. I did not have to defend my pain to him. He believed me. He reiterated that there were no new therapies. "I think it might help if we change your pain meds. Have you ever been tried on methadone?"

CHAPTER THIRTY-TWO

I was as afraid of the methadone as I had been of the opium. This is used as a substitute for heroin. Pretty scary.

No, it was not. It did not make me feel strange. I had no hallucinations or feelings of euphoria. I did not "nod off," which actually might have helped. If I was napping all the time, I would not feel the pain.

I remained in the hospital for two weeks. I still had the basic pain. None of the drugs, including the methadone, had changed it.

My eye was not bad enough to need the tarsorrharphy. It was not white, either. Dr. Schatz and others examined it under the slit lamp machine. Each time they did, they saw areas of drying out and little punctates. Not gargantuan amounts, but enough to be responsible for the pain being worse.

After two weeks, Dr. Schatz decided there was no reason for me to stay there. There was nothing else to try. He did not discharge me back to my home. Instead, he arranged for me to go directly to the Wills Eye Short Procedure Unit. They put me "out." They washed my face. A few hours later, I awakened, my eye white, my face clean and shiny. I always had more pain after the washings. They had to scrub which made the area swell. Once it subsided, so, too, did the extra pain.

Despite the lack of benefit from the methadone, I returned home with a two-week supply. Dr. Friedman had given me the name of a doctor in Manhattan. "I was one of his students. He'll give you the prescriptions for it."

I saw Dr. Corter in his office two weeks later. A tall gentleman, probably in his fifties, he wore a nice dark blue suit jacket and white shirt. There was very little chitchat. He looked over the records I had brought with me. He asked me a couple of routine questions. He reached a conclusion fairly quickly. "I really have nothing to suggest or offer you." That was okay with me. I had only made the appointment, so I could get the methadone prescription. "Oh no," he said. "I won't give you any prescriptions for that."

It had not helped me anyway. I was not adverse to the idea of not taking it anymore. Unfortunately, my body was.

I knew it was addictive. I had often heard it touted in the news as the drug given to heroin addicts. It was taken to wean them from their addiction. And yet, methadone is as addicting, if not more so, than heroin. After years of taking the codeine, I did not seem to be addicted to it. I had been taking the methadone for less than a month. I did not think that was a long-enough time to become addicted.

I was wrong. After not taking it for a day, I felt physically uncomfortable. My body ached. My nose alternated between feeling horribly stuffy and running. I felt like I had a very bad cold. I had seen addicts on television with their noses running. It was an awful thought, but I realized that might be me. I took a pill that evening. I felt better. I decided that I would continually cut the dose in half during the next week until I had no dose left to take. By the end of the week, I felt fine. I did not need it anymore.

The increase in the pain that had prompted my visit to Dr. Arentsen and my admission to the hospital had abated. The explanations were plentiful. My eye was better. My face had been washed. Being in the hospital kept me from going outside. I was not forcing myself to do things that make the pain worse. Whichever one(s) was/were right, it did not matter. All that counted was that the pain was no longer worse than usual.

I went back to the codeine and Dr. Muncey. I began to prepare myself, once more, for death. Dr. Muncey was very intrigued by my stay in the hospital. "I was away and you went into the hospital. Why do you think you did that?"

"I've been thinking about that," I said. "I realized that if I hadn't been seeing you, I would have called Dr. Schatz much sooner. I'm seeing you and the pain gets worse. Automatically, I decide it's got to be psychological. That's why it never occurred to me to call Dr. Schatz."

Being in therapy led me into the trap I had escaped from for a number of years: blaming the increase in pain on my emotional needs and dis-ease. Being in the hospital had given me the distance I needed to re-realize that the problem was not psychiatric. The pain is physical. I need physical, medical help, not psychological.

I saved all my unused medications. Opium, Demerol, Percodan, anticonvulsants, antidepressants, antihypertensives. To these, I added the methadone. Every once in a while, I cleared out all the old drugs. It was important that the ones in my stash not be expired and devoid of potency. I wanted to return to my former sense of calm and acceptance. The feelings I had after leaving Mensana. The sense of peace that had deserted me during and after my stay at MGH. I needed to be sure that death was only a side effect of my effort to end the pain. Of stopping the agony. That could be the only reason for me to take my life.

Each doctor, new or old, reinforced the certainty that there was nothing left for them to try. Any drug I asked for, I got. Often, the dose was for more or at a higher dosage than the one for which I had asked. A doctor did not do that unless a case was hopeless. I knew I would not accept any more doctors or therapies. It was time to rest.

Walking home from a session with Dr. Muncey, I noticed two teenagers walking behind me. They matched my pace. They were very loud, and very rude. I remembered hearing somewhere that confronting people who were annoying you was not something they would expect. They might feel humiliated or embarrassed. It was an effective way to get them to stop.

I turned to face them. One of them looked back at me. His eyes went to my forehead. He saw the build up of dirt. It was a solid yellowish-green clump. He pointed at me. He started running away. He ran into the street, missing a car by only a few feet. "She's got AIDS! She's got AIDS!"

I was the one who felt humiliated. The one who was embarrassed. I would have hoped the ground would open up and swallow me. Except for the fact that this was not the first time this had happened.

I was in Penn Station. It had been a few weeks before. I was walking towards the exit. Suddenly, a group of eight boys, about ten years old, circled around me. "Oooh. Look at her face. What's wrong with you?"

I tried to ignore them. I kept on walking. The boys stayed in their circle, walking along with me. Next thing I knew, I was being serenaded. They chanted, in a singsong voice, "She's goo-oot AaaaIDS. She's goo-oot AaaaIDS."

I stopped walking. I reached over and down. I put my hand around the elbow of the apparent leader. My face and his were only inches apart.

"I had an operation, and the doctor made a mistake. He paralyzed my face when he operated on me." I only addressed the disfigurement. I did not intend to explain about the dirt. They would never understand someone saying they could not tolerate touch to their face. He stopped the song. Just like a kid, he immediately changed his tune. "Did you sue him?" he asked me, grinning. Then he turned away, the others following his lead. They ran off, not waiting for an answer.

Kids are like that. In a group, they can often turn mean. The second incident could not be dismissed so simply. I could see how easy it might be for a fearful and ignorant person to mistake the dirt for Kaposi's sarcoma, the cancer that can hit AIDS patients. They had to be ill informed to make that mistake. The sarcoma's visual signs are purplish, irregular lesions. Nothing at all like the way the dirt looked.

Even though I understood why they acted in the way they had, it did not change how I felt. For three days, I was distraught. The two incidents set off all the rage I had been holding in. All the anger and bitterness I tried to keep hidden. Not only from others but from myself. Hatred at all those who stared at me. Hurt and pain from the ones who asked, "What's wrong with your face?" Anguish from and loathing towards all those who had hurt me so badly, physically and emotionally, since the pain had started.

Devastating rage and ravaging despair waged war within me. The pain, the dirt, the disfigurement, the reactions—they devastated me. On the fourth day, I took myself in hand. *Enough is enough. I can't let a stupid person on the street make my decisions for me. Either I have to take some action or let it go.* The choice was the same I had to make after leaving MGH. I could let the emotions engendered by the stupidities of a bunch of people get the better of me. Or, I could make the effort to return to a state where I felt comfortable within myself and my reasoning.

I felt helpless and hopeless. It was from the pain. It was from depression, which was mostly from the pain. It was also from what those men had said and done.

I was in no position to change the latter. Only to change my thoughts and reactions to it. *They were stupid. They had no right to say what they did or act the way they did.* I continued this ode to myself until it stuck. I would not let the men in the street force my hand. Suicide is only "rational" when all the emotional causes are pared away. Only when it is the reality that tells you nothing more can be done.

Hmmmm. Maybe I should call Dr. Osterholm. He fixed me the first time. I bet he could do it again. Well, maybe. I often thought of talking with him. I hesitated because of the lawsuit I had had against Dr. Martinez.

My father agreed to pay my lawyer, Ms. Lecky, for the out-of-pocket expenses. She and I had a contingency agreement where she would receive forty percent of the settlement or winning amount (if the case went that way).

Things were going along well, so I thought. He was paying her $600.00 here, $1,000.00 there as her bills arrived.

I was happy to see her being paid. We talked fairly often. Each time, she assured me she was working diligently on the case.

Then things fell apart. My father decided he did not want to pay her any more money. She and I spoke about the amount that was owed to her. "Carol, I can't keep doing this without your father paying what he owes."

"Okay," I said. "I'll tell you what. Don't do anything else until he pays you." After all, she said she was working hard on the case. She would not do anything to jeopardize it. She only made a profit if the case went to a (winning) resolution.

I talked with my father on the phone. "Charlie, you said you would pay Kate. I don't understand why you won't do it anymore."

"Well, she told me they were willing to settle the case for $10,000.00. So, you should just take that."

"I don't know how you got that idea. No one has made any offer. And even if they did, you think $10,000.00 would cover what he did to me? You think that would pay for all the eye care I'm going to continue to need?"

"I am not going to give her any more money. That's final."

No. It was not.

I filed a case against my father in Small Claims Court. I had no choice. I could not pay Kate. He had made a commitment to both of us. He had to live up to his word. Even if it took a judge to make him honor his contract.

The judge made us meet together in a small room outside the courtroom. "I want you to sit in here and come up with a way to solve this."

My mother was inside with us. She sat there. She added nothing to the "conversation."

"Charlie, you gave your word to Kate that you would pay her. I would never have had to bring this into court if you just did what you promised you would do."

He raised his voice. "You're not getting any more money from me for her. That's it."

"I don't understand you. I thought you wanted the people who hurt me to pay for it. I thought you wanted to help me. I thought you wanted to honor your word. I truly don't get it." I worked to keep my voice under control. I would definitely not let him see any tears.

I continued to try and get him to see what he had done was wrong. He argued back, never giving a reason for his behavior. Only refusing to even compromise on the amount.

The district magistrate returned to the room. "Have you worked this out?" My father looked at him with seething eyes. "No. And we're not going to."

"Okay, then. I did not want to have to hear this case, but I guess I will have to."

I am so silly. No matter what my experiences, I think justice will prevail. People will own up to their mistakes.

I came to the stand. "My father agreed to pay Ms. Lecky." I had copies of canceled checks he had written to her. He had sent them to me when they cleared, so I would know she had been paid and how much. I also brought with me a copy of her ledger that showed payments, amount, and from whom. My father's name was prominent.

I handed these to the judge. "This is the proof that my father has paid Ms. Lecky. He was honoring his commitment that he had made before I signed with her; that the out-of-pocket costs would be covered by him."

He took the proffered checks and papers and looked them over. "Thank you. Now, Mr. Levy, I want you to come to the stand."

My father rose and walked over to the witness seat. Before sitting, he, as had I, swore to tell the truth.

The judge asked him, "Did you agree to pay Ms. Lecky the fees your daughter says you did?"

"No." What? How could he lie on the stand, in front of a judge? I could not believe my ears.

"Did you ever pay any money to Ms. Lecky?" Well, the judge had the proof in his hands. The check letterhead was in his name. It was Charles J. Levy that had signed the check. It was his handwriting.

"No. I never paid her anything."

Well, he lied. That is the kind of person he is, I guess. The court has the written documents. It was not what I wanted to have happen, but the court would have to rule in my favor because there was nothing else it could do.

The letter came four weeks later. The decision was in favor of the defendant, Charles Levy.

I could not believe it. I called the judge's office. "How could he rule in favor of the defendant when I proved perjury?" The receptionist said, "The judge will not discuss any case he has decided. You cannot talk to him." I was so angry. *Now what should I do?*

I had no option. The case would have to go to the Court of Common Pleas. A much bigger deal than Small Claims Court. A place where it was more likely than not that perjury would be unacceptable and held against the defendant.

The time for redress from that court had expired. A special request had to be made, an appeal nunc pro tunc.

I wrote out the reasons why the court should allow this case to be heard despite the regulatory time allotted having expired. I filed the papers and, within two weeks, received a reply. The court agreed to allow the case to come forward.

My father had spoken with a lawyer before the Small Claims Court case was heard. He spoke with him again after the higher court gave their response. Suddenly, the issue was moot. "I'll give Kate her money," he said the next time he called me.

This was good. I called Kate. "Charlie is going to pay you. Now you can work on the suit some more."

Despite the issues with the money and my father, no lawyer would ever let a case get away from them by ignoring the things that needed to be done in a timely fashion, would they?

Kate called me a few days later. "I've got bad news for you. The case was thrown out of court. I'm sorry."

"What!" I yelled into the phone. "What do you mean? How could that happen without us knowing? I don't understand!"

"I called opposing counsel yesterday. I told him we would be going forward now. He said, 'Didn't you know the case was dismissed six months ago?'"

"How could that be? How could you not know that?"

"Well, the decision was published in the *Intelligentser*, the court newspaper. I'm afraid I missed the notice."

"Well, there must be something you can do?"

"I'm going to ask for a reversal. The problem is the statute of limitations for an appeal has ended."

Oh boy. "All right. I'll wait to hear from you."

In Kate's papers, she stated that the post office had not sent the court's decision to the right address. That was why she was unaware of the ruling against us.

The court responded that you can't blame the post office when you make a mistake. All Ms. Lecky needed to do, it declared, was read the paper every day. A lawyer had a responsibility to do this in order to assure he or she knew if a case had been decided. They disallowed a new hearing.

My father and my lawyer. People you are supposed to be able to trust. Both allowed Dr. Martinez to get away with what he had done to me.

Isn't there anyone who won't hurt me? I asked myself.

CHAPTER THIRTY-THREE

I had to do something. I had to find a way to feel like I was in control—of the pain, of my emotions, of my life. I trusted Dr. Osterholm. He had never lied to me. He had stopped the pain. He was the answer.

I called his office. "I'm not sure if he'll see me. It's been a very long time since I last saw him. Would you check with him to make sure?" I asked the receptionist. I did not want to specifically mention Dr. Martinez. Why stir the pot unnecessarily? "I'll ask him for you. In the meantime," she said, "why don't we make the appointment? You, or we, can always cancel it."

In November 1986, Dr. Osterholm and I met again. The issue of the litigation was never mentioned. We talked for about an hour. The meeting ended in the way I expected and hoped it would not. "I don't have anything to offer you." "Couldn't you just go in there and cut the nerve?" He replied with the same words he had in 1979. "It's too dangerous a procedure. Besides," he added, "you've had so much surgery now that the nerve has been burnt and cut already."

I started to get up from the chair. I sighed. "Well, I guess that's it then."

No, it was not.

"I think it might be a good idea if you see Dr. Barolat. He's another surgeon in the practice. He does a lot of surgery on chronic pain patients. Let me talk to him about you. Call me in a week about whether or not to set up an appointment with him."

Part of me wanted him to say, "Yes, I have something for you." The other part wanted him to be definite that nothing more could be done. The one thing I did not want was uncertainty. Once more, I got a "maybe." My mind, unable to stop itself, went directly into a hope mode.

It took a month before I could get through to the office to make an appointment. The first one available was four months away.

I was very nervous about seeing him. I had a hard time dealing with the wait. The week before Christmas, I got a terrific surprise. It was one that helped me get through what was to happen in the next few months.

My mother called me. "If you could have absolutely anything at all for Christmas, what would you want?" Maria, the foreign exchange student, my Brazilian sister as I called her, who had lived with us in 1970, the woman with whom I had lost touch but who was never far from my mind . . . she was always my answer.

I was pretty sure my mother was not going to stake me to a trip to Brazil. Nonetheless, I gave the only answer I had. "Maria." "You got it," she announced with glee. "She's living in Maryland. She just called me. She wants to come up for Christmas. Here's her phone number." When she and I talked, ten minutes later, it was as though it had not been thirteen years since we had last seen each other. I was happy to be talking with her on the phone. She was one of the last people I wanted to see me in person. Now that I looked the way I did.

"How come you're here? What have you been doing? How are the kids? How is Teo [her husband]?" I asked everything I could think of to keep her questions away from me. She started to answer. She made almost no headway before falling back into the conversational ritual we had first developed in high school. "You tell me first." "No, you tell me." Again and again she asked, "What have you been doing? How are things with you?" I put it off as long as I could.

My fantasy had always been that when we talked, I would only have good things to say. Instead, I had to tell the truth.

"Well, umm, I've been disabled for the past ten years." I gritted my teeth, my mind fighting to keep the words from coming out. "Since we are going to see each other, I have to tell you. The left half of my face is paralyzed. It's really awful. And, part of my left eye is sewn shut."

She was the Maria I remembered. Her accent was still heavy, but her English was somewhat better. "Things happen to people. I'm so sorry things have not been going well. It doesn't matter. I can't wait to see you."

She and her two sons, Fabio and Bernardo, took an Amtrak train to Philadelphia. I rode the local train from Erdenheim and met them there. The three of us got back on another train and rode back to the Chestnut Hill Station, near my parents' home.

To my great relief, it was going to be okay. No one winced when they saw me. It was a great visit. It was the first merry Christmas for me in a long, long time.

Maria and I went shopping, wrapped presents, filled hosiery. We talked and talked, and then talked some more. The children awakened to Christmas stockings at the foot of their bed for the first time in their lives. (The Brazilian tradition was to leave shoes near the tree. In the morning, Papa Noel would have them filled with wrapped candies.) It was almost like a real life for me. I had the pain. I took my codeine. But I had a sister who cared.

They left after a week. As they stepped into the train to go back home to Maryland, Maria and I assured each other we would stay in touch.

I kept my appointment with Dr. Barolat.

I wasn't sure I wanted to see him. I had not heard of him before. He was the third partner in Dr. Osterholm's practice. He had a pronounced accent. Dr. Martinez had also been the third partner. I had not heard of him before. He had an accent. I had a strong, unpleasant, sense of déjà vu. If he did have something to offer me, I feared it would turn out just as poorly as Dr. Martinez's had. But, if he had something to offer, I had no choice but to hear him out.

My first impression let me know I did not have to fear him as a Dr. Martinez clone. A short man, with short, neatly parted, light brown hair, he wore a greenish suit. He appeared to be in his forties. His face was open and friendly.

He asked me a few questions. Then he turned to read the history Dr. Osterholm had written from my visit in November. "Holy s—t," he said. Before he could explain, his beeper went off. "I'm sorry I have to go. I'll be back as soon as I can." He put my chart down on the desk before he left the room.

I could not understand his reaction. His absence gave me plenty of time to think up reasons.

I did not think it could be related to the medical information. The note must have mentioned my lawsuit or psychiatric history.

Why imagine? I picked up my chart. I was very surprised. The page he had been reading contained only two paragraphs. The first described the anatomical reasons for my pain. The second listed what had been done neurosurgically. I was reassured. I was appalled.

When he returned, we talked some more. After some thought, he said, "There is something.

"I think we could try an implant."

An implant? The machine I had seen and rejected when I watched *The Bold Ones* TV program in 1971? The thing I had refused in California? The same system proposed by Dr. Hosobuchi? The one he said he could not do if I went with the tractotomy? The thing I swore I would never let anyone put in me? I did not think so.

He explained that insertion would be a two-step process. "In the first part of the operation, I will place the electrodes. I'd be putting them in the back of your neck. A week later, I'll go back in. A battery will be put in your chest, under the skin, like a pacemaker. It is then attached to the wire leads from the electrodes. It's rather benign. If it doesn't work, and I'm not sure that it will, I can take it out."

"I don't want an implant." An unintended sigh of capitulation left my mouth. "But I'm game. If you think it's worth a try, let's go ahead." The same thought as always: *How can I refuse?*

Either the pain is so bad, so disabling, so debilitating, that I will agree to the thing that has been the most abhorrent, or it is not. It was. If he thought it could help me, I had no choice. Saying it was easier than accepting the reality that I had agreed to more surgery. Particularly, this one. He showed me two things before I left his office. The first was a gigantic, donut-shaped, blue magnet. If, for any reason, the unit needed to be turned off, all you had to do was hold the magnet up against the battery (through your clothing). That immediately turned it off.

The second was a large, black, heavy briefcase. In it was a handheld computer that allows the patient to turn the unit off and on herself/himself. It allows you to do, or undo, what you might have done using the magnet. In addition, it is possible for the unit to be turned off by elevators, large machinery, and unknown magnets, etc. The handheld lets you turn it back on in those instances, too.

It also enables the user to change the amount and rate of the stimulation. That made the idea of an implant even worse. The last thing I wanted was to have to carry a case all the time, constantly reminding me of the implant.

On my way out, I noticed a woman in the waiting room. She carried one of the briefcases. "Excuse me. You have an implant? Do you mind if I ask you how long you have had it?" I was almost scared to ask my next question. Frightened of a "yes" or a "no." "Does it work?"

"My pain's in my arm. I have had it for years. Before the implant, I was virtually housebound. Since Dr. Barolat put in the implant, I am almost completely pain free." I was happy for her. I fought with myself. *If it helped her, then it must work. Geez. There is no excuse to refuse it, then.*

"Do you always have to carry the case with you?"

"No, but I don't need to have the implant on all the time.

Only if I'm going to go out and do something that I know will make the pain worse. Then, I do take it with me."

There was no way I could ignore her smile. She beamed. The smile only someone who knew pain and finally had relief, could wear. *Maybe,* I thought, *it might not be such a bad thing.*

I talked to Dr. Muncey about it. "If something's been offered to me, I'm in no position to refuse. It's not a matter of choice. I have to accept anything they offer."

It was the same as when I had spoken with Linda about her recommendation of Dr. Barrett, and the patients who had benefited at the clinic. The woman's arm pain and improvement were not my face pain. Maybe it would help, maybe it would not. Dr. Muncey and I debated the validity of my position. He felt there must be a middle ground. As far as I was concerned, that meant compromising with the pain. I could not, and would not, do that. It had to be either relief by treatment or relief by death. After much thought and conversation, I knew I had to go ahead. If benign, then the risk was minimal. If it worked, I would be free. If not, I had everything that was in my medicine cabinet.

If suicide did turn out to be the answer, I was concerned about doing something so drastic while Maria lived in the States. By the same token, I could not let her presence deter me from doing what I felt had to be done. She worked as a psychodramatist in Brazil. The American Society of Psychodramatists was meeting for a week in Manhattan. She stayed in my apartment while she attended the convention. The second night of her visit, I took her out to a Chinese restaurant.

We finished our meal of egg rolls and entrees. The teapot was full, the fortune cookies yet to be opened.

"Maria, I have to tell you something." I continued to put the words together in my head. I wanted her to understand, and not feel threatened, or frightened. She knew about the pain. She saw me take my pills. I explained that it was very bad. I told her about all the operations and treatments that had been tried. She is very smart. Nevertheless, I did not know if she really understood the depth of my suffering. Or how desperate I was to get rid of it.

"I've thought long and hard about what I'm going to say. I'm going to have the surgery. I hope it works. If it doesn't, I'm planning to commit suicide. I want you to know so that if I have to do it, it doesn't come as a surprise. I also want to be sure, and need to be sure, that you understand why I may have to do it."

To my relief, she did not become visibly upset. That was one reason why I think I decided to tell her in a public place.

She said, of course, what everyone else said, "They're always doing research. You don't know what they might come up with." She seemed to realize that this was not something I could easily, if at all, be talked out of. "I want to talk to one of the therapists at the convention about what you're telling me, about your situation. Will you see him if he agrees?" "Yes," I said, and let the subject drop.

Some time later, I had a similar discussion with Jay. She and Maria were the two people I most wanted not to hurt. Jay had been there for me almost every step of the way. Although it had been years since we had been together, Maria, in person or in thought, supported me. Neither of them could stop me, if it came to my death, but I did want them to know. It only seemed fair.

Maria's colleague, Bob, said he would talk with me. I went to his office on 23rd Street. We discussed my medical situation. We talked about my potential suicide. Kind and compassionate, looking like a therapist with his white beard and casual outfit of beige jeans and button-down shirt, he said he did not want to see me die. "I can understand why you feel this way. I would like to talk with you more about it if you're willing." I was. I saw him for two more sessions. He did not have much to offer other than a kind shoulder and compassion, which was a lot. I was still seeing Dr. Muncey. Bob and I agreed I should wait and see where things were going before setting any more appointments with him.

The surgery was scheduled for May 17, 1986. Dr. Muncey finished his residency in June. We decided to terminate therapy in the beginning of May. It was Dr. Muncey who suggested that we stop before I had the surgery.

I felt a sense of abandonment. I also felt that he was more comfortable terminating before the surgery, so he would not know if it did not work. I think he knew how serious I was about my suicide.

I did not want to go ahead with the surgery. Since I did not feel I had an option, I would not have minded if someone, or something, else forced me to cancel.

Six years had passed since Dr. Hosobuchi had operated on me in San Francisco. That was in 1981. During the surgery, I received two units of blood.

I had not been feeling well for a while. A number of my lymph nodes were swollen. I felt very fatigued. The resident at the Internal Medicine clinic at St. Vincent's suggested that, if any more symptoms occurred, I be tested for the AIDS virus. Coincidentally, Dr. Koop, then surgeon general of the U.S., suggested that people who had received blood before 1982 be tested for AIDS. Once I heard him say that, I decided not to wait. I went to the Department of Public Health, where the test was offered. They took a blood sample. I was told to come back in three weeks for the result.

When I returned as instructed, the counselor was smiling. "Good news, you don't have the virus."

"Oh," I said, downcast. "I'm sorry it's negative." He looked at me in horror.

"You want to have AIDS?" he asked, bewildered.

"No, no, of course not."

"It's just that if I had ARC, the pre-AIDS virus, you know the one that doesn't have to turn into AIDS? I'm going to have brain surgery that I would rather not have. If I had ARC, it wouldn't have to turn into AIDS, but I would have to cancel the operation. I couldn't take a chance of giving it to my surgeon."

He continued to give me a look that showed how crazy he

must have thought I was. "Well . . . okay. Good luck to you then."

He was right. It was a crazy thought. I wanted to have the decision taken out of my hands. This would have done it.

As it turned out, I was glad I had taken the test. Approximately two months later, I received a letter from the California hospital suggesting, "As someone who had received blood . . . I talk to my physician about being tested for AIDS."

"The third time's the charm," so the cliché goes. Back into the Thomas Jefferson University Hospital I went. Monday, May, 18, 1987. The day of my third operation there.

I hoped Dr. Barolat would prove the cliché to be true.

CHAPTER THIRTY-FOUR

Monday morning. I awoke with my nerves frayed.

I was scheduled to go to the OR as a "TF"—to follow. That meant when they were finished with all the other surgeries. Sometimes a wait of three or four hours. The waiting was made more bearable by Maria. She had come up from Maryland for the day. It was procedure number seven. It was only the second time I did not have to wait alone.

We sat on my bed. We stood in my room. We walked around the room. Maria left a few times to go outside and smoke. We waited and waited some more. At around 1:00 P.M., a nurse came into the room. "It shouldn't be too much longer, I hope. We want you to stay in your room so you'll be ready."

Maria was starting to get nervous. She had to leave no later than 6:00 P.M. to get back to Maryland for a meeting. "I don't want to go before you come back from the operation. I hope they get you soon." "Me too," I replied.

I was not allowed to eat. Hunger started to gnaw at me. Liquids were forbidden. My tongue felt as dry as a desert. Maria left the room again. She came back a few minutes later. When she opened her mouth to speak, I knew it was not a scent hallucination. I smelled food on her breath.

The wait was hard. Maria and I started to run out of things to talk about. There was a pink elephant in the room, the surgery. We tried to talk around and by it.

Afternoon became early evening. At 5:00 P.M., Dr. Barolat walked into the room. "I'm sorry, Carol. We are not ready for you yet." I was sitting on the bed. My body sank into itself. "Is it going to be done today?" I asked whiningly. "Yes. Definitely. I will be doing it today."

Maria asked him if he had any idea when. "Soon is all I can say." He walked out. Maria turned to me. "I want to stay, but you know I have to leave in an hour." I knew. *Finally, I had someone to be there when they rolled me away, and I still may end up going downstairs alone.*

She waited until the last possible minute. At 6:30 P.M., she was the one without a choice. She gave me a kiss on the cheek and a long hard hug. "I wish I could stay." Both of us held back tears as she walked out of the room and my vision. I lay back on my bed and swallowed my hurt and frustration.

Dr. Barolat walked into my room at 7:00 P.M. He brought a litter with him. "The OR's free. I'm going to take you down myself." I got on the litter. Dr. Barolat chauffeured. It was nice to have something that made me laugh. A doctor driving a litter. Not something you see every day, or even any day.

Usually, the pre-op room is busy with nurses and assistants, anaesthetists and anaesthesiologists, patients and their doctors. It is noisy, very bright, and very active.

At this time of night, it was me, Dr. Barolat, a nurse or two, and the anaesthesiologist. The latter put an IV in my arm and then a nurse took over the driving duty and wheeled me to the OR.

The drugs dripped into my arm and fast "asleep" I went. Dr. Barolat, so it was explained, made an incision in the back of my neck. He inserted the electrode wiring and hooked it up to the uppermost part of my spine.

I did not awaken, or become awake and aware, until sometime in the middle of the night. When I did, I found myself in a private room in the neurosurgical intermediate care unit.

I was totally unprepared for the pain. Normally, the one nice thing about brain surgery is that the brain itself does not feel pain. Only the incision is uncomfortable.

I never realized how much a neck is used in moving around. Any time I wanted to shift my position or sit up, I had to manually lift my head using my hands. It hurt, a lot. For the first time ever, I had to ask for pain medication because of the surgical pain. I felt better within two days. The nurses let me move back to the regular unit.

It took a few days longer to overcome the remaining post-op pain and weakness. Then, the most important part of the procedure started.

Beth, Dr. Barolat's nurse, came into my room. She wore a long white doctor's coat. Her blonde hair was clipped back off her face. She held something in her hand. She held it out to me "This is the TENS unit."

It was similar to a radio-like transistor. It was rectangular, about three by six inches. She safety pinned it to the front of my pajamas. She hooked it up to the two leads that were accessible through two small puncture-like areas in my back.

Beth pointed to various dials, explaining about each in turn. One allowed her and me, if it worked, to change the rate and strength of the current that was sent by the unit to my spine through the electrodes.

Once or twice a day, Beth, and sometimes Nickie*, a former patient of Dr. Barolat, would come in to work with me on finding the proper selections. Nickie, a beautiful, blue-eyed, tall woman, with very erect posture and obvious health, looked like she should be working as a model. Looks are deceiving. She could walk and move because her implant, put in a few years before, gave her the ability to walk and stand tall. She was a living advertisement for the surgery. As we sat, I would experience jolts, wavelike sensations, sizzles, or nothing as one of them changed the width of the pulse (whether it was a quick jolt or a drawn-out sensation), one parameter of the stimulation. Strange sensations would happen as the time between the stimulations was changed. It had a positive and a negative pole. As the polarities were changed, so, too, would my reactions. The possible combinations were enormous. Beth, Nickie, Dr. Barolat and I would not give up until we found just the right one.

I could feel the stimulation in my neck and in some parts of my face. They were not always pleasant. Again, some of the bad things that happened to me became good. Because of the numbness in my face, I felt it only when I turned my head, which placed more pressure on the wires.

I did not expect to have any relief, at least not that first week. It was strictly a preparatory period. It took many sessions and changes in polarity, width, timing, and force. Day after day, the meetings ended with me shaking my head. "No. None of them helped." Beth and Nickie were my Don Quixotes. They refused to stop looking for the elusive combination. And, lo and behold, they found it.

Most patients know when it is right because they can feel the stimulation in the pain area. We decided which was right by my feeling it in the general area of pain when I turned my head. It was time to put it in permanently.

As I lay in the pre-anaesthesia room, I started to cry. I tried to stop. The tears had been kept in too long. They flowed and flowed. Dr. Barolat came in to say hello. He stopped at my litter. "Carol, what's wrong?"

"This is closure, isn't it?" With a somewhat quizzical look, he answered, "Yes. It is." I repeated myself, "Once the battery is in, it's closure." I continued to cry. He looked upset. "I'll see you in the OR in a few minutes," he said and walked away.

He did not understand, I am sure, what I meant by "closure." His "yes" meant the procedure. Once he put in the battery and attached everything, the process is complete. I used "closure" to mean that I had reached the end. There were absolutely no more options. It closed off any other chance of relief. My tears were the tears of grief. I cried because there were no more doors after this. I wept because the end of the surgery might begin my death.

The deed was done. I knew not to expect an immediate

change. Dr. Barolat made it clear that it might take some time. I waited, but nothing happened. I was still afraid to touch my face. When it was touched by accident or mistake, the pain came. There was no change in the eye-movement-induced pain.

A few days later, my eye went bad. I walked down to the Ophthalmology Department. As soon as the resident called me into the exam room, I gave him a warning. "When you touch my face, you're going to cause me pain. Gentle touch is worse than hard, so don't be gentle. It has to be examined, so don't worry about hurting me."

This was the same speech I had given to every eye doctor for the past twelve years. I prepared myself for his touch. My stomach curled into itself. I felt the same fear I always felt when I knew I would have to place my face against the forehead barrier of the slit lamp machine. "You have to bring your head closer than that," he instructed. He cupped my chin with his hand. He gently pulled my head forward.

I watched as he picked up a cotton swab. I clenched my teeth. "I have to wipe away some of the lubricant." He lifted it up. He moved it closer and closer to my eye. *Oh, just do it already*, I thought. *Let's get this over with!*

I held my breath, waiting for the touch. Anticipating the onslaught of pain.

Finally, he held it against my eye and . . .

"Do that again," I commanded.
He did.
"Son of a gun!" I exclaimed. "It's not that bad. Son of a gun."
I must have repeated it ten times.

I still had the pain when he touched me. But, it was not the same intensity. Normally, it was so bad it literally took my voice away. It usually brought on nausea. It did not this time! Son of a gun! The implant worked

Cindy*, my roommate, told me she overheard two residents talking as they walked down the hall. "Did you hear about the miracle in room 9081?" she heard them say. "She can touch her face."

I went home after two weeks. Nothing else got better. I was very depressed. I had no more benefit. The implant physically disgusted me. Down the back of my neck ran a long scar. Beth had shown me the battery before the surgery. Seeing it outside my chest had not prepared for the way it would look once it was inside me.

I looked down at my chest. What I saw sickened me. There was a hunk of metal lying under my skin. It looked, to me, as though it was five inches long. In reality, it was only two and a half by two inches. I am a somewhat small woman, so it looked much larger. I got chills every time my hand brushed against it by mistake. Even with the warmth of my skin, I could feel the hard coldness of the metal.

I saw Dr. Barolat for a follow-up appointment a month later. I told him nothing had improved. "That's that, then," he said.

He saw no point in keeping the unit in. At the first touch, when I realized there was an improvement, excitement took over. Once the novelty wore off, I was able to more realistically assess the level of benefit. My clean face was mostly from the washing during surgery. A month later, I was dirty again. There was no reason to keep the unit in. Medically, it did not have to be taken out. As repulsive as it was, I did not want any more surgery. "Give me a call in a couple of months. You can decide then what you want to do."

Even if I chose not to have the unit removed, I did not have to keep it on. It could be turned off in one of two ways. It was easy to turn off. I had to carry the large blue magnet with me at all times. In case of an emergency, the stimulation changing or discomfort, for instance, holding it up against the battery turned it off.

I kept it on. I do not know why. I suppose it just seemed like too much effort to turn it off. It was kind of silly since it was not making a real difference in my activities, in my life. The breeze, wind, a touch, nothing at all, continued to set me off. I averaged up to eight grains of codeine a day.

Another month went by. Nothing changed.

One morning, I was standing in the shower. As I washed my hair, I realized I was not turning the left side of my head away from the water. It was streaming over and down the left side of my face.

I stood stock-still. Afraid to move. Afraid to break the moment. Not like the first time. When the pain had come out of nowhere. Not like so many years ago, when I was afraid to move and set off the pain. If I moved now, at all, in the shower, standing under the water, maybe I would not feel what I was not feeling now. And what was it that I was not feeling? I was not feeling pain!

I decided to try and shampoo the left side of my scalp. *IT DOESN'T HURT!* I washed my left face. *THERE'S NO PAIN!*

I could not believe it. Another day passed. The constant pain, it was gone!

I counted the amount of codeine I had taken the day before. It had been only three. The day before that, I had taken eight. That day, the pain had been bad. Within a day, not counting the weeks gone by without benefit, the implant started working.

I no longer needed the codeine.

I had been taking it for ten years. I consumed up to fourteen grains a day. My average was eight per day. I had to be addicted. I hated the way it made me feel, but a narcotic is addictive. That is part of the definition of narcotic.

"The heck with it," I said out loud. I picked up the bottle. I put it on the farthest back corner of the top shelf in the medicine cabinet. "Good-bye, codeine," I said. I had no reason to take any more of it. Stopping it was no problem. I had no withdrawal symptoms at all. It was done with. Yeah!

There was no reason to take any of the drugs that remained in the apartment.

I walked into the bathroom. I took out every pill, capsule, and liquid I had saved. One by one, then handful by handful, they went into the toilet. For the first time in—I did not know how long—I was not thinking of suicide. Death was the last thing I wanted. Even the battery did not seem quite as bad.

The implant set me free. All I wanted was life. With the exception of Dr. Barolat, I liberated myself from the medical community. I needed no more drugs, tests, or treatments. The battery was only good for a few months to a year, depending on how I used it. But, until the battery died, the pain would not return. It might recur then, but the placement of a new battery required only minimal surgery. With that exception, I was finally out of their clutches.

Well, not completely. But my eye was the only cause of the medical care I continued to need. Whether from my face being clean or the unit itself, my eye went bad only twice in the seven months before the first battery died.

The one thing the machine did not affect was the lightning pains in my lower cheek. They had returned in 1985. I went back on the drug Tegretol, the one that had stopped the lightning before. It worked again. The lightning stopped.

For the next few months, I just enjoyed my life. I went shopping. I bought new clothes. I found myself picking bright yellows, oranges, and reds. The colors that spoke of joy. I bought long hanging earrings. The kind that had hurt me because they pulled on my face. I could wear them now, no matter what they weighed. They were no longer a signal of depression. They were a sign of feeling good. I went swimming. My eye still needed to be protected, so I had to wear goggles. I could even tolerate them.

One day, I went to Wills Eye Hospital. I wanted to thank the people at the Day Surgery Unit for all the face washings. As I rode in the elevator, I received the best compliment of all.

A familiar-looking resident entered the car. We smiled at each other. Then we both realized he had been the eye doctor who saw me after the implant. As we reached his floor, he said, "You look very good." That was an all-purpose line. The comment that made my day came a few minutes later, when we passed each other in the hall.

He stopped me. "I know what the difference is. You don't look like you're in pain anymore."

I was not completely pain free. I still had the eye movement pain. It, too, improved, but only a little. I could now read for twenty to thirty minutes instead of only ten to fifteen before the pain became too bad. Other than that, I felt fine.

I was so entranced by my ability to touch my face that the fact that I could not work, even with the implant, did not get through to me for a few months. Then, I surprised both myself and Dr. Barolat. "I will never let them put a box in me!" became "Would you put in another one so that I can read and work?" I asked him the same question each time we talked. His answer never varied. "It cannot be done. The nerve that may be causing that aspect of the pain is too deep in the brain. It's too danger- ous." Even that did not dampen my enthusiasm. I figured if I asked him enough, he would become so annoyed with me he would have to agree.

I was imprisoned no longer. I embraced my freedom. My isolation had been all encompassing. I felt I needed to learn how to be back in society. Bob, the psychodramatist, suggested I join one of his group therapies.

I worried about how people would react to my story. I was particularly concerned about the way they would respond to the way I looked. At least, with the members of the group, it was no problem. It would take some time for me not to hesitate and look at the floor when someone asked me, "What do you do?" but I knew I would get there.

There was one other thing I needed to do. I decided I would honor my commitment to Mary and write a book. There had always been one major reason for me not to work on it: My story would not have a happy ending. Now, I could do it without worrying about how it would affect other people. Now that it has a happy ending.

Because it is not the end.

It is the beginning.

NOTES

1. Roy, R., ADV., DIP, S.W., and E. Tunks, M.D., F.R.C.P. *Chronic Pain: Psychosocial Factors in Rehabilitation.* London: Williams and Wilkins, 1982, page 23.

2. Neal, Helen. *The Politics of Pain.* New York: McGraw-Hill, 1978, page 88.

3. Hendler, op. cit. pages 104–108.